THE SUPREM

The Supremes' story was a beautiful fairy tale and a dream come true. I cannot idly stand by as Diane, Motown, and Berry Gordy, Jr., try to crush all I have worked so hard to preserve. Everywhere I go, people tell me what the Supremes meant to them, and I am gratified to know that we touched millions of lives. They remind me of what Diane and Berry seem to have forgotten: that the world first fell in love with *three* young black girls from the Detroit projects, not just one. Yes, there was Diana Ross, and before that Diana Ross and the Supremes. But it all began with the Supremes. It reminds me of the old question: What came first, the chicken or the egg? Well, I'm one chick who is damn proud of the egg she came from.

Whatever happened to the Supremes? What went wrong? These are questions I've been asked time and again, but which I've never been able to answer fully. Until now.

—*Mary Wilson*

SUPREME FAITH

Someday We'll Be Together

MARY WILSON

AND PATRICIA ROMANOWSKI

To Valerie & Darsey

[signed] Mary Wilson Supremes 2008

HarperPaperbacks

A Division of HarperCollins Publishers

HarperPaperbacks *A Division of* HarperCollins*Publishers*
10 East 53rd Street, New York, N.Y. 10022

*I dedicate this book to my four children—Turkessa,
Pedro, Jr., Rafael, and Willie—and to all the people
who have come in and out of my life,
giving me the love that is my soul's existence*

In Memory of

Florence Ballard (Supremes)
Paul Williams (Temptations)
Tammi Terrell
Marvin Gaye
Sandra Tilley (Vandellas)
Georgeanna Dobbins (Marvelettes)
Hubert Johnson (Contours)
Shorty Long ("Function at the Junction")

ACKNOWLEDGMENTS

Through the grace of God, I have lived a full and contented life even though many of the hurdles I had to jump over came fast and unpredictably. But during all the hard times, there have been people there, when I have reached out to them.

First of all, I thank my children, Turkessa, Pedro Jr., and Rafael, for giving me the space to take on such a huge project. To my publicist Jay Schwartz: I truly owe my public image to him, for it was he who directed that part of my career and kept me in the limelight. Gill Trodd from England was the best road manager, nanny, chauffeur, and wardrobe mistress any star could have. She was invaluable. Work has never been a problem for me; I have Ira Okum, Abby Hoffer, and Barry and Jenny of Marshall Arts to thank for booking me all over the world in the seventies and eighties.

I'd like to thank my thousands of English fans—like Kevin Medville, Terry and friends, Steve, Doug, John, Lee John, and Pat Ross (for loaning me all her scrapbooks); Paul

Delapeñna and friends, who made me feel welcome while on tour there; Margie Wooden and Tony Turner for taking great care of my gowns and hair on the road; Greg whom I can't find and who styled all those wigs we carried around in wig boxes; Howard Porter for chasing all around London to find my *Dreamgirl* manuscript, which I had left in the back of a cab while enroute to Heathrow Airport. Can you believe he found it? Thanks to my godson Allen Poe, for always being there for me, and designing all my eighties gowns. Thanks Angela.

To Anthony for his creative Christmas cards, and to my chauffeur, Kenny, for his wonderful dependability.

A very special thanks to Hazel Bethke Kragulac for her contribution to my life. To Glenn McGuire for coming up with that divine subtitle "Someday We'll Be Together." Ted LeMaster for the wonderful portraits. Norwin Simmons for giving me his entire Supremes collection (sans Diana Ross). And special thanks to Charlie Murdock. A huge thanks to Maxine Powell, Cholly Atkins, Maurice King, and Gil Askey who gave the Supremes the class and charm that helped them become a class act.

The Supremes have thousands of fans all over the world, many of whom have sent me photos and clippings for my research for both books. I feel very grateful for the fans who do not appear in this book but who have sent cards and letters, and who supported us throughout the years during ups and downs, changing members, and hit records. To put every single name on these pages would leave no room for the story, so forgive me, but you are here, in every line, in every thought, and in my heart. My love to my new brother and sister, Duke and Lynda Greene, and to Mr. Boone for inspiring me to write.

All artists are indebted to their fan clubs, and I too have my fan club, under the direction of Carl Feuerbacher. I want to thank him, along with a few folks like Tom Ingrassia and Nick Strange, for their day to day assistance.

My heartfelt thanks to Mark Bego, my assistant, for sitting and working along with me to remember all those happy and tragic moments of the seventies and eighties. And, last but not least, to my manager, Chip Lightman, for taking a chance on managing me.

PREFACE

n January 1988 I stood on the stage of the Waldorf-Astoria Hotel's grand ballroom, proudly accepting an award for the Supremes. We were being inducted into the Rock and Roll Hall of Fame, alongside the Drifters, the Beach Boys, Bob Dylan, and the Beatles. Again it was me and me alone representing my group.

For the past two decades I had made it my job to keep the legend and the memory of the Supremes alive. Florence Ballard had died tragically a dozen years before, and my other singing partner, Diana Ross, had decided that she was far too busy to even acknowledge the group that had made her a household word. Like our millions of fans worldwide, I was proud of the Supremes and our accomplishments. I believed and feared that no one would ever care as much about the Supremes as I did. Today, over two decades later, I know that for a fact.

As I accepted the crowning honor of my long and exciting career as a Supreme, I found myself apologizing for Diane's unexpected absence. But I wasn't totally surprised. Since she left the group in 1970 to become the legendary "Miss Ross," she's gone out of her way to pretend that the Supremes never existed and that our phenomenal success was hers alone. Diane, Motown Records, and its founder, Berry Gordy, Jr., thought they could just sweep the Supremes under the rug, and the world would forget us. But the world did not. This pitiful charade was an insult, not only to me but to everyone who loved the Supremes.

The Supremes' story was a beautiful fairy tale and a dream come true. I cannot idly stand by as Diane, Motown, and Berry try to crush all I have worked so hard to preserve. Everywhere I go, people tell me what the Supremes meant to them, and I am gratified to know that we touched millions of lives. They remind me of what Diane and Berry seem to have forgotten: that the world first fell in love with *three* young black girls from the Detroit projects, not just one. Yes, there was Diana Ross, and before that Diana Ross and the Supremes. But it all began with the Supremes. It reminds me of the old question: Which came first, the chicken or the egg? Well, I'm one chick who is damn proud of the egg she came from.

Whatever happened to the Supremes? What went wrong? What killed the promise, and the group? These are questions I've been asked time and again, but which I've never been able to fully answer. Until now.

Contrary to popular belief, or Motown's version of the story, the Supremes didn't just wither after Diane left. In spite of Motown's deliberate lack of support and its scheming against us, we had several hit records and continued to be a top draw around the world. In those years I was the group's manager, the sole original member, and along with several talented young ladies, I kept the group alive.

In 1979 I took the long-overdue plunge into my solo

career. I set about discovering who I was, both publicly and privately. My discovery process hasn't always been pleasant. While I strove to keep the Supremes on top, I faced other personal challenges: enduring a physically abusive marriage, raising my adopted son and my three natural children, regaining my self-esteem, being a working mother. I realized that not all of my enemies were external. Some were deep inside of me. There were insecurities and fears that for years my success had eclipsed and repressed, but never erased.

When I began singing I was just a happy, confident little girl. Bit by bit certain events and people began chipping away at what I felt was the real Mary Wilson. The way I thought about things like success, money, and fame were different from the way other people I encountered in show business thought about them. Many of them based their self-image on the money they earned or the trappings of success they collected. Inside, some of them were really sad and lonely people.

If I'm already a happy person, I thought, *I don't need all of these things to make me happy.* Many people, particularly at Motown, interpreted my attitude as ambivalence. Because I didn't assume the lead singer's role right after Diane left and instead did what I felt was best for the group, some saw me as unambitious. Since I grew up with the Motown family, I listened to these people and saw myself through their eyes. As my self-confidence plummeted, fear took its place.

When I finally took charge of the group in the mid-seventies, I became mired in petty squabbles and group politics. Although I was sorry to call it quits with the Supremes, I knew that it was time. Not only did I have my eye on recording as a soloist, but I also began taking acting classes and eventually performed in movies and the theater. Through all my trials and endeavors, one thing has never faltered: what I call my "Supreme Faith." I prayed to God for a life filled with challenges, lessons, and happiness, and I have gotten just that.

When my first book, *Dreamgirl: My Life as a Supreme*, became a huge success in 1986, it made me truly realize how important the Supremes were to so many people. I also realized how much the public longed for a real reunion of the Supremes. Motown's corporate machinery robbed our fans of a proper worldwide farewell tour, or a satisfactory end to our glorious career together. I too have dreamed that, as our song says, "Someday We'll Be Together." While the odds on that remain somewhat questionable, my hope and faith—though sorely tested—never falter. As I've learned, anything is possible.

The hope that Diane and I might again be friends is only a spark of a dream I once had. In 1983, during the Supremes' highly publicized reunion at the "Motown 25: Yesterday, Today, Forever" TV taping, I was the victim of Diane's volatile temper. I stood shocked as she tried to push my microphone down and then shoved me onstage during the only song we sang together that night. When the television special aired, Motown included mere seconds of the so-called reunion. It had to protect the "Motown family" image and hide Diane's shameless shenanigans.

Since then and my book's publication, Diane's behavior toward me has alternated between warmly cordial and maliciously cold. When I have attended Diane's concerts and attempted to wish her well backstage, she's rudely snubbed me. The frosting on the cake came in 1989 while Diane was on her "Working Overtime" tour. She refused to set foot outside her dressing room until I had been expelled. I never dreamed that Diane, my daughter's godmother, could be so vindictive. Typically, I publicly apologized for *her* immature behavior.

I can no longer pretend that these incidents haven't occurred. While Diane hurt me deeply on a personal level, Berry and Motown caused me endless pain by deliberately misleading me, and causing me to relinquish my rights to the group name.

Two decades later, I'm still fighting for the Supremes, even though they are long, long gone. Until Diane left, I'd never thought about the business side of my career. My knowledge was limited to the music, the stage, the recording studio, the wonderful people I'd met, and the great places I'd been. I signed my contracts, did my job, had my fun, never once even considering that there was something else making the wheels of Motown spin besides talent, camaraderie, and love. In my heart I—and my fellow performers— were just adults blessed with the ability to continue living in the dreamworlds we'd spun as teenagers when we watched our favorite acts on the stage of Detroit's Graystone Ballroom. We had music and magic and success. To me, that was a beautiful miracle, a blessing.

What turned everything so sour in the seventies? Did Motown actively conspire to kill the Supremes? Were all of the company's efforts centered so totally on Diane's career that it felt compelled to destroy my group? In reality, the dream that was the Supremes began to unravel the very night that Diane left. I'll never forget that emotion-filled evening of January 14, 1970, a night that really put my supreme faith to the test.

Although I wouldn't realize it for many years, that night I began a very hard journey. On it I learned that Motown's heart didn't beat to the driving backbeat the world danced to. Corporate politics and the bottom line called the tune. I'd put my faith in Motown not just because of what it had stood for, but for what it was; the most successful black enterprise in history. Of course, other labels treated their artists badly; we all knew that. We also thought Motown was different.

Once upon a time, I believed that machine worked for me. In truth, my talent—along with almost everyone else's at Motown—was just the grist for that mill.

CHAPTER 1

*P*ass me your lipstick," I said to Cindy Birdsong, glancing into the dressing-room mirror. "Are you wearing that curly wig tonight? I sure wish I had brought my blond wig."

"I can't seem to make up my mind," she replied, sipping from her glass of champagne.

Just then someone knocked on the dressing-room door.

"Who is it?" I asked.

"Gil Askey," our musical director replied.

"Come on in, Gil."

"Hey girls, what's going on? Is everything all right? You guys should see out front—every star from Hollywood is out there! Marvin Gaye, Bill Russell, Steve Allen and Jayne Meadows, Smokey Robinson, Lou Rawls, Dick Clark . . ."

Behind Gil walked a delivery man with another bouquet of flowers to add to the dozens already there. Our huge makeup mirror was encircled with congratulatory telegrams from around the world.

Another knock: "Five minutes, Miss Wilson and Miss Birdsong!"

Diana Ross and the Supremes' final farewell performance took place at Las Vegas's Frontier Hotel, beginning near midnight on January 14, 1970, and ending in the wee hours of the following morning. Coincidentally, January 15 also marked the ninth anniversary of the original Supremes signing our first contract with Motown. As I wrote in my first book, *Dreamgirl: My Life as a Supreme*, what appeared to be an emotional send-off was a true show in every sense of the word. Yes, Diane's leaving signaled the end of an era; no one could deny that. But after having spent the last several months working whenever possible with her replacement— Jean Terrell—and Cindy Birdsong, I felt nothing but optimism and hope.

The final show started with "T.C.B.," a rousing opener, segueing into a hurried greatest-hits medley, followed by "The Lady Is a Tramp," "Let's Get Away from It All," "Love Is Here and Now You're Gone," and "I'm Gonna Make You Love Me." I then sang my solo, "Can't Take My Eyes off of You," after which Diane playfully said, "Thank you very much—now get back to your microphone!" Everyone laughed.

We sang "Reflections," and then Diane had two solo numbers, "My Man" and "Didn't We." Cindy and I returned for "It's All Right with Me," "Big Spender," "Falling in Love with Love" (from our *Rodgers and Hart* LP), and "Love Child." Next came "Aquarius/Let the Sunshine In" from the musical *Hair*. Diane moved through the room, coaxing celebrities in the audience to sing along. Smokey Robinson and his wife, Claudette, Dick Clark, Lou Rawls, Steve Allen, and other stars good-naturedly joined in on what nearly became a marathon sing-along. The show hurtled to a close with "The Impossible Dream" and, fittingly, "Someday We'll Be Together."

Toward the end of the last show, Diane officially introduced Jean as the next Supreme. Then Nevada Senator Howard Cannon read aloud a beautiful congratulatory telegram from Ed Sullivan, in which he praised us for having made it "without backstabbing and hypocrisy" and "working as a team." (If only he knew . . .) He continued, "As of tonight, one of the greatest attractions of the sixties becomes *two* of the greatest attractions of the seventies." How I hoped he was right. Everyone cheered, tears were shed, and we were presented with huge bouquets of roses. Then it was over.

A huge, crowded party was held in one of the hotel's private lounges. After putting in an appearance there, I moved to the casino. Sitting at the blackjack table, I gave one of the greatest performances of my life. I'd left the farewell celebration because I couldn't stand being the forgotten star. It was really Diane's moment. Inside, it hurt me more than anyone knew. That I could feel such pain and yet happiness all at once surprised me even though I've always believed that because of my Piscean nature, I'm able to see both sides of an issue and to feel two seemingly contradictory emotions simultaneously.

"Hit me," I said. The dealer turned up my five of hearts. I looked at my cards; I had ten in the hole.

"Mary, you'd better stay in!" someone shouted from the side of the table. The casino was buzzing with excitement. I looked at my hand and knew my staying days were over. A fifteen would mean that I'd lose this hand of blackjack. I took a chance.

"Hit me." The dealer turned up a six. Blackjack! Everyone cheered.

"Mare, how are you doing?" It was our manager Shelly Berger's wife, Eleanor.

"Winning," I replied with a smile. Looking up I saw a tall, handsome man step out from the crowd. "That was a great show you girls put on tonight. Why aren't you back in there at the party with everyone else?"

I didn't answer but smiled politely. Most everyone was still inside, toasting Berry and his star Diane, congratulating them on their success and wishing her the best in her solo career. I was happier right where I was, being myself, having a great time.

"Hey, baby." It was my friend Marvin Gaye. As always, he had that shy, sexy smile. He touched my shoulder gently and gave me a kiss. "You were really jammin' up there tonight," he said softly. He was right. While Diane was in the audience, I was wailing loudly, as is very evident on our live farewell LP.

"Yeah, well, you really tore up the place when Diane gave you the microphone," I replied. Marvin had sung a chorus of "Let the Sunshine In" so beautifully that I, like every other woman in the room, thought we'd die. It had come toward the end of Diane's last performance with the Supremes, a tremendous moment. It also marked the end of the most exciting part of my musical career. But that isn't what I was thinking about then. I was looking ahead, ready for whatever came my way.

Lots of people assume that Diane's departure hurt me or made me bitter, but that's not how it was. Motown began engineering the change as far back as four years earlier. Despite Diane's persistent claims that she, Cindy, and I "discussed" her going solo, it was never mentioned. In fact, I first learned of Motown's plans while the Supremes were touring Europe in 1968. I'd seen the stories in the press, and after Berry changed the group name to Diana Ross and the

Supremes, speculation as to when she would leave swelled. Maybe I was naive, but it didn't occur to me that these were more than rumors until a reporter from an English music paper asked me point-blank, "What about Diana Ross leaving? What are you going to do?" He looked at me as if I knew what he meant.

"As far as I know," I replied honestly, "she's *not* leaving."

I thought back to spring 1967, when Berry said, "Mary, changing the name doesn't really mean anything, except that you girls will be making twice as much money. It won't affect your position in the group." As we stood in a recording studio, Berry had his arm around my shoulder and spoke in an even, paternal tone. "Now we have two entities: Diana Ross, and the Supremes. And people will pay more money to see you girls."

He had just fired Flo (though, to be honest, it was her fault too). Knowing that she and I were close friends, Berry wisely tried to assuage my fears and draw me back into the fold. His charming grin reminded me of a mischievous little boy. "And I want you to remember, Mary: no matter what happens, I will always take care of you."

In the last dozen years I'd lived two lifetimes, the first between 1958 and 1964, when Flo, Diane, and I became friends. We started singing together and, in our homemade stage costumes, set our hearts on a dream. This was the happiest time of my life. We were learning our profession, on the road, in clubs, and in the recording studio. It was like being in school. In 1964, when "Where Did Our Love Go" went to Number One, it was like we had graduated at the top of our class. Another life began for us, one of promise, wealth, and security. We toured the world, meeting everyone from ardent fans to royalty. Like most young people, we lived for today and thought it would last forever.

When Berry replaced Flo with Cindy, I began to grow up. I started to see that the world wasn't always good, life wasn't always happy. And being happy today didn't guarantee that you would be happy tomorrow, or ever again. Yet I did not really understand that the Supremes' success was about much more than simple dreams. There were also unchecked ambition, hard work, money, greed, and company politics. I was too much in the middle of it all to see how this would ever affect or change me.

Once I knew for sure that Diane would go, I experienced a whole range of emotions: anger, hurt, sadness, and, finally, acceptance. My decision to carry on with the Supremes and replace Diane was logical and right. The Supremes obviously needed a third member. And Motown, which had invested countless millions in creating both a group institution and a solo star, knew there was still money to be made from both acts. To the public, the Supremes were more than the label's flagship, the personification of Motown. We led the roster in Number One hits, commanded top personal-appearance fees, and continued to maintain our still-undisputed position as the most successful female singing group in history. Diane's leaving changed none of that. Even before Jean Terrell was introduced to the public, we were booked well into the next year, all prestigious rooms in Las Vegas, New York, San Juan, and Miami.

Motown officially announced Diane's plans in late 1969, and everyone wondered who would take her place. Reporters kept asking, "When will you step up to the front, Miss Wilson?" That seemed a natural move, but the mere thought of it filled me with fear. For years I'd done my solo spot in the show, "Can't Take My Eyes off of You," and always to enthusiastic applause. But as I've learned, having the voice to sing and having the talent to be a lead singer are two vastly different things. After years of being pushed into the background, told I lacked drive and a voice, I'd started believing it. I could have taken over the lead if I'd asked Berry, but I decided to put the group first. A new lead singer who could really handle the job was best for the Supremes, and that's what I wanted.

Fan magazines ran contests asking readers to nominate singers for the job. It was rumored that Florence Ballard might rejoin as a lead singer, something Motown would never have gone for. Other nominees were Tammi Terrell, by then suffering from the brain tumor that would claim her life the following year, and Syreeta Wright, a singer under contract to Motown. Because Syreeta's style and voice were similar to Diane's, she seemed an obvious choice to Motown, but I thought the "obvious choice" was a mistake. Everyone knew that Syreeta wanted a solo career, and I refused to bring in someone who saw the Supremes as a stepping stone. The Supremes had to be a team again. Berry decided on a singer he'd happened to hear in a Miami showroom in mid-1969, Jean Terrell.

Motown was following the standard procedure for replacing group members, except that unlike with the more quiet personnel changes—Flo's ouster from our group, David Ruffin's departure from the Temptations—it made this a grand occasion. This was what Diane wanted and what Berry wanted, but amid all the hoopla, *Motown* was the star. In Berry's mind, no single member was greater than any act, and no act was greater than the label. Not Flo, not me, and in the very end, not even Diane.

Today people say it was obvious that Diane was unique, that she had done all she could with the Supremes. But in fact, both within and outside the industry, many—including some people at Motown—predicted she would fail when she went solo. Not me. I believed in Diane and knew that anything she set her sights on would be hers. And while this might surprise you, I also thought she deserved it.

That night at the blackjack table, I flashed back in time to Hitsville, the original Motown building on West Grand Boulevard in Detroit. It was September 1961, nine months after we'd signed our first recording contract. Diane, Flo, and I had just finished a Smokey Robinson song called "Those D.J. Shows," a hard-driving, soulful track with a wailing sax and Flo and me singing out clearly in the background. The three of us tumbled out of the studio, laughing and hugging one another, and ran through the hallway singing, "I'm gonna be diggin' that rock and roll . . . If I don't, I'll go insane, when I'm too old to walk around with a cane, I'll still turn on those DJ shows." We really did think we'd still be singing rock and roll as a trio even when we were ninety. Now Flo was gone, and soon Diane would be too. Only I remained to hold the Supremes together.

Once, when I was very, very young, I prayed to God that he would make the Supremes a success, and my prayers were answered. Did I dare to dream again? The realization that I was no longer a carefree young girl struck me time and again. Here I was, a twenty-five-year-old woman, the single adoptive mother of a young boy, my son Willie, and the sole support of my wonderful mother, Johnnie Mae. Being the last original member of the Supremes also brought new challenges. I loved the Supremes and what we stood for. We were at the pinnacle of our career, and I was determined to keep us there.

The world in 1970 was very different from five years before. Politically, socially, musically, everything was changing. The Supremes would have to keep in step with the times, something we'd had a little trouble doing the previous two years. When Diane left, we had a Number One hit, "Someday We'll Be Together." How funny to say "we"; the record featured only Diane and Motown's house background singers, the Andantes. Despite that, this song became our anthem, because it expresses the Supremes' spirit.

As much as the Supremes were loved all around the world, the last couple of years with Diane we'd lost something of our winning form on the singles chart. Our historic run of five consecutive Number One hits was three years behind us. While "Love Child" and "I'm Livin' in Shame" were big hits, there were disappointments too: 1968's "Forever Came Today" and "Some Things You Never Get Used To," and 1969's "The Composer" and "No Matter What Sign You Are," none of which made the Top 25. For an act so often in the Top 10, those records hinted at an imminent commercial decline.

When I couldn't stand smiling anymore, I left the casino and went up to my suite with my best girlfriend, Margie Haber. I had champagne on ice, and we sat up for hours, drinking, talking, and laughing. Every once in a while, the phone rang. "You're being paged downstairs, Miss Wilson." I'd just laugh and hang up. Margie, who is Jewish, told me that I was "meshugana"—Yiddish for "crazy." I finally fell asleep around four-thirty in the morning.

A few hours later I was startled awake by the shrill ring of the telephone. I was so tired that when I opened my eyes, I couldn't even recall where I was.

"Mary? Mary? This is Berry."

"What?" Didn't this man ever sleep? It always irritated me that Berry called very early in the morning to discuss important matters, knowing he would probably wake me out of a sound sleep.

"I don't like Jean Terrell," he stated abruptly. "I don't think Jean is right."

I bolted up in bed, pushing my hair out of my face. Was this a nightmare? "What are you talking about? Didn't we just tell the world that the Supremes had accepted Jean as our new lead singer?"

"I've worked with Jean and talked with her," Berry replied, ignoring my questions, "and I am sure she won't work out." My head spun as I thought of all the work of the past half-year. By day Cindy, Jean, and I rehearsed, recorded, had gown fittings and photo sessions. By night Cindy and I sang all over the world with Diane.

"I want Syreeta Wright in the group."

I couldn't believe he was saying this. We were booked to make our national television and live-concert debuts with Jean in just weeks. I was speechless, feeling angry and betrayed. If Berry really didn't want Jean, he should have known it before. Just a few hours before, I had known, for the first time in years, where I was going and with whom. Now with a wave of his hand, Berry threatened to destroy everything.

"No way!" I answered. "Jean stays."

For a few seconds, Berry was quiet, probably as surprised as I was to hear me stand up to him. Berry Gordy might have been the lord of the manor, he might have made me a star, and he certainly could do lots of things for me. But he wasn't snatching this away.

"Mary, do you hear me?" Berry demanded. "I said Jean is wrong for the group, and I want her out."

"I heard you. And the answer is no!"

"All right," Berry replied sternly, "then I wash my hands of the group!" He hung up. I looked around my luxurious hotel suite and began to cry.

CHAPTER 2

I left Las Vegas certain Berry would call any minute to say that Jean Terrell had to leave the group. Oddly, neither he nor anyone else at Motown ever mentioned the subject again. Still, I did fear that when Berry said he was washing his hands of the Supremes, he meant it.

Just days after the "farewell" show in Vegas, we were in the studio recording as the "new" Supremes. I found myself standing in front of the microphone with Jean and Cindy. As I looked at this new grouping of world-famous Supremes, I reflected on the first time Diane, Florence, and I were together in the studio. It dawned on me how much the three of us had accomplished. At first it felt very odd without Diane, but I realized that my life must go on and that there was no sense dwelling in the past. Jean, Cindy, and I were recording "Up the Ladder to the Roof," our first single together. Our producer, Frank Wilson, had already recorded the music for three songs: "Up the Ladder," "But I Love

You More," and "Everybody's Got the Right to Love," all for our first album, *Right On*.

As the three of us listened to the instrumental tracks over the huge studio monitor speakers, we beamed with happiness. We'd spent part of the past six months working with several great producers, but no one had created a sound as fresh and well-suited to us as this. Cindy, who had been in the Supremes since spring 1967, was smiling broadly, her eyes twinkling, and Jean looked like she couldn't wait to start singing. We knew this was going to be something very different for the Supremes, and we were ecstatic.

That day, Frank said, "Mary, you know Suzanne dePasse [Berry's chief assistant] has been pushing the idea of Motown developing more concepts for our albums. So I've come up with this for you girls. It's a world-peace concept, a higher ideal about humanity."

I was delighted that Motown was working with us to give the new Supremes an exciting new sound.

"If the few songs I produce on this LP are hits," Frank continued, "I'll have a chance to produce your next LP." I had known Frank since he joined Motown in the mid-sixties, and we were good friends. Frank's work, like that of his fellow Motown producer Norman Whitfield, represented a very clear departure for Motown and the Supremes.

In song selection and performance, *Right On* was very strong. It opened with our first gold single, "Up the Ladder to the Roof," an invitation to love, and closed with Smokey Robinson's beautiful "The Loving Country," which also expressed Frank's love concept. These new songs were more soulful than earlier Supremes tracks. As you can hear on "Up the Ladder," Frank favored an almost ethereal vocal sound, with layered voices and harmonies far more complex than in our later work with Diane, but all driven by a pulsating, bass-heavy groove. He also experimented with modern studio effects, such as the electronically phased vocals on "Nathan Jones."

One of the most exciting things for us was Frank's approach to our singing. Not only did he come up with great chord structures and harmonies that went beyond the typical I-III-V progression, but he also had Jean singing background, which gave the songs a richer vocal sound. This was something we had not done since our early days with Diane.

By the end of the session, we were flying. I sat down in the control room while Frank discussed a few points with Jean. "This is a very straight song," he said. "You don't have to oversing it." With Cindy sitting beside me, we listened as Jean glided through the harmonies we'd just put down. She made one vocal run so glorious that when I closed my eyes I thought I was back listening to a soloist at the First Baptist Church in Detroit.

Frank pushed a button, and the music stopped. "Jean, I want you to keep it simple. You're making it too soulful." When I talked to Frank later, he confessed that he hated doing that, but he had no choice. Frank didn't ascribe to the company's long-standing attitude that artists were the least important link in the creative chain. He would fight for what he believed was right for his artists and their records. He made great strides on our behalf, but even he observed certain limits and kept to the established Motown Sound.

Jean seemed a little confused, so Frank went into the studio and sang the part for her. He was so patient and good to work with. Jean, whose recording experience was limited, tended to do a lot of runs, which are the long notes singers hold while running up or down the scale. These are common in r&b because they do add soul. I was disappointed that these were being cut, but I knew what we had was perfect.

Our new sound not only celebrated the refined pop the Supremes were known for, but was more contemporary and soulful—in other words, black.

How Jean came to the Supremes is a Cinderella story. It was early 1969, and Berry and our manager, Shelly Berger, were in Miami. One evening they wandered into the Fontainebleau Hotel and caught a show by Ernie Terrell and His Heavyweights. Ernie, the former World Boxing Association heavyweight champ, had retired in 1967 and put together the five-piece group, which included two of his brothers. The lead singer was his twenty-one-year-old younger sister, Jean. As she later told me, "Berry immediately began taking notes on me, and after the show Ernie and I talked to Berry and Shelly until morning." Clearly, Berry was impressed with Jean's silken soprano, as anyone who heard her would be.

Several months later Jean and Ernie traveled to Detroit, where they met with Motown, but for whatever reason, nothing happened. That April Berry called Jean and asked that she come out to Hollywood, and there, the following month, she signed with Motown. Not to slight Jean, but it struck me as odd that the search for Diane's replacement would end so quickly, especially considering what was at stake: the continued success of Motown's top group. There had to be hundreds, or at least dozens, of young women who might have been Supremes. But Berry saw Jean Terrell and chose her.

Even after nine years with Motown, I still knew too little about the actual business of our career. Jean's contract was a solo contract, and from this point on Motown signed each successive Supreme individually. In effect, the label was "subletting" memberships, a development that would create problems for us in the years to come. This was another variation on Motown's "divide and conquer" method of control.

When Berry happily announced to me that he had found Diane's replacement, I was very surprised at how excited he seemed. "Mary, she's great," he enthused. "You'll love her." For a while I hadn't been so sure that he wanted the Supremes to continue without Diane. I didn't trust Motown completely but decided to wait and see. When I heard how enthusiastic Berry was, I was relieved. If Berry was behind something, then everyone at Motown was behind it too. Berry's office called to set up a time for Cindy and me to meet Jean. Berry played us a tape, and I was impressed immediately with her voice.

Jean was Diane's complete opposite. At five feet six, she was taller than both Cindy and I. In her conservative outfit, medium-length Afro, and minimal makeup, Jean was anything but a kittenish glamour girl. Instead, she projected strength and confidence. Though not beautiful in the classic sense, she had undeniable presence. Everything about her, the way she spoke and carried herself, seemed to say, "I am proud to be a black woman."

This is wonderful, I thought. Some critics regarded the Supremes as a "white" group; why, I'll never know. Although many of the business people and our social acquaintances were white, my success had drawn me closer to black people and black ideals. I embraced the burgeoning awareness of black culture, history, and pride. Like many blacks of my generation, I felt it important to show my blackness in every aspect of my life, especially our music. Cindy felt the same. Jean's presence provided a refreshing change.

Berry asked me my opinion of Jean. I agreed he'd found the right person, and I could see he was happy that I liked her. Over the years I'd known Berry, we'd differed many times. He knew that the group meant more to me than anything else and that my loyalty would always be to my girls and not to him or to Motown. I first made this clear to him back in 1960, when the fourth Primette (as we were originally known), Barbara Martin, wrecked his Cadillac and everyone—except one person (I've always suspected Diane)—told Berry the lie we had all agreed on.

When Berry called me on the lie, I said, "My loyalty is to my group. My girls are the most important thing in the world to me." I was sixteen, and I was crying my eyes out. From then on, Berry liked and respected me but never felt that I was, as he often said, "on his side."

The Supremes were a real group again, three equal partners all committed to a goal, just like in the beginning. Not only did we work well professionally, but personally we all got along beautifully. For me this was a rebirth.

Cindy had been a Supreme for two and a half years. An original member of Patti LaBelle and the Bluebelles, she knew Diane, Flo, and me from our days touring the black chitlin circuit. Cindy was always the consummate professional, a hard worker, cooperative and flexible. *Everyone* likes her. She also had a great deal of self-confidence and brought her unflagging enthusiasm to everything she did. Cindy never had a negative thing to say about anything, which, when you're out on the road working the way we were, is a tremendous asset. Our fans thought she was the greatest. In the beginning, some people thought she was trying too hard to be like Flo, but Cindy eventually found her place in the group and became one of the public's favorite Supremes. Today people still ask me, "Where is that Birdsong girl?"

When she first joined, Cindy, like most people, naturally assumed that because Diane was lead singer, she was also boss. It was a while before I convinced Cindy that, business-wise, we were three equals. (Unless Diane threatened, "I'm gonna tell Berry on you.") I was still very sad over Flo's departure, and I'm sure this colored my attitude toward Cindy at first. As time passed, though, we got to know each other well. She soon found that no matter how much she tried buttering up Diane, by then "Miss Ross" didn't pay much attention to either of us.

Cindy helped so much with Jean, showing her the dance steps, taking extra time with her, drawing her out. Like every young woman who would join the Supremes, Jean was both excited and awed by her new position. To be suddenly thrust to the top was a little disconcerting. Before, Jean had lived and worked in relative obscurity; now everyone would be watching every move she made, both onstage and off.

In many ways Jean was different from Cindy and me. She was one of ten children born to Lovick and Annie Terrell, who moved to Chicago from rural Mississippi when Jean was six years old. Jean's family had much in common with Flo Ballard's. Both were large, and in each everyone stuck closely together and was wary of "outsiders." Unlike Flo, Jean often spoke to reporters about her family's closeness and the fact that her older brother Ernie and her mother inspired each of her siblings to have and work toward a goal.

Anyone could see that Jean Terrell had a mind of her own. Having worked all my life with strong, outspoken women, like Diane and Flo, I respected that.

One of the happiest times I recall from these early days was when we were trying on our gowns. Jean, Cindy, and I laughed and joked as we took turns seeing which costumes fit whom. At up to $2,000 each, the gowns represented a sizable investment, and we weren't about to replace all of them. Jean joked about Diane being so thin, and Cindy said, "Mary, I guess you'll have to wear hers." Cindy struggled into my dresses, Jean ended up in Cindy's, and I took Diane's.

These were all the newer designer gowns we'd had made since Flo's departure. What happened to all the gowns before Cindy joined the Supremes is a mystery. When Diane left in

1970, all music and gowns were to be turned over to me. I am still looking for them.

Our fans finally got to "meet" Jean when we appeared on *The Ed Sullivan Show,* Sunday, February 15, 1970. Having been on this program with the Supremes approximately twenty times since late 1964, I'd come to think of the CBS studios in New York City as a home away from home. Jean had never done network television and was nervous, as we all were. But I believed our true fans and the public would love us.

Before the show, several fans came backstage. From inside our dressing room, we could hear them shouting for us to come out and sign autographs. Most were in their young teens, and we knew many by name. No matter how big the Supremes got, we always made time for our fans, because they were important to us. I'm happy to say that loyalty continues today. As fans go, ours were different; opinionated, outspoken, they let us know if they thought we were doing something wrong. One fan said, "Mary, I'm sorry, but I don't like Jean Terrell at all."

"Please just give her a chance," I replied. "Maybe we can change your mind."

I figured he was one of the fans who decided they weren't going to like anyone taking Diane's place, no matter what. Diane's leaving had split our fans into three camps: those who followed us, those who followed her, and those who loved both Diane and the new Supremes.

For this important appearance, we followed a format we and Motown had established years before: sing a standard, or a medley of standards, to show that our repertoire extended beyond our hits; then debut our next record, which, thanks to this broad-based exposure, would most likely become a hit. Motown's acts were such popular guests on any number of television variety shows that records were usually premiered sometimes just hours before release.

Dressed in identical red-sequined pantsuits, Cindy and I stood in the wings while Jean took her place onstage and began singing, "If they could see me now, that dear old gang of mine, eating fancy chow and drinking fancy wine." We joined her after the first few lines of the medley, which included "Nothing Can Stop Us Now," and fell into the routine as if we'd been doing it together forever. Jean appeared serene and confident, and Cindy and I felt more certain about her with every note.

Next we lip-synched, or mouthed the words, to the prerecorded track of "Up the Ladder to the Roof," set for release the following day. As we glided and swayed, the studio audience rocked in their seats. Even before the rapturous applause swept over us, I knew we'd won them over.

Mr. Sullivan then called us over for one of his "chats." He introduced Cindy as "Cindy Birdstone" and for a moment looked as if he wasn't sure which of us was Jean. I "helped" him out and thanked him for the beautiful telegram he'd sent us in Vegas. Mr. Sullivan wished us good luck, and as we waved good-bye, the audience went wild. The next day we got word that "Up the Ladder to the Roof" was selling out at record stores across the country. Things couldn't have been better.

By week's end we were opening at the Fairmont Hotel in Dallas. The Fairmont chain was prestigious, and we had always enjoyed working there with Diane. It also had the greatest china of any hotel we'd ever stayed in, so each time we played there, we "augmented" our "collections." Cindy had the most extensive by far, and in later years, when I had trouble booking my solo act there, I wondered if someone had gotten hip to the disappearing dishware.

As always, Motown provided a small army of professionals—arrangers, choreographers, designers, musicians, writers—to put together our new act. But as good as we were in rehearsals, it was impossible to predict the live audience's response. Audiences could be quite fickle, as indiscriminate in their approval as in their criticism. Even with Diane in the group, I knew there were nights when we weren't "on." Notes fell flat, cues were missed, and we were not at our best. Yet most people only had to hear the opening chords to one of our hits, and we could do no wrong.

This engagement was important for other reasons besides it being our live debut. The Supremes now were regarded as more than a mere pop act. We had become what our detractors called a "Vegas act," a term that didn't bother me. Back then there were few venues for black artists outside the chitlin circuit. With greater success, we moved up in show business, and that meant moving into better clubs.

The Supremes were among the first rock and roll acts to appeal to adult club-goers, and we brought black audiences to these clubs. In 1965 we broke racial and stylistic barriers by playing New York's Copacabana. At the time, nightclubs were *the* hip places to be. While conquering the club circuit was part of Motown's overall strategy to attract a more adult audience, we wanted to achieve that as well. It meant status, money, and career longevity. The Supremes' ascent dovetailed with Berry's plans to push Diane further to the front of the group and then out on her own. Everyone benefited, but to some critics, fans, and the record industry, club success was a handicap, mainly because clubs attract adults, and adults don't buy as many records as teenagers. We were fortunate that as a rock and roll act, we were loved by *both* the older generation and the younger record buyers.

By nature, club acts are extravagant and showy. Glamour and the Supremes were by then synonymous, so we had no qualms about the sequined gowns, the elaborately coiffed wigs, and the glittery chandelier earrings. It was a part of performing I especially enjoyed. I loved being a woman and a star, and I loved all the dazzling trappings. Now, that's not to say it wasn't a lot of hard work. Some of those gowns weighed up to forty pounds each, and you could fry under the wigs and the stage lights. Fans expected all the glitz, and we happily obliged. From the start, it was the Supremes who demanded the gowns, not Motown. We wouldn't have had it any other way.

But what was considered an admirable accomplishment in the mid-sixties—three black girls from Detroit's inner city conquering the Copa, Las Vegas, London's Talk of the Town—now seemed like a sellout. To younger people especially, glitz plus glamour equaled white equaled phony.

With Jean and *Right On*, we expanded the Supremes' image, keeping the sequins but reviving the soulfulness some people thought we'd lost since the early records. The distinctly black rhythm & blues influence in our music was so much stronger prior to "Where Did Our Love Go," and you could really hear it in Flo's singing. Sadly, few people heard her before Berry appointed Diane lead singer. Thank God for recordings, because today people can hear Flo's wonderful voice on "Ain't That Good News" (*We Remember Sam Cooke*), *The Supremes Sing Country & Western*, and the recently released "Silent Night" (now on the CD *Never Before Released Masters*).

As I viewed our itinerary for the coming year, I saw it was filled with the same great venues we had played in the past and was every bit as hectic. Our new live act still included our two Supremes medleys with all our hits. Plus we sang "Reflections," "You Keep Me Hangin' On," and our new hit, "Up the Ladder to the Roof," as well as such standards as "Once in a Lifetime," "MacArthur Park," "Something," and "If They Could See Me Now." We threw in a few surprises: Janis Joplin's "Mercedes Benz" and a country-and-western-style medley of songs about Texas.

What excited the fans was that the formula of our act had changed. Instead of there being only one lead singer, Jean and I now shared leads. *Why shouldn't a group have more than one lead singer?* I wondered. Over the years there had been many groups that did, such as the Temptations, the Pointer Sisters, and the O'Jays.

Inevitably this lineup was compared to its predecessor, and Jean compared to Diane. Jean anticipated reporters' questions about Diane: "How do you feel about taking her place?" "What do you think of her?" "Are you and Miss Ross friends?" Their interest was understandable. Berry and Motown had been vigorously promoting Diane as the first superstar of the seventies. As uncomfortable as it may have made Jean, it couldn't be avoided.

Because it was opening night, and the crowd was dominated by show-business people and writers, we were a little nervous. Some industry people believed that Diane was making a big mistake by leaving us, and others felt that we were making a big mistake by going on without her. It seemed unthinkable to them that both the Supremes and Diane could continue successfully. I didn't see it that way at all. She was great, we were great, and there was plenty of room for us both. From the moment we swirled onstage, the audience loved Jean. As we took our bows to a standing ovation, I saw Jean smile, and I felt her anxiety about comparisons to Diane dissolve.

In those two hours, the Supremes seemed to have stepped out of Diane's shadow. But during our second show that night, the emcee announced, "Please welcome Miss Diana Ross!" A spotlight found her, Diane rose from her seat in the audience, and the crowd applauded wildly. Every newspaper made a big deal out of the "reunion of Miss Ross and her former partners." Apparently Diane had checked into the hotel that afternoon under an assumed name. Inexplicably, she never contacted me or anyone else in the group; the only time we saw her was during the show.

In April Motown released *Farewell,* a lavish, boxed, double-album documentary of Diane's last show with us. Charting at just Number 46, it wasn't one of our top-selling LPs. A couple of months later, our first album with Jean, *Right On,* was on its way to a solid Number 25; not the best showing the Supremes ever had, but certainly better than our last releases before Diane left.

The next big date looming for us was New York's Copacabana. It was so inspiring to stand on the stage where the Supremes had made history, and to feel we could do it again. Dionne Warwick, a good friend for many, many years, Glen Campbell, and Flip Wilson, whom I'd begun dating, were among the celebrities attending our opening night. We had critics eating out of our hands. The consensus was that Jean was certainly different from Diane, but it was a welcome difference. In most comparisons, Jean came out on top, especially as a singer; they felt her stage presence was more natural.

Over the next few weeks we appeared before sellout crowds in Washington, D.C., and San Francisco. A writer for the *Miami Herald* stated the general critical view of us: "Miss Ross has been replaced by Jean Terrell, a singer who, if not quite so unique, is a much better singer. . . . For the first time in years there is a true attempt to produce a really elegant harmony. And the two remaining members . . . [are] no longer merely hooting owls for a lead singer." This was what the Supremes were in the very beginning, and I couldn't help wondering how things might have been different if we'd returned to this format before Flo left. This is not to say that I objected to Diane as lead singer; I am happy for all the hits with her as lead. We should have been allowed, however, to share more on album cuts and in concerts.

Another reviewer applauded Motown's taking us in a new direction: "Instead of slipping in a Xerox copy [of Diane], Motown has mainlined quality and class into the act, mostly abandoning the old Supremes sound and creating an entirely new concept instead." Although only a handful of writers came out and said it, what they meant was that with Jean the Supremes were once again "black enough."

Considering all the positive signs, I almost forgot about Berry's threat to wash his hands of the Supremes. In only a few months we had proved ourselves on television, on stage, and on the charts. "Up the Ladder to the Roof" was on its way to Number 10 here and Number 6 in England. I felt stronger every day. *No,* I thought, *nothing—not even Berry—can stop us now.*

CHAPTER 3

$\mathcal{N}$ ew York City and Los Angeles are the centers of the entertainment world, and as the original Supremes started doing more television work, we often found ourselves on the West Coast for weeks at a time. Motown even established an office there in 1965. My main reason for moving west in 1969 was to have a private life away from Motown and its chaperones. Initially, Cindy and I stayed at the Beverly Comstock Hotel; we felt like two kids running away from home.

In 1965, when Diane, Flo, and I each bought our first house on Detroit's west side, I never imagined that I wouldn't live there for the rest of my life. This was my home. But when the Detroit riots hit, everything changed. I came home one day from a tour to see the city in flames. I was driving on the Edsel Ford Expressway when an Army truck packed with armed soldiers pulled alongside my car. Through a bull-horn one announced: "Please get off the streets! No one is allowed in the streets!" I hurried home.

From my kitchen window I watched in disbelief as men, women, and little children carried radios, televisions, stereos—even stoves and refrigerators—they had taken from the burning stores. All day long gunshots crackled in the distance. The hometown I loved was dying.

Flo stopped by to visit that day; her house was just two blocks down the street from mine. She had only recently left the Supremes. I told her that I planned to move to California soon, and she replied, "Mary, girl, if I could, I would too. But I've got my family, and I belong here with them."

As much as I hated to leave my hometown, my mind was made up. We were stars, and I was going where the other stars lived. Though I had to leave my family and friends, in late 1968 I happily packed all my belongings and watched the van as it disappeared down the street—heading west.

I initially rented a house in Nichols Canyon, in the Hollywood Hills. Isolated by trees, it felt like you were living out in the country, and I loved the solitude. I'd grown up idolizing Doris Day and in love with Hollywood, and the very idea that I now lived there thrilled me. The very look of the place was exciting. The sun always shone, so you never had to wear winter coats and boots. I saw palm trees instead of smokestacks, flowers in the winter instead of snow, rolling hills instead of skyscrapers. To me this was paradise, and I swore I'd never leave.

On any given day, you could run into stars on the streets in Hollywood, or in Beverly Hills. It was a haven for fun and drama in those days. In Los Angeles I discovered a whole community of people who did the same kind of work I did, who understood this lifestyle. I loved it from the beginning and started making new friends very quickly. Today Hollywood is much more casual about its stars; but when I moved there it was every bit as glamorous as what I'd seen in the movies.

Everything about my new life was so eye-opening. People were walking around in shorts, conscious of their health, and on self-improvement kicks. I too joined in, immediately taking Yoga and acting classes, becoming a vegetarian, and reading self-awareness books. I had my astrological charts done, and read about nutrition and different philosophies. Everyone wanted to improve their lives, and I did too. I loved this new freedom. The lure of Hollywood had gotten to me: driving up and down Sunset Boulevard, stopping into Schwab's Drug Store, shopping on Rodeo Drive, and basking in the sun year-round. I had arrived in "Surf City U.S.A." And, if I had been the local party giver in Detroit, I really blossomed in L.A. Since the Supremes were the rage, people flocked to my parties in the Hollywood Hills, to see what the Supreme glamour and glitz was all about.

Part of my new lifestyle included perfecting my craft. Probably the single most important thing I did was to start taking vocal lessons. Back in Detroit, none of us ever thought about taking voice lessons, but in L.A. it was the thing to do. My first teacher was Seth Riggs, with whom I made great improvements in just a short time. But, one night I went backstage to see my friend Freda Payne. She told me about her teacher Giuseppe Belestrieri, whom everyone calls "the Maestro." He is responsible for turning my voice into the strong instrument it is today. Once I learned from him how much of my singing problems could be solved simply through physically strengthening my vocal cords, my confidence began to return.

Less than six months after moving west and living in a rented house, I found my dream home, tucked away in the Hollywood Hills on Rising Glen Road. It was a beautiful ranch-style house that overlooked the entire city. The view of Hollywood was fantastic, and on a clear day you could see all the way to Catalina Island. It was truly a dream come true. I particularly loved the gigantic swimming pool. Between that, the fireplace, and the sauna I was sold. I set about designing everything in the home to suit my casual personality. There were only two actual chairs to sit in; everything else consisted of huge pillows, low coffee tables, plush green velvet draperies throughout, and a mirror-lined hallway that was twenty feet long. Often I would sit there and meditate when I wanted to be alone. My bedroom was all done in red velvet draperies and red carpeting, to match the oversized round bed that I bought—to make sure that I never woke up on the wrong side of the bed. Because we had done so much traveling in Japan in the sixties, I fashioned my kitchen in an oriental style. Guests were always amazed that they had to sit on the floor when I invited them over for dinner. Also in true Japanese style, I requested that everyone remove their shoes upon entering my house.

It was a fantastic house, and at first I filled it with dogs and cats and friends. Now that I had a secure, promising future, I longed for someone to care for, someone with whom I could share the life I'd built, a husband and children. At the time, my older cousin Christine had several children. Her eldest son Willie was eleven and seemed to need more attention than her other kids. Whenever I was in Detroit, I'd make the rounds, visiting all my extended family. Willie's grandmother told me that he had a discipline problem and that they were considering placing him in a reform school.

I firmly believe that in Willie, God gave me a chance to do something for someone in my own family. So I asked Christine if I could perhaps have Willie come live with me, so that I could give him the attention he needed. Because I had seen so many children in my travels around the world whom I would have loved to adopt, I felt that here in my own family was someone who needed some special care and could benefit from the love that I wanted to give. In California he would live in a more pleasant environment, attend special schools, and experience a different life than what he knew in Detroit. Although I never adopted him legally, Willie was, and is, my son. I believed that I could really help him through the sheer force of my love.

He moved out to California with me, and I assembled a household staff that included a woman to take care of him while I was away. Having grown up poor, I knew nothing about having maids or other servants, except for what I'd seen on television. In Detroit I'd always done my own housekeeping, with my mother or cousin Josephine helping, but now I was living the life of a star. I hired a wonderful young manservant/personal secretary named Harry Pondichelli, who waited on me hand and foot. A single woman would never dream of having a manservant in Detroit. Hollywood was just different.

The situation with Willie paralleled my own early childhood. Because my natural mother was unable to care for me, when I was three her sister, my Aunt I.V., and her husband, John L. Pippin, took me to Detroit. I lived with them until I was ten. In a way, I tried to re-create for Willie the good parts of my experience with I.V. and John. I showered him with love and many of the luxuries he didn't have at home. Willie's bedroom in the Rising Glen house was decorated with a big bed that looked like a stagecoach, and he had a pet boa constrictor, which kept unwanted visitors away. The rare times when I was home, we spent hours together, lying by the fireplace and playing chess. He was wonderful, playful, and sweet when I was around. But like most kids, he resented my being away. Being a career woman and a mother was hard at first, but I loved the new responsibility.

I found "instant motherhood" fulfilling. Caring for Willie gave my life balance. No matter what else you've accomplished, learning to handle a child is a unique, rewarding challenge. Not all of it was easy. I was a single working mother with many hats—or in my case, wigs—to juggle. Whenever possible, I took Willie along with me. He had some wonderful experiences, such as meeting royalty in England and counting among his friends some of the Jackson 5. However, growing up in Hollywood had its drawbacks too, and I'm afraid that he was also exposed to things most kids don't see until their late teens. Like any working mother, I wondered if I was doing the right thing for my son by continuing my career instead of staying home.

When I was growing up I had always heard about wild Hollywood parties. I started frequenting popular exclusive private clubs in Beverly Hills, such as the Candy Store, the Daisy, and Pips, where on any given night you could run into Peter Lawford, Liz Taylor, Tom Jones, Joe Namath, and countless others. It was at this time that I really got into the Hollywood night scene. I loved entertaining friends. Soon my house was filled with people like Diahann Carroll, the Dells, the Pointer Sisters, Ron Ely (TV's "Tarzan"), Brock Peters and his wife, Lola Falana, Glynn Turman (who later married Aretha Franklin), and Lincoln Kilpatrick, just to name a few.

When I threw parties, I always did my own cooking. I would go down to Chalet Gourmet for beluga caviar and stock up on cases of champagne and white wine—which were very "in" at the time. Hard liquor was un-chic, because everyone was on such a health kick. Often the parties were impromptu get-togethers after an evening of dining and dancing at the Candy Store. If someone like Frank Sinatra was holding court there, just getting into clubs like this—of which I was a paying member—was a hassle. It was bizarre to see celebrities waiting in line for hours just to get in. The Candy Store was set up like a 1920s speakeasy, with a peephole for the doorman to see the patrons.

I had been protected from the devastation of the psychedelic drugs that were prevalent in the late sixties and became so popular with the counterculture. The Supremes were considered goodie two shoes compared to Jimi Hendrix, Sly and the Family Stone, and Janis Joplin. Because marijuana had gradually crept into all walks of life, it was something that I would tolerate, but had no desire to indulge in. Even doctors and lawyers would smoke a joint after a hectic day. One day in early 1969 I told one member of a very popular singing group, "If you have to smoke that, go out in the backyard, because I do not want it in my house." I was square!

To say that I was naive about drugs is an understatement. For several months I dated a guy who—unbeknownst to me—smoked marijuana regularly. I never understood why he simply smiled at me whenever I offered him a drink and told him to "loosen up." When I ran into him a few years later, he laughed because he said, "It was so funny. I used to just die laughing, because you were trying to loosen me up with a drink, and I was already mellow from the joint I'd just smoked!"

One night, while I still lived in my rented house, some friends and I decided to play Bullshit. This is a verbal game that we used to play with our Motown cronies like Gladys Knight and the Pips while touring. However, as the night got later and the drinks flowed, we turned this already crazy game into an even hotter and more exciting event. This time around my roommate, Gina, said, "Why don't we make each person who loses strip?" I hesitated, while Marvin Gaye stammered and blushed profusely. So, it was agreed that we would remove only our outer garments—like shirts, pants, and skirts. No, it didn't get any further.

When I did encounter drugs in Hollywood sometime in the early seventies, it was not as I'd imagined. Marijuana usage had long been widely accepted. Cocaine was another story. However, the way it was presented in the Hollywood scene, it wasn't perceived as something done in a back room or a dark alleyway, or by junkies.

It was usually served in a private study or bedroom. The best parties were usually given by movie producers, and a group of elite partygoers would be invited to indulge. It was served with the formality of having champagne in a champagne bucket.

When I first started attending Hollywood parties I wasn't aware of what went on behind closed doors. There was always the general party and then a more exclusive "private" party going on in another room. After I'd been in Hollywood a while, I was allowed to enter those back rooms.

There, cocaine was served on a Waterford crystal dish with a sterling silver spoon, like an exotic spice to be indulged in by the elite. It wasn't presented like the taboo and degrading substance I had heard about. It was the crème de la crème of Hollywood indulging in its own opulence, and most of us didn't realize the danger that it would hold in the future because of the glamour that surrounded the scene. We had all been convinced that we were enjoying a better, safer high than pot or champagne—myself included. It had gotten to the point where people were wearing expensive "coke spoons" on gold chains around their necks. In the coming years, too many people would be ruined by the very things we thought were so harmless in that era.

For years in the sixties Berry warned me that I was "too available" to the public in general and to men in particular. "If you keep more to yourself and stay in your hotel room instead of going out, you'll have more of a star mystique," he would say. "Be more like Diane."

I saw his point, but I wasn't out there only to be a star; I was out to live my life too. I knew how men were, and that's what *I* would call loose. They slept with as many women as they could handle physically. When the Supremes were on tour, we saw women prowling backstage, in hotel lobbies, and in hallways—everywhere—for male stars. Men don't run after women like women run after men. As a woman in show business, I had precious few opportunities to meet men.

Stars from the music business now mixed with people in film and with sports figures as well. The handsome football player-turned-actor Jim Brown lived just up the street from me. I'd known Jim for a couple of years, and it was he who introduced me to Mike Warren around 1969. Mike was then a star basketball player for UCLA. Mike and I started dating. He and I danced many nights away at the Daisy in Beverly Hills, and he took me to all of the UCLA games where I watched him, as the team's captain, play with Kareem Abdul-Jabbar (then Lew Alcindor) and Magic Johnson in their last years of college basketball.

After my relationship with Mike Warren ended, I met and fell in love with Mike's best friend, actor Jack Lucarelli. He was very gregarious and fun. Jack and I took acting classes together and he was wonderful with Willie. Jack invited himself to move in with me, which was fine, but I learned from this experience that I was naturally sort of laid back when it came to assertive men. I needed to speak up for myself more, but how? It was something I vowed to work on.

Not all the men I met were lovers. One of the first people I encountered after moving there was Dr. Hurbert Avery, a successful black physician a few years older than me. He and I checked each other out, but we decided that being friends would be better than being lovers. We have remained friends all these years, and he not only delivered all three of my children in the seventies but was always someone I could turn to. It was Hurbert who helped me when I suffered a bout of depression when I learned Diane would be leaving the Supremes, and he stood by me when I was going through the last stages of my affairs with Tom Jones and the Four Tops' Duke Fakir. When he married, his wife, Mauna Loa, and I became best friends too.

The men I did fall in love with were often other stars. In the mid-sixties I had ended my long relationship with Duke Fakir. I suppose because in my first book I wrote so much about Tom Jones, people assume that he was *the* love of my life. He was certainly one, but the real one was Duke. We still saw each other on and off through the late sixties and early seventies. He is a wonderful person. And by then, my affair with Tom was over, even though we remained friends.

Hollywood offered many more opportunities to meet men, and I'm not ashamed to admit that by the 1970s I was definitely husband hunting. I was at a Hollywood party with Bob Jones, Motown's publicity director, when across the room I spotted actor Steve McQueen. Deep inside I was still an old-fashioned girl, and so I often asked a male friend to introduce me to another man. Even in that era of changing mores, I felt awkward approaching strangers.

After sneaking a few glances Steve's way, I was certain he was looking at me too. Bob introduced us, and we hit it off from the start. He had undeniable charisma. Like many movie stars, Steve was interested in and intrigued by people from the music business.

Despite Steve's reputation for being wild, he was very, very quiet and didn't like being around too many people. He was very gentle, sensitive, and could spend hours talking about anything: animals, comic books, the music business, or weighty philosophical issues. He could be very childlike and sweet. We usually met at his house in Malibu, where we smoked grass on the beach. Steve kept our relationship a secret. It was more an intense friendship than an affair, but there was a physical side to it. He called me his "exotic doll."

Even though I was looking for a husband, several otherwise good relationships ended whenever the subject of marriage came up. This is what happened with Flip Wilson. I first met him in the sixties, when we were playing Leo's Casino, a popular Cleveland club and chitlin-circuit landmark. At the time the Supremes had a couple of hits. Flip was a stand-up comedian in the Redd Foxx mold, performing and recording sexually explicit material.

One evening at Leo's, Diane, Flo, and I were standing in the wings, blushing at Flip's act. After the show, Berry, who was always very protective of "his girls," cornered Flip backstage. "Listen, man, you're going to have to clean up your act, because my girls are good girls. We can't be on a show with acts like yours." The three of us stood out of sight, giggling as Berry threatened to cancel our dates there if Flip didn't tone down his material.

Flip did clean up his act enough to finish the gig, but Berry kept us away from him as much as he could. Flo, Diane, and I still snuck out to see Flip between shows, though. Our paths crossed dozens of times over the next few years, and Berry's warnings aside, we hung out with Flip whenever we worked together. At the time, Flip and I became close friends, but nothing serious. I just thought he was a terrific guy.

Like most people, I'd always thought of Flip as a very funny man. But as I got to know him, I learned that he rarely cracked a joke offstage. At first I found this strange, but I grew to respect his ability to separate private life from public life. I've always been drawn to creative men, but few are secure enough to share their creativity with a woman.

You wouldn't necessarily look at Flip and say, "Hey,

he's sexy," but I can tell you he really was. Flip was terribly romantic and loved women, not just for their bodies or their feminine qualities, but for their intelligence. That was something I always liked in my male friends, and to have it in a love relationship made it even more special.

Flip would sit for hours, writing jokes and working out different situations for material, then say, "What do you think of this?" He'd perform the material for me as if he were on stage. I'd be nearly convulsed with laughter, and with a totally straight face, he'd ask, "What do you think?"

"That was hilarious, Flip!"

"Oh. Okay. Great." Then he'd resume his writing.

After I moved to Los Angeles, Flip and I spent more time together. Willie liked Flip a lot too. He would talk and joke around with Willie, and was a very positive influence.

Flip and I took long, quiet walks, and I loved cooking for him. He would call me up and say, "Make sure you have my dinner ready." One day I decided to make him my famous lemon meringue pie and ended up severing a finger tendon trying to catch the glass pie plate as it fell off the counter. My finger still doesn't straighten out completely. If anyone asks, I say that Flip cut my finger. Or the devil made me do it.

At the time, black people were pulling together, socially and politically, but intermarriage between successful blacks and whites was on the rise. Interracial dating was basically accepted, but any mixed couple would always get second looks wherever they went. Many blacks, myself included, felt it was important to marry within the race. I thought that marrying a black man would complete my life. I was proud of being black and believed that as a black public figure I should set an example. Many black men I knew felt the same way. It wasn't only because of the times; I saw it as a very natural impulse, an expression of blackness.

Flip and I had finished dinner one evening when he became very serious and said, "Will you marry me?" Though I cared for him deeply, I had to say no. There was real love between us, but not the kind I thought went into a marriage. When I told Flip that I didn't think we should marry, he became very upset. "You black women," he grumbled, "when you find a good man, you turn around and marry a white guy."

"Flip, I really do want to marry a black man, but I can't marry you just because you are black."

"I'm a nice guy. I've made something of myself," he implored. "I love you."

I don't know if Flip understood that I was as hurt as he was, but I couldn't see us having a solid marriage. I thought then that only a passionate, all-consuming love could make a marriage. Today, I know differently. Unfortunately, I didn't convey my thoughts to Flip as clearly as I might have. For several months he was very angry, and I respected him for reaching out for the same ideal I too was searching for. Eventually we got to be friends again, but not without some awkwardness.

On May 24, 1970, Cindy became the first Supreme to marry while still in the group. Her husband was a debonair white guy named Charles Hewlett. They met a couple years earlier when he came backstage to see us in Las Vegas. The ceremony took place in the Crystal Room of the San Francisco Fairmont Hotel during one of our engagements. It was a small wedding, with just close friends and family, as well as our band and other people we worked with. The reverend said some beautiful words, very much in the spirit of the times—"God, help us to be groovy people so that our minds will be open"—and read from Kahlil Gibran's *The Prophet*. I was so happy for Cindy and believed in my heart that I would find that same happiness for myself. Someday.

Cindy, Jean, and I were having a ball traveling the country. Our friendship was growing, and everything looked bright for the new Supremes. Throughout the summer we performed live and on television. Prime-time variety shows were still a staple of TV programming, and we appeared regularly on most of them (*The Flip Wilson Show, The Ed Sullivan Show, Glen Campbell's Goodtime Hour,* and later, *The Sonny and Cher Comedy Hour*). In addition, we were popular guests on television specials hosted by Bob Hope, Kate Smith, and other stars, and on talk shows such as David Frost's.

I particularly remember a summer appearance in Central Park, one of our best dates ever. We had special stylists, and a young black designer named Stephen Burrows created for us short, stretchy, white gowns. As Stephen dressed us, he remarked, "Everyone's going to just die when they see you ladies slither out onstage with these sexy dresses. They even get to see your legs!"

Rather than wear our usual elaborate wigs, we had our own hair styled very simply, just pulled straight back off the face and adorned with silver hair ornaments. Standing in the wings, Jean, Cindy, and I looked at one another. We did look fabulous. *And yes,* I thought, *we're going to do it all over again.*

When we strode onstage, the audience went wild. I guess it had been many years since anyone saw a Supreme in anything but a flowing gown or an elegant pantsuit. The sun was just setting; grand old trees surrounded the entire Wollman skating arena; and behind us loomed the old, graceful buildings of Manhattan's Central Park South. It was one of those thrilling moments when everything a performer gives out comes right back tenfold. The ecstatic crowd wouldn't let us leave.

We returned to the Frontier in Las Vegas, scene of the big farewell eight months earlier. Comedian George Carlin opened for us. George wasn't the only comedian we worked with in those days. Rodney Dangerfield, Herb Eden, and Stiller and Meara were just a few of the great ones who were our opening acts.

This particular night in Vegas was fantastic. Ed Sullivan and his wife visited us in our dressing room, and exclaimed how great the group was. Sensing that he still wasn't sure who was who, I said, "Hello, Mr. Sullivan. Mary Wilson." He looked relieved to see that I was one of the girls he'd known since 1964, and that he wouldn't have to guess who was Cindy and who was Jean.

We now knew that the early enthusiastic reviews weren't just flukes. One critic wrote, "The Supremes with Diana Ross were great; without her they're just as good, sometimes better." When we got home from a series of one-nighters through Texas and the South, I was tired but very pleased.

Because I led such a hectic life, I found it comforting to write in the diary I'd kept since I was a teenager. My diary was like my best friend, and in it I expressed a quieter, more vulnerable side of myself than the world usually sees. I wrote:

November 3, 1970

The tour is over, and I am glad. It was one of those decadent tours (private jets, private dinner affairs, etc.), but working in Texas was hell. For example, one show was in a jet hangar. It was over 100° on stage every night, and it was all one-nighters. Sometimes when you're building a career as we are, you have to do extra work. I thank God for this chance to accomplish great things again.

We don't hear more cracks about Diane when we're onstage, so they have accepted us without her. But we need a smash to put us directly on top again. I think "Stoned Love" and the LP will do it.

I put all my hopes on our second album, *New Ways ... but Love Stays.* The performances were uniformly strong, especially our Top 10 hit "Stoned Love." The dramatic orchestrated intro dissolved into a gritty, danceable groove, topped by strings and joyful harmonies. It and many of the other songs on this album captured us as we presented ourselves live: three identifiable vocalists. The record includes beautiful versions of Simon and Garfunkel's "Bridge Over Troubled Water" and the Beatles' "Come Together."

Frank Wilson's contribution to the Supremes at this point was invaluable, and in many ways analogous to Holland-Dozier-Holland's work with the original group. Though the Supremes recorded with several producers before and after H-D-H, it was their songs that initially defined our sound: "Baby Love," "Where Did Our Love Go," "Come See About Me," "I Hear a Symphony," "Stop! In the Name of Love," "You Can't Hurry Love," "You Keep Me Hangin' On," "Back in My Arms Again," "Love Is Here and Now You're Gone," "My World Is Empty Without You," and others. The team's defection from Motown in 1967 was a major blow to the label, but no group felt its impact as acutely as the Supremes.

Frank was one of Motown's younger producer-writers. Along with Berry, Hank Cosby, Deke Richards, and R. Dean Taylor, he had coproduced "Love Child" and "I'm Livin' in Shame," both of which he also cowrote. Aside from his work with us, Frank is best known for producing ex-Temptation Eddie Kendricks ("Boogie Down" and "Keep On Truckin' "), the Four Tops ("Still Water [Love]"), and the young Michael Jackson ("Got to Be There"). Although Frank was not as well known outside of Motown as were some other writers and producers, he was an influential figure. Marvin Gaye credited the Tops' album *Still Waters Run Deep* as the inspiration for his *What's Going On*.

In those days Motown always recorded us on the run. We made our first records with Frank in the little time we could grab between shows. We hurried into the studio, learned the songs, rehearsed them, then recorded our vocals over a prerecorded instrumental track. Today I regret not always being more involved with the writing of our records, especially our albums.

The original Supremes made it when singles counted most, and albums generally consisted of a hit or two, plus eight to ten tracks of "filler." By the early seventies, however, LP sales had become more important. Yet except for albums by writer-artists Marvin Gaye and Stevie Wonder and Norman Whitfield's work with the Temptations, Motown still relied on hit singles. Those of us who didn't compose our own material had less input when it came to our albums. That isn't to say we made no creative contributions (even in the sixties, Diane, Flo, and I helped arrange some of our harmonies), but it wasn't enough.

Cindy, Jean, and I posed for a group portrait in naturals, scant makeup, and black turtleneck sweaters. It was simple, classy, and the shot that I strongly believed should have been the album's front cover. What Motown put out instead was a hodgepodge of little round pictures of us in various stage costumes. At this point in our career, every aspect of our presentation was critical. The baby-pink background with hot-pink girlish type looked outdated: the wrong image at the wrong time.

Even worse, Motown decided the LP couldn't be titled *Stoned Love*. Yes, albums were important, but it took smash singles to draw public attention to them. The country was then in the midst of an antidrug hysteria, with self-appointed experts "discovering" drug references wherever they looked, even in the old Peter, Paul and Mary children's song, "Puff the Magic Dragon"! Our singing "Stoned Love" was actually edited out of a national television show for this reason. Sure, there were drug references in music, but not in *our* music.

When Frank wrote of a stoned love, he meant a real love, a solid love. Just one listen to "Stoned Love," and you knew that it was about love, peace, and faith in God, not getting stoned on drugs. Strangely, Motown didn't hesitate to release the single "Stoned Love" into this hysterical climate, yet worried about an LP with the same title.

I still maintain this album should have been the record to put the Supremes back on top. I think that through its neglect and carelessness, Motown squandered our big chance. *New Ways* settled at a very disappointing Number 68, a poor showing for an album bearing a gold single.

My dismay with the label was eased by the Top 20 success of "River Deep—Mountain High," which we recorded with our friends the Four Tops. (The single came from *The Magnificent 7*, the first of three LPs our two groups did together.) Since Diana Ross and the Supremes enjoyed two phenomenal albums and two historic television specials with the Temptations in 1968 and 1969, pairing us with the Four Tops was a natural. "River Deep—Mountain High" was an exciting record, and Levi Stubbs's and Jean's voices a dynamic combination.

As 1970 ended, we could look back on our first year with pride: two gold singles, four Top 25 hits, and a tour schedule fully booked into 1972. Unfortunately for Diane, she hadn't made quite the solo splash she and Berry had counted on. Her first single, "Reach Out and Touch (Somebody's Hand)"—now her theme song—stopped at Number 20. (I've read that she previously recorded the song while with the Supremes, but that's not true. Even so, we often got requests to sing it; people thought it was a Supremes song.) That fall Diane's cover, or remake, of the Marvin Gaye–Tammi Terrell classic "Ain't No Mountain High Enough" went to Number One, but it would be nearly three years before another Top 10 single.

Partly, this was no doubt due to the fact that Diane's decision to leave the Supremes was not popular with everyone. Many people also blamed her personally for Flo's ouster. When Diane opened solo at the Frontier Hotel, the room wasn't even sold out. So much for the misconception that Diane rocketed to superstardom after leaving the Supremes, while we floundered. Berry must have been puzzled; this wasn't how it was supposed to be.

CHAPTER 4

No matter how enthusiastically the Supremes were received onstage or how many records the group sold, in the eyes of the corporate powers at Motown, we were employees, plain and simple. Except for Diane, none of us was treated like a star. As the Motown myth got retold and reinvented, Berry and the machine loomed larger and more important than the writers, producers, musicians, and performers. I noticed that with each year Motown assumed more credit for making the artists what they were. Whenever we were billed for a concert or television appearance, it wasn't "The Supremes," but "Motown Presents the Supremes" or "Motown's Supremes."

By the early seventies Motown began its transition from the local label, where everybody was family, to an impersonal business. Most people see the early-1968 crosstown move from the original Hitsville building on West Grand Boulevard to a large office building on Woodward Avenue as the big change, for Hitsville had been home.

In the late sixties, whenever we had a few days off in Detroit and found out the Tops or the Tempts were recording, Cindy and I went down to Hitsville and stayed all day. By the time we left, we'd seen everybody who was in town. Then a group of us would head over to my house for a party, where we'd dance, sing, and laugh all night. Motown's choreographer, Cholly Atkins, still lived in part of the duplex I owned. He'd be rehearsing some other acts in his basement, and so the party would grow. Some people believe the artists weren't as close as we thought we were. But whenever we got together, it was like a family reunion, and it's still like that today.

That first move symbolized a big change, but we would never guess how big. I was just becoming confident with my new life in California when I got the news. "Did you hear Motown is closing down its offices in Detroit and moving to Hollywood?" someone asked me. I couldn't believe it.

Without any emotions involved, it did make sense. Berry had moved there to live and found the West Coast preferable to Detroit. Business was in Los Angeles, and with Berry interested in television and movie production, the relocation made sense. The 1967 riots were a factor too.

Motown's West Coast move didn't become official until 1972, but our home base was already being dismantled. Not all those who had worked and made Motown their life were invited along; many were left in Detroit, where they had to find new jobs after years of service. Some stayed behind by choice. For the most part, the Motown family as we'd known it was over.

The biggest changes in Motown, however, were taking place behind closed doors. Once on the West Coast, Berry began turning over the day-to-day operation to handpicked assistants such as Suzanne dePasse, Ewart Abner, Barney Ales, and Mike Roshkind.

Supreme Faith

Suzanne dePasse, in her twenties, was the youngest. She'd been booking talent at a New York City club called the Cheetah and was introduced to Berry by Cindy in the late sixties. Suzanne moved up rapidly and before long was Berry's protégée. Once Berry appointed anyone, that was who everyone had to impress, even though they might talk about the person behind his or her back. Many of the old-timers wondered whether Suzanne could handle everything Berry threw her way, but she did. She also brought aboard a new way of thinking about artists and records. I must say that of anyone at the label, she seemed to be the person most behind the Supremes. Today she is the executive director of Motown Productions.

Ewart Abner, a short, fair-skinned black man, had been president of the Chicago-based independent Vee-Jay Records label. Initially he was director of Motown's management division, International Talent Management. Of all Berry's assistants, smooth, personable Abner had the best rapport with the artists, creating the impression that he was on their side. If you went to him, no matter how upset you were, he was reassuring and sympathetic, always saying that he would take care of it. Whether he actually did was an entirely different story.

Barney Ales, the head of sales, had worked with Berry almost from the beginning and in 1960 was appointed vice president of sales and distribution. Barney had a hand in writing "Buttered Popcorn," one of our early singles in which Flo sang lead.

Mike Roshkind joined Motown in 1966. Many artists referred to him as "Berry's hatchet man." On a personal level, Mike and I generally got along well. He was a very effective executive who knew how to get things done, and with Berry gradually abdicating his role as Motown's leader, the company badly needed someone like Mike. Tall and distinguished-looking, Mike, like many of Berry's upper-echelon people, was white. His friendly manner never compromised his directness, and he could turn ice-cold in an instant. Mike was the heavy, the iron fist in Motown's otherwise velvet glove.

In the early days, you always saw Berry around Hitsville and could call him on the phone. Now if you needed to reach Berry, you had to go through Mike. While Berry pled ignorance about whatever went on in his absence, we all suspected differently. Rather than delegating full authority to the executives and staffers, in truth, Berry still needed to control things. Accordingly, the new Motown was set up so that even those with titles and the trappings of power still needed Berry's approval. Everything came down to Berry Gordy. I think this was Motown's biggest problem: it relied on the personal vision of a leader who was largely out of the picture.

In Los Angeles Berry was among his peers—other big-time wheelers and dealers—and he fully enjoyed it. The first time I visited his new home, it was graphically clear that Berry was a success. His house, formerly owned by one of the Smothers Brothers, had underwater tunnels and bridges in and around the pool. Among his guests were the biggest stars in Hollywood. Berry was obviously very, very happy.

Berry's team—dePasse, Abner, Ales, and Roshkind—was pleasant enough to deal with. But it was becoming increasingly difficult to get the simplest thing taken care of. Not only was the family feeling gone, but the artists had to deal with strangers and a whole new set of rules. It was the beginning of the end for many of us. We'd come off a three-week tour and go straight from the plane to the studio, only to find that someone in charge was too tired to work or didn't feel like it. That *never* would have happened at Hitsville.

True to her word, Jean Terrell maintained her individuality and was always completely honest and forthright with the press. Motown had abandoned its long-standing policy of overseeing (basically controlling) press access, so we were freer to say what was really on our minds. And Jean did.

Like Flo, Jean was incapable of pretending to believe in something she didn't. She felt very strongly that entertainers should address political and social issues. This seemed quite a switch for a Supreme, and some people couldn't reconcile our female fantasy image with some of Jean's blunt statements. The funny thing was that Cindy and I also began commenting on political issues when appropriate, but because we were viewed as friendly and outgoing, the same statements were perceived a little differently. Maybe they didn't take us as seriously.

Jean knew that joining the group meant conforming to our image on *and* off the stage. Being a Supreme really was a twenty-four-hour-a-day job. You not only had to look your best wherever you went, you had to be your best. This meant always being a lady: dressing stylishly, being friendly to everyone, and never leaving the house without your eyelashes. After so many years, and having been a clotheshorse my whole life anyway, this was second nature to me, and to Cindy as well. Looking back, I'm amazed at how many column inches writers devoted to discussions of the big question: When would the Supremes stop wearing wigs and sport naturals, which to many symbolized black pride.

At first Jean found our whole glamour dimension fascinating, but it wasn't long before its thrill wore off. Little by little she took less of an interest in dressing up around the clock. If the three of us had to make a special appearance or go to an interview, Cindy and I wore clothes that were casual but chic. Jean, in contrast, preferred dressing simply, which was fine. It just wasn't what people expected. I saw no contradiction in being proud of my blackness and being glamorous. She did.

Jean admitted that some people interpreted her shyness and nervousness the wrong way. She didn't mean to appear unfriendly, but that was how many of our fans took her, which was too bad. If the three of us were together, Jean often sat by herself. She had a special friendship with Cindy, and I came to rely on Cindy and our wardrobe mistress, Jan Dochier, to communicate with her.

With the start of 1971, I resolved to take greater control of my life. As with most Motown artists, the label had always handled my business and personal finances. It rankled me to have to ask Motown's permission before I made major purchases. All I knew about how much money I had was what Motown told me; I never saw any statements.

When I finally hired outside accountants to look into my personal business and the Supremes', I was shocked to discover that the "hundreds of thousands of dollars" Berry and Motown had repeatedly assured me were in my account actually amounted to *one* hundred thousand. And when I asked that it be released to me, I was told I needed Berry's signature!

My first reaction was anger; I'd been betrayed, fooled. After I calmed down, I dialed Berry's number.

"Hello, Berry. This is Mary. Look, I want to handle all my own money now."

"What do you mean?" he asked, surprised. "Mary, you can't take it out. This is one hundred thousand tax-free dollars. My name is on it for your protection."

Protection from what? I wondered. I was also a little mystified by this "tax-free dollars" business. Of course at this point it was tax-free; I'd already paid the taxes on it years ago when I earned it!

Supreme Faith

Berry finally gave in reluctantly. This was a positive first step, but it still hurt me. Motown had always told us it was investing the money for our own good. What I had were a few stocks and an investment made purely for its tax write-off value. Before, I knew that I didn't fully understand my own business; now it hit me how much I didn't know. For example, I didn't know how many records the Supremes sold, what expenses we'd paid over the years, or what I was entitled to. People at Motown had led me to believe I had made millions, and why would I have doubted them? *After all,* I thought, *the Supremes have made Motown many millions.*

I remembered all the times journalists asked, "How are you girls set for the future?" I'd smile and proudly say, "Oh, Motown is investing for us. Plus all of our taxes are paid on time. We're being well taken care of." I guess the laugh was on me. Now, this isn't to say $100,000 is small change; it's not. But put it in perspective: an artist with a midlevel hit makes that amount on a single record. When I think about our twelve Number Ones—more than anyone in our time except the Beatles and Elvis Presley—plus the hit albums, the television specials and appearances, the sold-out concerts, and then see what I have to show for it all, it makes me sick, and, believe me, I was not a big spender.

As I probed more deeply into my finances, I realized I needed an expert's help. Chuck Barnett from the William Morris Agency told me of a young Englishwoman named Hazel Bethke who might fit the bill, and she did. Hazel brought order, friendship, and a spiritual love into my life that endured for many years. Although she left me in 1989, I will never forget her tireless efforts to keep my personal and professional lives running smoothly in the early days. She worked around the clock, was available for any emergency, whether it was taking care of Willie or dealing with the banks or Motown. With Hazel's help I could really begin to direct the

Supremes' career and oversee business details that would have been unthinkable otherwise.

On January 20, 1971, Diane married Robert Silberstein (known professionally as Bob Ellis), a white public-relations executive, in Las Vegas. It was a surprise to a lot of people. When I heard the announcement on the radio, I smiled to myself and recalled how Diane used to ask me, "Mary, what do you see in all those white guys you date?" She always thought she would wed Berry someday, so I guess the question of marrying a white man never crossed her mind back then. Exactly why she did not become Mrs. Berry Gordy has never been totally clear. Only a year before at the farewell show in Vegas, Diane had said from the stage, "I am now part of the Gordy family; I am a sister." But as much as Berry may have loved Diane romantically, his primary attraction to her was—and would always be—professional.

In February we began work on our last album with Frank Wilson, *Touch,* probably our most rock-oriented work and, I think, our best. We recorded it all over the country, wherever we happened to be performing. The first single, "Nathan Jones," was the most unusual hit of our career, with its unorthodox blues-based structure and unison lead singing. Jean's vocals are pulled out of the mix ever so slightly, then our three voices break into harmony. As with almost everything Frank did for us, we loved this the minute we heard it. The psychedelic electric guitar and electronically treated vocals made "Nathan Jones" a great, unique record, and it reached Number 16, our fifth consecutive single to go Top 25.

This album was the first Supremes LP to be reviewed by *Rolling Stone.* As much as I've always taken critics with a grain of salt, the review showed me that we could reach a new, wider audience. *"Touch* is an unqualified success and the final proof that the Supremes will continue without Diana

Ross," Jon Landau wrote. Other critics continued to note our new concept and direction.

For reasons I could only guess at then, Motown simply didn't push the LP or the follow-up single, "Touch." The latter was different for us, because while I was singing some leads on each album and in our shows, this was the first 45 we'd released with Jean and me sharing leads. The lyrics were very sexy; this was a real soul love ballad. Still, nothing. It was our first flop, stalling outside the Top 40. Perhaps Berry's threat was rearing its ugly head.

Not long after *Touch* we stopped seeing Frank Wilson around. He was deservedly proud of the three albums he'd made with the Supremes but understandably disappointed with how poorly they charted. Jean, Cindy, and I felt the same way. The unfortunate thing about Frank's not working with us again after *Touch* was that our new sound was finally beginning to evolve.

The Supremes' releases began having trouble just as black music was entering a state of flux. Even during the golden sixties, Motown's records could not have crossed over to white record buyers without airplay on rock-and-roll-dominated Top 40 AM radio stations. In the late sixties album-oriented "progressive" FM radio drew away millions of AM listeners. While the new FM rock stations might play records by Marvin Gaye and Stevie Wonder, most of Motown's current singles-oriented acts—us, Diane, the Jackson 5, the Four Tops—suddenly "didn't fit."

Radio, since the late fifties the great ground of musical racial integration, was again segregated. Disc jockeys, who in the fifties and sixties picked what they played, lost programming control to consultants. The reviving force of black radio would be disco, which, it turns out, was another nail in the coffin for those of us who believed there was more to black music than dance music.

Beginning with "Up the Ladder to the Roof," I noticed a distinct difference in what having a hit single meant. In the sixties a Top 20 hit was played everywhere, and people couldn't help but know about it. That all changed. Suddenly you could have a successful hit that an average audience would not immediately recognize, or, worse, might not have ever heard.

In the sixties, even though not everyone in our live audience bought all our records, at least they recognized the hits. Now we would perform one of our four million-sellers—"Up the Ladder to the Roof," "Stoned Love," "Nathan Jones," and later, "Floy Joy"—and maybe receive just lukewarm applause. They didn't know our songs anymore.

Another, more insidious, reason behind this was that Motown stopped promoting our records the way it had in the past. People assume that hits "just happen," but that's not true, not even for the biggest stars. Each year thousands of records are released, yet only a few hundred get heard at all. If two acts are equally talented, the biggest difference between the unknown and the star is promotion: radio play, advertising, television appearances, print publicity. In fact, besides manufacturing the record, promotion is a record company's key job. Record promotion to radio stations is so integral to artists' careers that the government investigates instances of its abuse: payola, or play for pay. A record without promotion is like the proverbial tree that falls in the woods. Without Motown's clout behind us, we drifted.

While the Supremes were starting to struggle, Flo's solo career had quickly gone down the drain. Since leaving the group, she kept in touch with me; we called and wrote whenever we could. She was still in Detroit, married to Tommy Chapman, and the mother of twin girls. ABC Records, which signed Flo in March 1968, dropped her after her first two singles failed. Her last moment in the spotlight was a performance at President Richard Nixon's 1968 inaugural. By March 1970, when she came to see us perform at the Elmwood Casino, across the bridge from Detroit in Windsor, Canada, it was the beginning of the end of her solo career.

Only a month before, Flo became the first Motown artist to publicly break rank. She filed a $8.7 million lawsuit against the label, charging, among other things, that her firing from the Supremes was part of a conspiracy. Among the codefendants were me, Diane, Berry, Mike Roshkind, Ralph Seltzer (another Motown executive), Cindy, and Jean. As part of her original 1968 settlement, Flo received about $160,000, but her attorney misappropriated all of it. The judge had no sympathy for Flo, ruling in late 1971 that because she was unable to return any of the money and hadn't "done what she should have done" under the law, her suit wouldn't even be tried.

Flo had to name me in the suit, but I didn't take it personally, as some people thought I should. When it comes to business and law, sometimes you must do things you may not want to. I understood this, and I wrote Flo a letter telling her so. The post office returned it to me, unopened, claiming it could not deliver the letter. Flo never saw it.

While the press focused on Flo's provocatively worded charge that Diane had "secretly, subversively, and maliciously plotted and planned" to run her out, the suit raised another point that would be of increasing interest to me as the years passed: the issue of who owned the Supremes' name. Her attorneys contended that because she coined the name *Supremes*, she was entitled to share in its commercialization. They stood by this claim, even though part of the settlement she worked out with Mike Roshkind forbade her to ever identify herself as a former member of the group. For example, the word *Supremes* could not appear in her artist's biography from her new label. In addition to the $8.7 million, Flo's suit called for the Supremes name to be taken off the market.

Flo and I talked about the suit. She was extremely angry and knew that she had been terribly wronged. With little else happening in her professional life, she focused on her fight against Berry. I worried that her anger would consume her, but I also understood that you can't keep your pride and self-respect when people treat you this badly. Despite the suit's charges and all Flo's talk, she never wanted to hurt any of us, and, surprisingly, least of all Diane. Berry was a different story. She hated what he had done to her, and I don't blame her. Because now, slowly, it was happening to us.

I tried to help Flo channel her anger constructively. My main concern was that she do things right: research everything, find the right attorney, know what's going on. Instead she seemed obsessed with the very idea that she was suing Motown. She couldn't see the kinds of games they were playing, and believed that right would take care of itself.

Throughout the summer we kept up our frenzied pace, criss-crossing the country. Because the Supremes lacked a monster hit, initial enthusiasm for us started to fade. Sometimes standing onstage, even amid the cheers and applause, I sensed the skepticism of some people in the crowd. It was as if we had to prove ourselves, over and over again. There always seemed to be someone sitting out there in the dark, arms crossed, whose face said, "Show me." I fully believed we could.

For years I had been begging Berry and our managers to devise some kind of long-range plan for us. Especially once I took in Willie and Cindy married, we needed schedules where we worked six months a year, with the rest off. But now we depended more on touring to make up the money we weren't earning from records. It was a vicious cycle with just one way out: a Number One record. If we had that hit, it would be like getting sprinkled with fairy dust. Cindy and I had experienced years of professional ups and downs; we understood the business. For Jean, however, it must have felt like her gilded carriage was turning into a pumpkin before she got halfway to the ball. By mid-1971 all three of us were doing something unimaginable in Motown's earlier days: complaining publicly about our record company.

In August we teamed up with the Four Tops for a run at the Carter Barron Amphitheatre in Washington, D.C. One goal was to promote our second joint album, *The Return of the Magnificent Seven,* but, as it turned out, the album got no higher than Number 154—an embarrassment for all of us. Its successor, *Dynamite,* placed six positions lower. Within the year the Tops would be among the first of Motown's major groups to abandon Berry and his gang for another label. As Duke Fakir said, "We left Motown because we felt they were killing us, and we wanted to survive."

On opening night in Washington we made our standard fake exit and then waited in the wings, expecting the applause that would bring us back for the last number. Nothing. After a few seconds, we returned to the stage and stepped into a performer's nightmare: the audience was out of their seats, heading for the door. Jean announced, "We've got one more song we'd like to do," then we went into our rendition of the theme from *Exodus.* It was a painful, mortifying moment. How could this happen to the Supremes?

I still hadn't found Mr. Right, so although I was dating less, I was looking. In Las Vegas I met and had a brief flirtation with Bill Medley of the Righteous Brothers. Bill always struck me as a very sexy guy. He is also one of the kindest, gentlest men around. We remain friends. In fact, in 1989 he and I shot a pilot for a possible television series.

Even when we weren't working Vegas, I'd go there on

weekends and see friends' shows around town. Diahann Carroll was performing, so I caught her show. I'd known her for many years. To the public, she is a classy, beautiful woman, but among her friends she's also very friendly, soulful, and down to earth. At this time, she was dating David Frost, the English talk-show host. Seated at our table was George Hamilton. Later George and I went out on the town and had a wild time. I'd always thought he would be smug and square, but take it from me, he was anything but.

In November we embarked on a triumphant tour of Great Britain. Ever since the first transatlantic Motown Revue hit England in 1965, it's been one of my favorite places in the world. I've always appreciated that the British respect performers for what they have to offer, with or without current hits. That's why countless performers move or spend large parts of each year there and in Europe.

Our stateside lack of the elusive big hit did not diminish our British fans' love for us. In fact, as many British writers pointed out, Diane's leaving mattered very little there, and our records always charted higher and did much better in the U.K. than they did in the U.S. This was interesting, because with Diane, only one of our singles went to Number One there, compared to twelve here, and of those, only half made the British Top 10. Our track record there since Jean had joined was great: "Up the Ladder," Number 6; "Stoned Love," Number 3; "Nathan Jones," Number 5.

We played sold-out houses everywhere, which was very heartening. The highlight was a show at the Royal Albert Hall before Princess Margaret and Lord Snowdon. It was a charity event, with the Four Tops headlining. I had met Princess Margaret before, and so at the after-show party, Obie Benson of the Tops and I chatted with her at length about politics. This was one of the tours I took Willie on. Everywhere we went, he was the perfect little gentleman.

When we returned to the States in December, it marked the end of almost eighteen continuous months on the road. I decided to work even harder. Jean became more critical of Motown. She declared that she would no longer record whatever she was given but would "veto" and refuse to sing material she did not like. Some of her remarks sounded quite defensive, and writers ate it right up. She told one English reporter, "The Supremes were a status group before I came in, and my joining them didn't take away any of the status, as far as I'm concerned. But maybe in people's minds it did."

We were also growing weary of answering the same questions about Diane. Were we still friends? How often did we see her? How did it feel to go on without her? How did Jean feel stepping into her shoes? I loved and cherished the connection to the old Supremes and our—*my*—past, but I was torn. I had to be loyal to the new group, or they would feel I was a traitor. Through no fault of Diane's, her spectre still hung over us like a dark shadow.

Considering this, it came as no surprise that Jean began withdrawing from us and stating her position more strongly. Sometimes when I heard her comments or later read them, I winced. There was nothing the press loved better than a feud.

When Jean first came in she made it clear to everyone that she was not about to be one of three singing puppets. She was a true individualist, and this was why Berry wanted her out of the group following the farewell show. But instead of continuing to insist that we replace her or just firing her outright—which he could have done—he played it cool. He seemed to know that if he gave the Supremes enough rope, we might hang ourselves. Without realizing it, Jean grabbed it and ran, and so did I.

CHAPTER 5

"O kay, baby," Smokey said, "try it like this."

I sang, "Floy, floy, floy—floy joy, you're the man. I hope in some way, form or fashion I fit in your plans." He smiled. "That's great, Mary."

Cindy, Jean, and I were recording our fourth album, *Floy Joy*, with Smokey Robinson. Besides singing with his group, the Miracles, Smokey is one of the world's greatest songwriters and producers. He also has been a vice president at Motown since the early sixties. I was so surprised and thrilled when I learned we'd be working with him.

Things had come full circle. Smokey was one of the first producers to record the original Supremes; the song was "Who's Loving You," a ballad. I'll never forget the moment in 1960 when Smokey handed the lead sheet to Diane and not to me. I'd always sung our ballads and was sure I'd be doing this one too. (This was even before Berry designated Diane lead singer.) My heart broke, but I put aside my personal feelings, something I'd do a lot over the years.

While from 1964 on Holland-Dozier-Holland pretty much had the Supremes to themselves, we recorded a number of Smokey's songs, especially in the beginning. Though none was a big hit, Smokey remains one of my favorite producers to work with. He was always perfectly organized and had everything—the arrangements, the lyrics—worked out down to the tiniest detail. Being a performer himself, he really understood singers. He also gave me a great surprise: Smokey had written the album's title track with me in mind. During the sessions, he was so supportive and patient, guiding me through my lead lines on "Floy Joy." It was an experience and a kindness I will never forget.

Smokey came up with some beautiful, sexy, close harmonies, especially for "Floy Joy," and the album really sparkled. Suprisingly, while "Floy Joy" became a Top 20 hit in spring 1972 and remains a perennial favorite among our fans, few people know that it was a duet between Jean and me. A second single, "Automatically Sunshine," on which I sang lead, didn't do as well, though it did hit Number One in some local markets, including Washington, D.C., and Honolulu.

Because it was the first time I'd been in a studio with Smokey since the early sixties, we did a lot of talking, about Diane and her career (we both agreed she deserved all the good things that came her way) and about everybody else we knew, but mostly about what was going on at Motown with the Supremes. Thinking that Smokey would be more understanding than the corporate people, since he was an artist as well as an executive, I gave it a shot.

"You know, Smokey, I don't understand what it is. We're making good records and working hard, but Motown isn't giving us the push," I said. "I just don't know what we should do about it. I feel like we're getting good material but going nowhere."

Smokey thought for a minute, then said, "Why don't you talk to Berry about it? I'm sure if you do, he'll take care of it. Everything will be all right."

Smokey meant well, but he was like Diane: totally blinded by Berry's razzle-dazzle. Because Berry always treated Smokey and Diane differently than the rest of us, they see him differently than we do. Unlike most everyone else at Motown, Smokey and Diane could take Berry at his word. It wasn't Smokey's fault.

Everything about *Floy Joy* gave me hope. These tracks were the realization of what I'd felt the Supremes should be. Smokey achieved a beautiful blend of our voices, especially on "Automatically Sunshine." Again I was sure that we'd found a match as perfect for the Supremes as Holland-Dozier-Holland were in the sixties. And after losing Frank Wilson, having Smokey now was the best thing that could happen to us, and I wanted him to be our producer forever.

Cindy was expecting her first child in the fall and didn't plan to return to the group after that. She had always been very open about whatever was on her mind, and many times she mentioned that she might leave. Still, it was a surprise when she finally announced she was going. Whatever Cindy was into, she gave it her all. Her new family was no exception. Cindy's husband Charles often traveled with us, and they really enjoyed the show-business life. But once a baby enters the picture, things get complicated.

One evening in Washington, D.C., the three of us caught Stevie Wonder's show and noticed a great singer in his backing vocal group, Wonderlove. Sandra Tucker came to audition for us in Detroit and brought along her sister Lynda, whom we'd also seen in Wonderlove. Once we saw Lynda we realized that even though Sandra was a great singer, Lynda was who we wanted in the group. (Coincidentally, Sandra had replaced Cindy Birdsong in Patti LaBelle and the Bluebelles when Cindy left them to join the Supremes in 1967.)

The three of us had an instant rapport. Lynda was very outgoing and lively. When she was around, someone was always laughing. Her basic attitude was extremely positive, and that was something we desperately needed.

"You know, Mary," she said, "we have a friend in common."

"Oh, who?"

"Cholly Atkins."

As it turned out, she had rehearsed with Cholly at my house many times. Then she said, "I'm a Pisces," and I said, "I am too." That sealed it for me. When I learned that her father was Ira Tucker of the esteemed gospel group the Dixie Hummingbirds, I told her about how on our early bus tours the Temptations often broke into Hummingbirds songs a cappella. All this seemed to point to Lynda being the girl I was looking for.

Lynda adopted the stage name Lynda Laurence (or Lawrence; she later married musician Trevor Lawrence). A native of Philadelphia, she began performing with her father's group as a child. In her teens she formed a band with her brother and two friends, and then moved to Detroit, where she performed as a solo artist. Lynda met Stevie Wonder, and along with her sister Sandra and a cousin joined Stevie's backup group. Her first recording with Stevie was his 1970 hit "Signed, Sealed, Delivered." The trio, later rechristened Wonderlove, remained with Stevie until we "discovered" Lynda.

As Lynda told reporters afterward, she was thrilled to be a Supreme. We began rehearsing her immediately, and she worked every day with Cholly Atkins to learn the steps. Lynda came to our shows in Windsor, Canada, and studied tapes of us. We were scheduled to embark on an extensive tour of Australia soon, and I wanted her to go with us.

The shows in Windsor went well, and many people came to see us, including Berry and Flo. I was very happy that Flo was out, because she'd started withdrawing from the world ever since a judge threw out her lawsuit against Motown in November 1971. When Flo met Lynda backstage, she said, "That girl is really going to be good. She'll add some personality to the group."

The night Berry attended was one of the very few times he returned to the Detroit area after moving to Los Angeles. Back in the dressing room, he remarked, "I'm really pleasantly surprised at how good your show is." Then we got on to the subject of his new film venture, and he boasted, "Diana and I are going to make it."

"Berry," I said, "I know you and Diane are going to make it, but I am too."

"Yeah, but Diana and me are going to *fly*, and you'll have to go door-to-door."

Heart-to-heart talks between Berry and me were rare these days. When we did have them, there seemed to be another motive at work on his part. As he spoke proudly about his future plans, I recalled playing blackjack with him to pass the time on the road many years before. Once, in 1965, we stopped a game, and he owed me $4,000. "Oh, Berry," I said, "you know you don't have to pay me. It's just a game." His face lit up with relief.

"Okay, Mary, great!"

A few days later Berry beat me hand after hand. We kept score in dollars, but I really didn't think that he was playing for real. Finally, when I was in the hole $6,200, Berry said, "Okay, pay up. Give me my money."

"But Berry, the other day I let you go—"

"That was *you*, Mary," Berry interrupted. "It's a lesson

you have to learn." I ended up paying him every cent of the $6,200 over time. I suppose he wanted to teach me that not everyone was like me; certainly not Berry Gordy.

Around this time we started recording with Jimmy Webb. Though Lynda wasn't yet officially in the group, she sang on this album. (Some people assume she was on *Floy Joy* because Lynda is pictured on the cover, not Cindy. Due to her pregnancy and imminent departure, Cindy declined to appear in that photo.) I remember Jean, Lynda, and I staying up almost all night at my place after a session and talking. I was so happy and felt that we were on our way. Again.

Jimmy was the Supremes' first non-Motown producer, and it struck some people as an unusual pairing. Working with Jimmy was the idea of our latest manager, Wayne Weisbart, assigned to us by Motown. I was surprised but thrilled that the label let us use an outside producer. Jimmy had written such hits as "Up, Up and Away," "MacArthur Park," "By the Time I Get to Phoenix," "Wichita Lineman," and "Galveston," and produced Thelma Houston's beautiful album *Sunshower.* Interestingly, he had also worked briefly as a house writer for Motown's song-publishing division, Jobete Music, some years before. Jimmy released a few solo albums, but his performing career was eclipsed by his outstanding work as a writer and producer.

Jimmy was extremely quiet, and we got along very well. He struck me as one of those rare people who don't just make music, but have the music inside them, much like Marvin Gaye. One thing we liked about Jimmy was that he respected us and listened to our opinions. His approach differed from what we were used to. While he worked out all the musical details beforehand like most Motown producers, Jimmy encouraged our input. He taught you the melody, but then expected you to do your own thing.

The resulting LP, *The Supremes Produced and Arranged by Jimmy Webb* (originally titled *Beyond Myself*), was radically different from *Floy Joy*. Once again we were back to being a lead singer with two backup vocalists. I did sing one song, "I Keep It Hid." (In 1989 Linda Ronstadt covered this on her album *Cry Like a Rainstorm*.) The other selections included Joni Mitchell's "All I Want," Harry Nilsson's "Paradise," and the rock oldie "Tossin' and Turnin'." Stephen Schwartz's "I Guess I'll Miss the Man" from the Motown-financed Broadway musical *Pippin* was the first single. It was the LP's only cut not produced by Jimmy.

As much as I loved this album, several things about it were not in the Supremes' best interest. For example, Jimmy brought in additional background vocalists. After Smokey's having achieved that perfect vocal blend, I saw this as another big step backward. Except for Jean, the group on *Floy Joy* and the group on *The Supremes* might have been two different entities. Still, *The Supremes* received many very positive reviews, all commending our willingness to experiment. It was a great disappointment when "I Guess I'll Miss the Man" sold poorly, and the album became only the second in the Supremes' history not to enter the Top 100 (the first had been 1968's *Funny Girl*).

We hadn't set a definite date for Cindy's departure, but proceeded with our schedule. She sang with us live, and Lynda recorded with us. We had some time off after the March date in Windsor and were looking forward to the upcoming April tour of Australia. Unfortunately, Willie and I had to attend my maternal grandmother's funeral in Mississippi. We got home the day we were to leave for Australia. The minute Willie and I walked in the house my housekeeper Geneva said, "Mary, there's some bad news. Jean is in the hospital." My friend Dr. Hurbert Avery was caring for her, and while it was not clear to me exactly what her problem was, he was emphatic that she not work for as long as eight weeks. Did that mean the tour was off?

After a couple minutes the magnitude of the crisis seeped in. I started crying. It seemed that whenever I thought that everything was fine, another problem arose. Willie put his arms around me protectively, and I plopped down on a large floor pillow and started making calls. Soon our staff people arrived to discuss our options.

Our manager Wayne had left for Australia earlier, assuming we would follow. When we finally reached him, I said, "Even without Jean, we should do the tour. Lynda's been recording with us, she knows the show, and she can step right in." Wayne disagreed and wanted to cancel but said he'd talk to the promoters and see what they thought. On Sunday, however, we were still in limbo. I visited Jean in the hospital. She was in good spirits, but her health was still in danger. "Jean, we're going to try to go ahead with Lynda singing lead," I said.

"Whatever you have to do is all right with me; I understand," she answered.

After talking to the rest of the staff and to Lynda I became excited; I knew we could do it. I phoned Mike Roshkind, who agreed it was best to go ahead and promised to get right to work on the details. Yet shortly after that, someone else called and said, "Mary, Mike has officially canceled the tour." I was devastated and confused. Over the next couple days I tried to put the tour back together, but Motown had decided, and that was it. We did, however, manage to do a couple of the tour's last few dates, in Hawaii, with Lynda, and she was great. Still, the idea that people who did not have my best interests in mind were controlling and making decisions about my life bothered me. They weren't paying my bills anymore; who were they to say whether we would perform or not? I knew I had to take more control, and I proceeded to do just that. I could no longer delude myself that Motown was on my side. It was me against them. They didn't care what happened to me, but I did. And I knew I had to survive.

Jean recovered sooner than expected, and we resumed our schedule, opening at New York's Copacabana on June 1. We were doing three shows a night, which was tiring but exhilarating. Toward the end of our first week, Lynda called. "Mary? Jean is very sick again, and she's on her way back to Los Angeles."

"She's what?"

"She's going back to Los Angeles. She's on her way to the airport now."

"What's wrong?" I asked.

"I don't know."

"Okay," I said, stunned. "I'll see you later."

I sat back in bed, feeling guilty for what I was thinking. This was beginning to strike me as a little bit fishy. No one would ever tell me exactly what Jean's health problem was. Coincidentally, it seemed to crop up when she was unhappy. I didn't really believe this, of course, but I couldn't help thinking it. Well, there was nothing I could do but put it out of my mind and tackle the problem at hand. Would we cancel the shows or go on, just Lynda and me, as a duo? Copa owner Jules Podell was not pleased with either choice, and Motown and our agent wanted to cancel.

Cindy came in and did the shows with us on Saturday and Sunday, with Lynda singing lead. We had only the gowns we'd brought with us, and Cindy's pregnancy was showing, so the fit wasn't perfect. Cindy was happy to be back, and I was thankful for her flying in on a moment's notice. Then on Tuesday, Jean was back, and I got sick, so for the first and only time the Supremes performed without a single original member on the stage. And I'm sorry to say, I doubt anyone in the audience noticed or cared. Were we really that interchangeable, after all?

Later that night, I wrote in my diary:

> I've always prided myself on being able to stay happy regardless of any misfortune. Maybe I was too young before to totally understand problems. Now when I look at people, I see things that I've never seen before.
>
> Tonight I realize that I cannot be totally happy through my career alone. It's been a long time since I've had a boyfriend. I decided that after my one love, I'd work hard on my career and give up my love life and stop being so free with the men I dated. I realize I cannot substitute my career for love. I even tried to use little Willie to be completely happy. My career was always enough to keep me happy.
>
> Actually, with Jean being ill on the last show, I should be in tears. Whatever was wrong has made her cancel out of tomorrow's press conference. Plus, the fans really missed her. Well, the day is over, and I lay here in the tub, soaking. After working these two shows, I reek like a truck driver. They just ran a lot of our old records on the TV oldies-but-goodies record commercial. I realize how much I have at stake.

In June we switched managers and started working again with Shelly Berger, who'd managed Diana Ross and the Supremes in the sixties. All during a meeting to discuss our upcoming summer tour with the Temptations, the managers and Motown people talked around Lynda, Jean, and me as if we weren't there. Then we discovered that not only were the Supremes the opening act, but we were billed under the Tempts. They were selling more records and had some big hits recently, like "Just My Imagination" and "Superstar," but still, this was a real blow to us. After we saw the itinerary, the only conclusion we could draw was that Motown was trying to kill us by working us to death.

We started rehearsals for the tour, and in some ways it was like old times, especially with Melvin Franklin and me. Melvin and I had crushes on each other when we were teens, and we've been dear friends ever since. But things were different, too. David Ruffin had left the group back in 1968, then Paul Williams and Eddie Kendricks in 1971. It was interesting, though, that despite all the changes, the Tempts still seemed stable. This I credit to cofounders Melvin and Otis Williams always supporting each other. Seeing them reminded me how much I missed Diane and Flo. I compared the Tempts' situation to my own: I would always be "outnumbered" by new girls.

We opened with the Temptations at the Now Grove in Los Angeles to great reviews. Many people from Motown attended the show, and afterward Berry invited us to a party at his home, but I declined. At the time, he and Diane were making *Lady Sings the Blues*, the film biography of singer Billie Holiday. "Hey," Berry suggested, "why don't you come down to the studio and see the rushes?"

My first impulse was to say no, but Berry insisted. We met at the Paramount lot, and he showed me some outtakes. I knew that Diane would be good, but I was surprised how great she was. I'd assumed you had to take acting lessons to know how to act. I was very proud of her and still think *Lady Sings the Blues* is the best thing she ever did.

The whole time with Berry I couldn't help but feel that he was doing more than just sharing his new work with me. He beamed as he talked about how great Diane was. His whole manner seemed to say, "I told you, you should have stuck with me." Berry was the winner, and he made sure that I knew it.

After Diane left the Supremes, I was always very proud of her and proud that she'd been a Supreme. Contrary to what most other stars might say publicly, there was scant support for Diane in Hollywood. Most of them said she would never make it alone, or if she did, she wouldn't be as big.

When word got out that she was going to portray Billie Holiday, some stars laughed at her behind her back, mimicking the way she hunched her shoulders and rolled her eyes when she sang, or the way the veins in her neck bulged as she reached for high notes. Part of this was anger and jealousy. There were many black performers who'd worked twenty or thirty years and could sing their butts off, but couldn't get the breaks Diane did.

One time Diane's name came up, and one star said, "That Diana is just too pushy for me. I mean, she acts like no one's important but her."

"Mary, I don't know how you put up with her all those years," another added. "You know that child is just a bitch."

This talk embarrassed me. It was like when people tell dirty jokes because they think you'll like them too. They were jealous of Diane and thought I should have been too. But I honestly wasn't.

August 1972

The review we received in D.C. was terrible. The critic said, "They lacked a gutsy, down-home sound." We "should give up giggling and act natural . . . background insufficient . . . parodies of a former time." But I'm not going to give up because something has gone wrong. We are going to make it work. We've got to get our people at Motown to see that music has changed, and we want to keep up, not die. Boy, we've been working our cans off. It's been almost two years now.

Replacing girls in the group has definitely hurt. But

when people feel they want to do other things, you can't stop them and say, "Hey, my life and career are at stake too." Flo, Diane, and Cindy? "Everyone's gone to the moon."

That summer and fall, nothing could distract me from the sadness and emptiness I felt. Since "Floy Joy" earlier in the year, our last three singles had fared progressively worse: "Automatically Sunshine," Number 37; "Your Wonderful, Sweet Sweet Love," Number 59; and the new "I Guess I'll Miss the Man," Number 85. Instead of making us a hit recording act that toured, Motown had let the Supremes become a road act without a hit. I felt like I was on a treadmill, running and running but getting nowhere.

I went back to Detroit to see my mother, as I did almost every fall. I loved my new life in California, but I also felt cut off from my roots: my Motown family, my blood relations, and friends. To compensate, I made extra efforts to keep in touch with childhood friends like Flo, Alice, and Ella, and to go home whenever I could.

It was so nice to sleep in my old round bed. After moving to California, I'd given my mother my house, and Willie's family and my Aunt Moneva moved into her old home. The drapes were drawn, so even though the sun was shining, inside my room was dark as night. I'd been out late, talking with Cholly's wife, Mae, and I needed my sleep. The phone rang.

"Mary, it's Flo!" my mother called. I picked up the phone.

"Hey, girl," she said happily, "come on over when you get up. The twins are waiting for you. I've told them all about their Aunt Mary."

"Okay, but first I have to get just one more hour's sleep."

Supreme Faith

71

"Oh, Mary, girl, get up. You sleep too much anyway. Girl, why do you sleep so much?"

"I have a lot on my mind, Flo. Sleep helps me work things out. But I promise I'll walk down to your house as soon as I get up."

Just then the smell of bacon, grits, and eggs cooking hit me. It was beginning to look like a conspiracy between my mother and Flo to get me up. I wandered into the kitchen and had a great home-cooked breakfast, then set out for Flo's house.

Whenever I walked through the old neighborhood, I recalled how Diane, Flo, and I each bought a house on this street and didn't even know it until after we'd closed our deals. That's how much alike the three of us were. Diane's house was directly across from Flo's, and mine was a couple blocks down the street.

When I rang the doorbell, Flo came flying down the stairs to open the front door. Her fair complexion was red, as it always was when she was excited. Her hair was now blond, so we both laughed when she opened the door and I blurted, "Blondie!" It was a nickname only her family, Diane, and close friends used, though I rarely did. Now it really fit. We hugged each other tightly.

Inside, the house was just as she'd originally decorated it, all blue, and her twins were all over the place. They were as different as night and day. Nicole was fair like Flo, and Michelle was chocolate brown like Flo's husband Tommy. I held them while we talked about babies. Flo was so proud of her children, and they loved her with that perfect love I believe only mothers know. It was the kind of accepting love Flo had never known before, and when she held her babies, it transformed her. All the friends and relatives I saw in Detroit kept asking me when I was going to have a baby; I wondered too.

Inevitably the conversation turned to Motown. "Mary, I've been hearing about your problems. I told you, girl, they weren't going to do anything for the group after Diane left. It's about time you woke up. Motown's only out for themselves."

Flo was right, but I changed the subject. I felt that my problems with Motown would only burden her. And this was a sore spot for both of us. Why Motown apparently wanted the Supremes to fail was beyond me. It hurt when anyone, including Flo, mentioned it. The situation was so depressing, I wanted to forget it for a while.

I sensed Flo's fear of where her life was going; she didn't want that to happen to me, too. I don't think Flo ever understood that while it was very easy for other people to say, "Leave the group," I fully understood that there was no place for me to go, just as there had been no place for Flo.

In October *Lady Sings the Blues* premiered in New York. It was the culmination of Diane and Berry's dream. Though they were no longer an item, he was as dedicated to her career as ever, if not more so. Diane was Berry's vehicle to his next conquest: Hollywood.

While some critics complained that too many liberties were taken with the facts of Holiday's tragic life, the film was a commercial success and a triumph for Diane, who chose to sing Holiday's music rather than lip-synch to the actual recordings. I particularly enjoyed Diane's singing, since most vocalists dream of singing jazz and blues like that. Later Diane was nominated for an Academy Award for Best Actress. The evening of the Oscars, I prayed she would win, but she didn't. Some in the industry believed that Berry, a Hollywood outsider, had overdone the pre-Awards publicity, and that Diane lost because of industry politics. Still, this was Diane's most definitive step to superstardom and away from all that had come before, including the Supremes.

That fall we played an all-star benefit for the Rev. Jesse Jackson's Operation PUSH. Taped in Chicago and later released as the feature film *Save the Children*, the show included Gladys Knight and the Pips, the Temptations, Marvin Gaye, the Staple Singers, the Jackson 5, the Chi-Lites, the Main Ingredient, the O'Jays, Bill Withers, Curtis Mayfield, Isaac Hayes, Smokey Robinson, Valerie Simpson, Roberta Flack, Jerry Butler, and Thelma Houston. The highlight was the young Jackson 5. Every one of us stayed to catch their set. No matter how many times I saw them, they were amazing. With four Number One hits behind them, they were now Motown's brightest stars.

We sang "Stoned Love" and "Up the Ladder to the Roof," among other songs, and got a wonderful response from the crowd. Everyone working on the film said we were great. Yet for some reason, our sequence got cut, something we didn't discover until the movie's release. I was crushed. Why did there always seem to be obstacles in our path? And who was placing them there?

In November we had a great run at New York's Apollo Theatre, where Eddie Kendricks appeared with us, and worked through the end of the year, even on Christmas Day. One highlight of the season was receiving the NAACP Image Award as Best Female Group. Diane won Best Actress, and several other Motown acts were also honored. For the first time since Diane left the group, we were honored as equally successful entities. This award meant a lot to me, since the original Supremes had never even won a Grammy.

While I had been worrying about the Supremes "missing something," we generally went over well live and had audiences dancing and shouting for more. Maybe my ideas about what the group should be were based on an unattainable ideal, the original Supremes. The realization of where we might be headed if I didn't keep my eyes open hit me when we arrived to play six days at a small Canadian club. It looked exactly like a Ramada Inn dining room, with a little portable stage. That was bad enough; then I learned that we were making $13,000 for the week, a far cry from the $30,000 to $50,000 we'd earned just months before at the Copa or in Vegas. Out of this our booking agents and Motown recouped their percentages, about one quarter of the gross, and expenses and payroll claimed anywhere from 50 percent to 90 percent of the remaining gross. Jean, Lynda, and I were paid out of whatever was left, which was unpredictable, sometimes amounting to just pennies.

It seemed pointless for us to be out on the road earning so little. It actually *cost* us money to play dates like this, when that time should have been spent at home, refining the act, cutting some good records, and, by our absence, creating a demand. Our contract with Motown was coming up for renewal. For the first time, I didn't automatically assume we would re-sign.

One morning Willie woke me up with the radio blasting. The disc jockey posed a trivia-contest question about the Supremes: "Who were the Grand Honorary Marshals in the Santa Claus Parade?" This was an old Hollywood tradition, where many stars appear in a Christmas parade down Hollywood Boulevard, and this year it had been the Supremes. It had been televised, and Jean, Lynda, and I had been thrilled to participate. We had ridden on a float, smiling and waving.

Great, I thought, *some more publicity*. But as I listened to the disc jockey chat with the winner, I couldn't believe my ears. He sarcastically remarked that we were "all new faces" in the Supremes, and "no one" knew who we were anymore, and where had we gone, anyway? Years later, after I saw

Rob Reiner's farce "rockumentary" about a fictional rock group on the skids, I'd classify this as one of those "*Spinal Tap* moments" in which even I saw the irony.

I couldn't control my anger. I phoned the station and after several tries finally got through. When the disc jockey answered, I snapped, "I'm Mary Wilson, and I am still in the Supremes, and have been since the very beginning. We are not all 'new faces.' "

"Miss Wilson, I'm so sorry," he said nervously, before apologizing profusely.

"Okay," I said. "Would you please then play something from our latest album, *The Supremes Produced and Arranged by Jimmy Webb*?"

After a second's silence, he answered, "Well, I don't think Motown sent it to us. Or maybe someone stole it. But if I find it, I'll play it."

"Thank you," I said. Half an hour later he played "Tossin' and Turnin' " and dedicated the Box Tops' "Sweet Cream Ladies" to the Supremes.

Even with all the work, our group shared some great, happy moments. Once we were in Mexico doing a photo shoot on top of some ancient ruins. Because it took so long to climb to the top, the three of us changed our outfits on one side of the pyramid, neatly laying down our clothes and undergarments on the stone. We were posing when a great gust of wind blew, and suddenly our bras, panties, slips, and stockings went flying through the air and fluttered down to the ground. Down below, several shocked tourists were amazed to witness this bizarre lingerie shower falling from the sky. We nearly fell off laughing, and the bewildered tourists continued to stare as we watched my bodyguard Benny chase our clothes.

Money was getting tighter. In December we opened in New Orleans to a half-filled room. It was getting harder and harder to maintain momentum. We never knew what we were going to find, and the unpredictability of it all began wearing on us. Jean took it the hardest, or at least showed it the most. There were nights onstage when she just wasn't into it, and the fans knew it. People remarked to me that she seemed cold and distant. Now I see that a lot of what she was experiencing was fear. She sometimes looked as if the weight of the Supremes was crushing her. Every once in a while a wiseguy in the audience yelled, "Hey, where's Diana Ross?" which would shake her confidence. (People still do this to me today.)

I was on Jean's side, but I still wonder if she realized how much I wanted her to stay and be happy—not just for the Supremes but for herself. If I tried talking to her about anything, such as being more discreet with the press, she took it personally. I wasn't attacking her or her beliefs, I was only trying to help her. If I asked her to just give in a little bit, she would say, "I can't do what they're asking. It's okay for you, Mary. But it's not good for me."

Lynda was still new enough to be excited just being there. I knew that whether there were ten thousand people in the audience or ten, you had to be "on." Each person in the room has to believe not only that you're happy to be there, but that you're happy to be there for him or her. It's a giving of yourself. Jean sometimes felt that simply being there was all she could give.

In early 1973 I went to the Now Grove to see the Four Tops, a group that I never miss seeing. They'd recently signed with ABC Records, and after two years of flop singles on Motown had a Top 10 hit with "Keeper of the Castle." Similarly,

Gladys Knight and the Pips bolted from Motown to Buddah Records and immediately went to Number One with "Midnight Train to Georgia," launching a string of gold records.

We wished them all the best, but until then no ex-Motowners ever did as well or better anyplace else. Among record companies, Motown was unique, and most of the artists who left found they needed its extensive support system. Mary Wells, Berry's first female star, had four Top 10 hits, including the Number One classic "My Guy," but after leaving Motown in the mid-sixties never had another. There's been lots of speculation why: some thought her head got too big; others contend that Motown's arms were too long. Whatever the reason, Motown pointed to her example whenever someone asked too many questions or got out of line.

For years most of us had overlooked or minimized how badly Motown treated us; as they say, you can't argue with success. But now the label's golden touch had started to tarnish. Acts that got attention, such as Diane, the Jackson 5, the Temptations, and Stevie Wonder, did well. As the Motown ship began sinking, the rest of us went down with it. In 1972 the label placed only four singles in the Top 10, a far cry from the heady success of the sixties. But few of us were brave enough to abandon "the family."

This night at the Grove everyone from the Four Tops' new label was out in force. You could see that ABC was behind them all the way. The Tops had two more hits on the heels of "Keeper of the Castle"—"Ain't No Woman (Like the One I've Got)" and "Are You Man Enough"—making 1973 their most prosperous year since the mid-sixties.

Jean, Lynda, and I began talking about what to me was unthinkable: leaving Motown. I admit I was very reluctant. They didn't really appreciate the value of the Supremes' name, which we might lose if we left. In the meantime, we arranged a meeting with Ewart Abner, now Motown president. Since

I'd always regarded Abner as the one company executive with some compassion for the artist, maybe there was a chance.

How strongly do Jean and Lynda feel about sticking with the Supremes and Motown? I wondered. I found out as I sat in my home with Abner, waiting for them to show up. They never did. As ever, I looked on the bright side. Frank Wilson had a song for us, Abner said, and top Philadelphia producer Thom Bell had flown in to discuss a possible future project. Either of these possibilities might work. If I could be optimistic, why couldn't they?

I served Abner a cocktail and we made small talk, then I said, "Abner, we are really tired of constantly touring. We are women out on the road. We all want a decent home life, like other women." Abner listened attentively.

"Motown has not followed up on any of our records to date," I continued, "and, Abner, you know we've made some very good records."

"Yes, Mar-ry," Abner replied, pronouncing my name as only he could. "I know you ladies have done a fine job of keeping this group together. But what do you want?"

I was a little confused; I thought it was obvious, but I repeated, "We need more and better promotion. *The fans* are doing a better job of promoting our records than Motown is."

"Yes, you're right, Mar-ry." Abner agreed with everything I said. Yes, they had to get us the right writers, and then Motown had to put the push behind us. Whereas Mike Roshkind would simply say, "We've done all we can do, and that's it," Abner assured me it would be taken care of.

Earlier that year Lynda, Jean, and I were discussing our trouble getting a decent record out, when Lynda suggested, "Why don't I talk to Stevie about it? We're still great buddies. He'll write us something." When Lynda proposed the idea to Stevie Wonder, he accepted immediately and gave us "Bad Weather."

Stevie had come a long way from the little boy who played harmonica on our bus rides in the sixties. In 1971, soon after his twenty-first birthday, he demanded Motown grant him full creative control or he would go to another label. He also became eligible to receive the monies Motown was holding in trust for him; the company turned over an astounding $1 million in royalties and advances. I can only imagine what went through Berry's mind as he wrote out that check.

Motown had lost performers before, but never anyone it really wanted to keep. In addition to his long line of hit singles, Stevie was one of the few Motown acts to develop a broader audience. The contract Stevie finally agreed to granted him the greatest freedom of any Motown artist. Not only was he freed artistically, but financially; for once, Motown permitted an artist to control his own publishing, the key source of income for songwriters. The album he'd worked on between contracts was the groundbreaking *Music of My Mind*, followed later in 1972 by *Talking Book*.

His new contract allowed him to produce other artists, enabling him to work with the Supremes. As he later told reporters about "Bad Weather," "I've been listening to Jean Terrell for a long while and feel the way she's been handled isn't right. She's got those certain riffs which sound great, but she's not been given the material on which to develop them."

Stevie was a dream to work with. He was very attentive, and he worked quickly and efficiently. We never felt rushed. As Stevie taught us the song, I thought, *He really is a genius.* I don't know if Stevie wrote it specifically for us, but the original title was perfect: "I Think I'm Going to Run into Bad Weather." When we heard its first few chords, with its unusual progressions and African beat, I knew this was our ticket. All Motown had to do was get behind it.

We recorded "Bad Weather" in Detroit during a run at the nearby Elmwood Casino. Believing this style would put us back in good standing with the disc jockeys, I encouraged Lynda and Jean to do some informal promotion, but they refused. I understood their thinking that Motown should be doing more. But it wasn't, and I figured that was all the more reason for us to get out there. Whether Motown was right or wrong wasn't the issue. Our careers were at stake.

I'd tried rekindling the offstage camaraderie I'd shared with Flo, and later, Cindy, but Jean was never one to go out, and Lynda declined my offers, saying she didn't feel she had the right clothes to wear, and so on. Further driving me apart from Jean and Lynda was their recent conversion to the Jehovah's Witness faith. Before, after, and between shows, the two of them closed themselves off and studied the Bible. Jean claimed that since she and Lynda had started reading the Bible, she was honest and guided by God. Like most Jehovah's Witnesses, Jean believed her way was *the* only true way, and that was that. I promised myself I would try to join them. Not only for whatever comfort it might bring me, but I was tired of being left out. Maybe this would help bring us together again as a singing group. Despite everything else, we still had a wonderful sound.

At this point, I guess you could say that I had everything, and I felt happy. Nothing really bothered me for more than a moment. As I got older, however, I realized that there were a few things in life I didn't have, like a husband and my own children. I was sure, though, that in time these things would be mine. I certainly didn't go around moping and thinking about what I was missing.

This eternally optimistic personality I'd developed as a

child helped me cope with the few problems I did have, just as it had seen me through the pain of having been given to my Aunt I.V. and Uncle John L. Pippin in Detroit while my mother remained down South with my younger sister, Cat, and brother, Roosevelt.

The Pippins treated me like a princess, dressing me in expensive, pretty dresses and making sure that I wanted for nothing. My Uncle John L. was a gentle, kind man, but my Aunt I.V. was strict and stern. I now understand that it was for my own good. She was only trying to raise me to be the best I could be. But deep inside, my little heart ached. I felt misunderstood and afraid. But strangely enough, I was still happy. Before I was even in my teens, I'd use my sunny, outgoing face for the world. I swore never to let anyone take that away from me. By the time my mother moved to Detroit to reclaim me at age ten, the die was cast.

My mother worked very hard to care for the three of us. She got no support from our natural father, Sam Wilson, who remained down South until he died in 1962. One of my few regrets is having never known any of my father's people. I know they must be out there somewhere. Despite being deprived of a decent education, my mother, Johnnie Mae, did a great job of raising me. One of our happiest days came in 1956 when we moved into our new home, in the Brewster Housing Projects.

Intellectually, I understood my life: growing up in the projects, loving to sing, meeting Florence and Diane, forming our little singing group, hanging around Motown, all the while praying to be noticed. Then the success of the Supremes, and how stardom changed my life and those of the people I'd grown up with, like Marvin Gaye, the Four Tops, the Temptations, the Marvelettes, and so many others. But once I moved to California, I began to see my childhood differently. I began to question the constantly happy person the world knew as Mary Wilson. Was I really always happy?

These are questions most people ask themselves in their teens or early twenties. I'd traded that part of my life for the success Diane, Flo, and I had been blessed with. From the moment the three of us, with our friend Betty McGlown (who was replaced by another friend, Barbara Martin), decided to form a group, my career consumed every waking moment. The Supremes were everything to me, more than just me and Diane and Flo. It was a separate entity, something greater and more important than any one of the three of us, and no matter what occurred—whether our records hit or missed, whether we flew or flopped—I dedicated myself to doing the best I could. There were rewards, of course, but there was also a price.

Around this time I often found myself thinking back to 1962, when I turned down marriage proposals because of my singing. What would my life be like now if I'd married my high-school sweethearts Willie Peeples or Ronnie Hammers then and had never known stardom? How many children would I have? While I wouldn't have traded my life for anyone's, I suppose it was only natural to wonder about the path not taken.

In 1973, when I was twenty-nine and still single, my mother's warnings—"Don't end up an old maid"; "When are you going to give me some grandchildren?"—began getting to me. Family has always been very important to me, and I desperately wanted to have children, but I also knew that I could never bear a child out of wedlock. I wanted to settle down, finally.

Opening night in Puerto Rico, I looked out from the stage of the Flamboyan Hotel and spotted the most handsome black man in the audience. It was funny, because I made it a point not to date fans and had never noticed anyone before when performing. But this man, with his deep brown eyes and gorgeous features, was different. We made eye contact several times, or at least it seemed that way to me. You never can tell at those distances.

After the show, the phone rang, and Lynda answered. "Mary," she said, "it's for you. It's a 'Pedro.' "

"I don't know anyone named Pedro. Ask him where I know him from."

"He says he met you in Las Vegas, but that he was at the show tonight too." I didn't recall meeting him, but that didn't mean it hadn't happened. He asked me to have a drink with him, and at first I hesitated. Jean and Lynda, both seriously dating their future husbands, egged me on. "I can't go out with a man I don't know," I protested. Yet for some strange reason, I said yes.

When we met face-to-face in the hotel lobby, I realized Pedro was the man in the audience. He said, "Hi," then French-kissed me. I couldn't believe any gentleman could be so forward! I was turned off . . . but somehow fascinated too. For one of the first times in my life I decided to take a chance. And as I wrote in my diary several days later, "He took me out, and that was it. We've been together ever since."

It was the beginning of a dream romance, except for one hitch: I had just started dating a wonderful man named Freddy, and I could see that for him the relationship was becoming serious. Here I'd gone all year worried because I had no one in my life, and now I had two men.

Freddy was stable, sincere, and not in show business. I met him in New Orleans, and we hit it off very well. He had visited me in Los Angeles, and Willie seemed to like him too. We met in Puerto Rico to discuss our future. He was very anxious for me to decide one way or another. Freddy and I enjoyed being together, but I wasn't sure it would work out. We were on different levels financially and from different social worlds. I explained to him that my career was taking up all my time and energy. He was understanding, but hurt. As he left Puerto Rico he warned me that someday I'd wake up all alone. It was something I'd thought about often myself and feared.

Pedro Ferrer told me that he came from a very wealthy, politically powerful Dominican family, and that his father, a Mr. Roig, was a banker in Puerto Rico. Pedro dressed impeccably, and was intelligent and articulate. All the friends he introduced me to were obviously from privileged backgrounds. Pedro grew up and was educated with children from the rich ruling class. He was a model child, incredibly bright and well adjusted. An excellent scholar, Pedro had an IQ of 150 and a burning ambition to make something of himself. I had never known anyone quite like him.

The next couple weeks Pedro and I were together almost twenty-four hours a day. I thought I was fairly sophisticated when it came to men, but a total stranger was sweeping me off my feet. Several years later I realized that the only men I really understood were entertainers. Other men were a great mystery to me, and I was far more naive about them and their motives than I knew. This fling was so strangely wonderful, right out of a romance novel. Having always read fairy tales as a child, I suppose I was always waiting for my knight to carry me away on his white steed.

The entire time I spent in Puerto Rico was pure ecstasy. Pedro drove me all over the island, impressing me with his knowledge of its culture and history. During one of our excursions he pointed out a gorgeous, expansive home and said, "My uncle lives there." He stopped the car, got out, and talked to the gardener, who seemed to know him. Yet Pedro never rang the doorbell or attempted to introduce me to his "uncle." It seemed odd, but I put it out of my mind. Maybe no one was home.

We were inseparable. He took me to the airport, and as he held me, I felt my heart break. When he kissed me good-bye, I knew this was the man for me. By the time I left Puerto Rico for New York, Pedro was talking about our getting married in two years. That didn't seem so unusual, but that I agreed to this plan was—at least for me. From the very first moment, I believed that being with Pedro was my fate, and I was so tired and feeling so beaten down and defeated, I wanted to believe in something. Whether this was going to be the love of my life, something permanent, I still didn't know. I just wanted to be happy.

CHAPTER 6

$\mathcal{F}$alling in love with Pedro made me so happy, but I still had the group to deal with. Cholly Atkins had been Motown's staff choreographer since the early days. Although his dance steps are an integral part of the Motown style, he had lived a whole life before coming to the label and never considered himself part of Motown like I did. Cholly was in his fifties by then and over the years had become something of an uncle to me. He was hip to everything and didn't say too much, but when he did, I listened. I could always count on him. After I told him of our problems and of how we had little money to hire people, he agreed to come with us for our next dates in Puerto Rico.

We were rehearsing one day when Cholly said, "Look, baby"—he always called me "baby" when about to offer some fatherly advice—"people are starting to talk about Lynda, saying she's too bossy and outspoken. Now, you know you're the leader of the group. You've got to take charge."

"Okay, Cholly, I will," I replied. "But I don't want the girls to feel I'm too bossy."

"Mary, you know that if you don't start acting like the boss, they will take over."

He was right. When I recalled how I felt when Diane threw her weight around, I cringed, but I knew that I had to do it. I knew that people—inside and out of the group—were taking advantage of me, and in my heart I hated it. I resented people for forcing me to be something I was not and never wanted to be. Honest, caring advice, like the kind Cholly offered, was rare around Motown. I appreciated his concern. Too many others who influenced my life worried more about kissing Motown's butt than looking out for me and the Supremes.

Once back in the states, Cholly rehearsed us on the choreography for "Bad Weather" between our shows with the Temptations at the Latin Casino in Cherry Hill, New Jersey. I thought about Pedro every moment. He phoned me at all hours. I knew he loved me, but I became a little peeved when he insisted on showing up in New Jersey—I honestly thought he was kidding. We spent six days together, and while the romantic aspects were wonderful, I was relieved when he went back home. To say the least, this romance was whirlwind; I couldn't figure out how things had heated up to this point so quickly.

I looked forward to our upcoming monthlong tour of England, on which I planned to take Willie. I was home so rarely these days because of the Supremes' hectic schedule that I wanted badly to spend more time with him, even if it was on the road. Willie was the one thing in my life that was truly real.

I liked taking my son overseas and exposing him to different cultures. Once there Hazel arranged for Willie to stay a few days with her mother in the village of Eye. There he learned the proper way to drink afternoon tea and to eat scones with clotted cream.

One evening after visiting one of Hazel's younger relatives, Willie decided to cut across a field on the way home. It was a small village, and the local constable knew everyone in town, so it's no wonder that the sight of a young black boy racing across the field caught his attention. The bobbies picked up Willie and detained him. When he explained that his mother was Mary Wilson of the Supremes, one officer replied, "Right. And I'm the king of England." It was all cleared up, but not before it made the papers.

England is my second home, and I had so many friends there that it wasn't long before the phone was ringing off the hook. David Frost invited me to join him for drinks. He was off to the Middle East and offered to bring me back some exquisite silk. We had a great time together, catching up on the latest news. The press reported that David and Diahann Carroll had broken up and that he and I were dating. Really, it was only one date, hardly the big romance columnists tried to make it. After that, however, we did see each other briefly.

Unfortunately, there weren't enough hours in the day for me or for Willie. And, as if I didn't have enough on my plate, one morning at five Pedro called, waking me.

"Mary, guess what. I'm coming to England to see you!" I almost dropped the phone. I protested, but he was so pushy; it annoyed me. "I'll be there on the third. And could you also make hotel reservations for some friends of mine?"

"Sure," I answered uncertainly.

"So give me a kiss," he said.

When I didn't comply right away, he hung up on me. For not giving him a kiss? I felt like I was being dragged away on a wild adventure.

March 1973

I love Willie; he's growing into a fine young man. I hope he can lose that deep, angry mess he has inside him. I thought this new life would help him. And I love Pedro. Thank God I've finally fallen in love. I see myself beginning to feel for real. It felt good. I think I must let my heart go to Pedro. He's everything I'd want in a man: he is handsome, dashing, warm, sexy, he has a large Afro, and he digs me. At first I went out on the trip that he's after my money. But that just seems obsolete now. I am not used to a man so persuasive. Anyway, regardless of all that, my common sense has been overruled. As in the case of T.J. [Tom Jones], I have decided to pursue the situation. I am sticking my neck out. Willie says he doesn't like Pedro, but Pedro will win him over. I talk like I have no doubts. I do . . . however, I am throwing away my inhibitions. I want to dash into this affair.

This week I saw Tom [Jones]. Although I still love him, and always will, I find that my feelings have changed. I no longer have the heartache of someone who has loved and lost. My love for him is now more of a loving friendship— which is perhaps what the relationship should have been to begin with—a beautiful friendship. Still, it was great seeing him again. This same thing happened to my affair with Duke Fakir. In both cases, I believed that I had found the love of my life. But I was wrong. With this realization came a little sadness but also a sense of security and peace. At one time I never would have imagined I would stop loving either of them, but that time has come.

Our elaborate beaded gowns were so famous that they were the the talk of seven continents. They were so legendary that they somehow inspired some of our most outrageous male fans to dabble in drag. In fact, during an engagement in San Francisco, while one of our designers, Pat Campano, was repairing one of our sets of sequined pantsuits, they mysteriously disappeared—never to be seen again.

During the English tour we were the victims of a widely reported theft. After doing interviews most of the day, Jean, Lynda, Hazel, Willie, and I went to the dressing room to prepare for the show. Jean, Lynda, and I were putting on our makeup when someone asked, "Where is the other gown? I see only two."

"It was there when we left last night after the show," Hazel said.

We turned the tiny dressing room upside down looking for the gown, but it was gone! Willie and our road manager complained to the club manager and Hazel called the police. These gowns cost over $2,000 each. Within several days, they tracked down the culprit, who was tried and fined five pounds. The thief turned out to be one of our flamboyant, ardent gay fans who'd come to the show with a group of his most outrageous friends. They brought each of us a beautiful bouquet. Over a dozen years later I received a letter from one of the young man's companions, now a schoolteacher. It remains one of my favorite fan letters:

Dear Mary:

When we got upstairs, you, Jean, and Lynda were having a meal. We went back to our table, where my friend appeared. He had a big smile on his face, and I said, "You look like the cat that's got the cream." He said, "I have," and from his lap pulled up one of those bags we had brought your bouquets in, and there was one of your gowns. He had managed to steal something that we were all secretly dying to possess one of those beautiful and priceless sequined gowns ... As we were sitting there, one of the waitresses spotted the dress, and my friend gave her £5 to keep quiet. Anyway, the dress came back to our home with us, and—it fitted us all perfectly!

Jean's attitude grew unbearable during this tour, poisoning everything. The Temptations were in England too, and we jumped at the chance to see them. All through the Temptations' concert Jean talked loudly and critically of them from the front row. Later, at a dinner given in their honor, she continued to behave rudely.

Later that week Jean refused to rehearse for our upcoming appearance on Great Britain's most influential pop-music television show, *Top of the Pops*. We were going to sing our new single, "Bad Weather." The show's producer held this incident against me and the Supremes for the next several years, long after Jean was gone.

Jean and I stopped speaking. Out of frustration, one evening between shows I scribbled her a note, saying we were scheduled for a quick photo session. Her back was turned, and after I handed it to her, she angrily threw it to the floor. I should have grabbed the broad by her bugle beads and throttled her! Around this time she also told us that she didn't like singing the old Supremes hits, either.

Despite Jean's taxing behavior, and her and Lynda's obvious intentions to exclude me from their lives offstage, onstage we were still the Supremes. We continued dealing with one another as business partners, and we all wanted what was best for our business. We agreed to seek new management with no connection to Motown. We interviewed new managers and companies, and were most impressed by Allan Carr, who managed Ann-Margret. He had great ideas and seemed excited by the prospect of working with us. Before long, however, he expressed concern over Jean's attitude. I couldn't blame him, yet I knew that with someone like him on our side, things might look up, and Jean would be happier.

Jean and Lynda still tried to convince me to leave Motown. The failure of "Bad Weather" was the last straw; despite glowing reviews, the record went nowhere. Even Stevie Wonder was upset. He complained to Abner, who promised the company would "get on it." The record had been out since March, and here it was May. The time to have "got on it" was long past. It was too late.

An impulsive break from Motown would surely fail. Jean, and to a lesser degree, Lynda, read my caution as indecisiveness. But I knew, better than anyone, what was at stake and how Motown would respond. The big problem, which would haunt me for years, was the name *Supremes* and who really owned it. Morally, it should have been ours, but it wasn't that simple.

Jean and Lynda couldn't have cared less about the name, and, as I soon saw, they resented it just as they resented the constant questions about Diane. Both believed we would do just as well, if not better, without the name. I remember thinking, *Just wait until you wise up and see how hard it is to make it out there without a gimmick or a name like the Supremes. You'll wish you hadn't given it up.* (Ironically, fifteen years later Lynda and Jean would be touring with another seventies Supreme, Scherrie Payne, as the FLOs: Former Ladies of the Supremes.)

Every day I was finding out more about my business, though never from anyone at Motown. During a short tour with Sammy Davis, Jr., he told me that he'd asked our managers to let us perform with him. No one ever told me about this or, as I would learn, similar offers from many other established stars.

The intergroup tensions were taking a toll. Opening night at the San Francisco Fairmont, we received one of the worst reviews of our career. As a matter of fact, I think it's one of the few times an act has ever called a press conference to reply to a review. Our press conference was also "reviewed," under a headline that read: WHEN THE SUPREMES GET ANGRY. The *San Francisco Examiner* graciously allowed us to address its critic's views, which boiled down to his feeling that we were "not black enough." This issue would remain a no-win for us.

S u p r e m e   F a i t h

At the press conference, I said, "I'll probably be disliked by whites and blacks alike for what I'm going to say, but I went into show business to entertain. I'm not saying, 'Hey, look at me, I'm black.' I'm saying, 'Hey, listen to me, I'm a singer.' I'm an artist first and a black woman second. I don't feel that the people who come and spend their money to see the Supremes perform should be primarily concerned with our blackness. They should be concerned with how much we are giving them for their entertainment dollar." Jean, not surprisingly, felt that she was representing "every black person."

Then my worst fear was realized when Jean announced privately, "I want out of the group." It became a race against time. Which would come first—a new deal, or Jean's leaving? Shortly thereafter, Lynda revealed she was expecting a baby; a few weeks later I had a false alarm.

June 1973

I called Diane to tell her I thought I was pregnant, but she had changed her number. An hour later she called me. That was really funny, because we hadn't talked to each other in over ten months.

"Hi, Mary!" Diane said brightly. "How are you doing? I'm going to Japan soon, and I know you've been there lately. Tell me, what's the style there? What's happening? And I need to borrow your huge wardrobe trunk.

"Also, there's that beaver hat I lent you years ago. Could you return it?"

"Diane, I'm sure I have returned it."

"No, you haven't." (Years later I found the hat stuffed behind some others in my closet.) "I know. Let's go out shopping together. Come over here."

Diane was upbeat and happy, as if we'd just spoken yesterday. We went shopping in Beverly Hills, the whole time making small talk. Diane breezed through one exclusive store after another; in one she tried on dozens of pairs of shoes. We talked about Motown and how poorly it was promoting the Supremes. It was like we were girlfriends again.

"You know, Diane," I said, "I'm glad we got together today. I feel that we're better friends now than we were before."

Diane turned to face me, her large brown eyes wide with disbelief. "Mary, we are *not*," she said. "I don't know how you could say that."

Stunned, I felt she'd taken what I'd said the wrong way. Her reaction was so strong, I didn't even try to explain myself. The rest of the day passed slowly. From then on, Diane made me feel that I was not her friend, but her dearest devoted fan.

Later that night I wrote:

> It was as I had expected: we still can't communicate or be honest with each other. It's not that we don't like each other. It's more that we're just on different planets since she grew up. She seems to always be pretending. If anyone knows her, I do. Still, she talks to me as if I am a stranger. Maybe time will help us to talk freely with each other. She still tries to compete. Why? She doesn't have to.

This is a classic example of what I found most frustrating about Diane: her ability to hurt me without even knowing it. I knew that if I said one word in my defense, she would feel that she had been wronged. As long as I'd known Diane, whenever I confronted her, she always took a defensive stance and acted like the innocent victim. Berry taught Diane everything she knew. The difference between the two of them was that Berry could charm a snake. No matter how he really felt, he could still pretend to like you. Diane could not. Even today people Berry's hurt still think he's basically a nice guy. I don't think Diane ever understood how Flo and I were hurt by her and Berry's shutting us out of their lives and using the Supremes to advance themselves. I knew our relationship wasn't going to be the real friendship of our teens, I just hoped we could be friends today. Years passed before I would stop reaching out for Diane.

That June Pedro visited me in Los Angeles. His flight was due in right after midnight, and I spent the whole day getting ready. I wore a beautiful dress to the airport and was all smiles until I saw Pedro come through the terminal with loads of luggage and a huge Saint Bernard named Sky. *It looks like he's doing more than coming for a visit,* I thought to myself. *It looks like he's moving in!* I was right.

We had pretty much agreed to marry in the near future, so at first I didn't mind. After just a couple weeks, however, we ran into trouble. He was a little too bossy with Willie and possessive of me. One day he announced he was going back home.

"I'm sorry. Mary, I do love you."

That might have been the end of it, but a strong attraction kept drawing us together. Two clichés pretty well sum up our relationship: "Love is blind," and "Oil and water don't mix." The more Pedro stayed around, the less sense it made. I saw his shortcomings, but I believed I could help him and that together we would make things work. He was the only person besides my family, friends, and fans who loved me and was on my side. Between Motown's abandoning the Supremes and the press virtually ignoring us, I felt like a failure. There had to be something I could succeed at. It would be love.

In July 1973 Jean called to inform me she was about to ask Berry for her contract back. Even though I wasn't totally surprised, I was nevertheless dismayed. I'd always wondered if Berry lured Jean into the Supremes with promises of a future solo career. As her unhappiness grew, Jean let little things slip out to the effect that he had. She was frustrated and angry; we all were. But couldn't she see I was trying to hold things together? From her tone of voice, her mind was made up.

Within the hour, who should call but Berry. We hadn't spoken in months. In the sixties he and I had been buddies. Now that the Supremes were no longer "his girls," we rarely saw each other.

"Mary, it's Berry," he announced chipperly. "Billy Davis told me you're getting married. I just wanted to say congratulations, and I'd really like to give you away at your wedding."

What? Here my career was crumbling, and Berry wanted to give me away at my wedding! "No thank you," I replied curtly. "My son is giving me away." What I wanted to say was something along the lines of "the nerve of you, Berry," but I couldn't. Something was up; I had to stay on my toes.

"Well, what's happening?" he asked. This was a typical Berry ploy. I found his condescending attitude so insulting, I went off on him.

"Berry, what's happening to our group? The records aren't being promoted, and we're being run ragged with this schedule."

"What do you mean? You're working, aren't you?" he asked.

"Yeah, Berry, I'm working—for pennies, so I have to go out there every day. I've already been working all my life, fighting for time off, and now I can't take a good vacation without worrying that there'll be nothing in my bank account when I get back."

"But you're planning to get married," Berry said. So that was it: Berry probably thought I was going to wed, retire, and get out of his hair. "Besides, Mary, I've done so much for you and the girls. What I've been doing—the movie [*Lady*

Sings the Blues]—is going to help you and all the other acts in the future."

Berry saw Motown Records as a chess game, and we were all just pawns. Sure, he could walk away and do something else until he was ready to start working the puzzle again. But he forgot that our lives and careers went on, whether he was there or not. Now that Berry was back on the scene, he felt I should be grateful for his interest.

"What about us now, Berry? We can't get into Vegas, we can't get a record played."

"Mary, I have priorities."

I thought back to Berry and his priorities. When the Supremes became hot, earlier "priorities" like Martha and the Vandellas and the Marvelettes dropped down on the list. Then we benefited; now the Supremes were topped on his list by the movie business and Diane.

"Priorities? Well, my priority is the Supremes," I said. "And I'm paying you fifteen percent of every penny to make us a priority."

Typically, Berry agreed on every point. This was his way of making people feel good without him actually having to do anything. He admitted I was right, but it didn't change what he thought about the Supremes: that we were finished, and if we weren't quite finished yet, we should be.

"You know, Mary, when you girls were all babies, I used to tell you, a little knowledge can be dangerous.'

Yes, I thought, *and you also said, "I'll take care of you."*

"Mary, we have an idea for an outside manager for you."

"Well, Berry, that's something I've been asking for for a while and something I've been working on now for several weeks."

"Oh, really?" He tried to sound surprised. He had to have heard that I'd taken over much of the group's business, that I was looking for an independent manager, that I was making demands at Motown. I felt that the real reason for this call was to see where I was at, to see whose side I was going to take. That night I wrote:

> I do hope this is a start for the Supremes to be free of Motown. Even though I am ready to walk away, I am not ready to just let Motown have the name *Supremes*. And that may force me to stay.
>
> Is Jean giving me a chance to step up and take the lead? I don't want to lose Jean. But supposing the choice is to go with Jean or to stay with Motown and the name *Supremes*? Being that those are the only two outs I have, looking deeper, I suppose this is the time I should just stop the Supremes. Sometimes I get angry with myself because I can't make a decision. Jean made a decision, right or wrong; Flo made a decision; Cindy made a decision; Diane made a decision. I am the only one still hanging on (pardon the pun). Or maybe I have made a decision: to stay.

"A little knowledge can be dangerous." Berry's words stuck in my mind. The Supremes were in this precarious position *because* I had no knowledge. Our new manager Bill Loeb's first job was to explore our options for leaving Motown and obtaining rights to the name. In each of our contracts since the very beginning, Motown's position was clear: it owned the name the *Supremes* and could replace members at will. But just because it had slipped that clause into the contract didn't necessarily mean it legally owned it. There had to be more to it.

I wondered, *Does somebody own a name just by virtue of saying they do and getting you to agree with them? Isn't there something else involved? If there isn't, does that mean a company like Motown—or anybody—can just say whatever it wants and make it so? Even if it's a lie?* Flo's agreeing to never refer to herself as a Supreme in her press once she left the label hurt her career tremendously. The name was Flo's idea, no one else's. More to the point, she was a Supreme, just as I was. The way Motown exploited Diane's connection with the Supremes all the time only proved that it understood its value.

This was something I needed to think about, but before long Pedro and his things—*all* of them—arrived from Puerto Rico. I was too surprised to protest. My choices were to either live alone or let him stay. At first I chose the latter. One day after an argument I told Pedro he should go back home, and when he tried to convince me otherwise, I lost control and slapped him. I'd never slapped anyone. He slapped me back, and I stood there stunned. No man had ever raised a hand to me before. I started hitting him back. For those moments I felt like a stranger standing outside my own body, watching it all happen. When it was over Pedro wrote me a long note, saying he was wrong and sorry. He wrote, "Let's try one more time."

There were so many positive things about Pedro, such as his kindness and his boyishly romantic ways. Almost every day he brought me flowers or penned sweet little love notes. In fact, most of the time Pedro was remarkably gentle and thoughtful.

He was one of the first people to convince me that I could accomplish whatever I set my mind to. He really believed in me. He taught me to be strong. It bothered him that I feared so many things, including, at times, him. He showed me that my contribution to the Supremes wasn't like Diane's or Flo's. What I had uniquely contributed to the group was my gentleness; my love. However, in the atmosphere after Flo left, I found myself deeply hurt and vulnerable, so I retreated within myself. I felt I must survive at all costs. As strange as it sounds, Pedro helped me to reclaim that part of myself Motown had beaten down.

I was relieved to go back to Detroit that weekend for Mary Wilson Day, on July 21. The event was set up by Dick Scott, one of the Supremes' managers in the sixties. During the ceremony, held at the newly redeveloped waterfront downtown, a city councilwoman praised me as an example of the power of black women everywhere. I gave a brief speech, thanking everyone, and introduced my mother. Then the singing group the Originals dedicated a song to me. I had a wonderful time, seeing so many old friends from the Brewster Projects days.

Late Sunday afternoon I went over to Flo's house. She said she was very happy for me, but that I needed a man in my life. Her twin girls climbed all over their "Auntie Mary," and one threw up on my shoulder. The rest of the day I could think only about how badly I wanted my own baby. I returned to the street fair and gave another speech, this time to black women, telling them how beautiful they were and how proud they should be. When I got home I read the Bible for a while, then fell asleep.

Eddie Kendricks came by the next day, and we drove over to visit David Ruffin. Eddie has always been one of my favorite people, and I was happy to see that both his and David's solo careers were taking off. Eddie and I were lovers for a brief time, but our relationship had evolved into an enduring friendship. Like any two Motown artists when they got together, we compared notes, talked about what was happening, and dished a few folks.

Eddie was a rebel who spoke his mind. When I told him what was happening to the Supremes and how I was beginning to take over the business, he said, "Mary, you have to keep at it and don't give up, no matter what happens."

Before I left for Los Angeles, Mom pulled me aside. Though she rarely interfered in my life, she said, "I like Pedro very much, but I don't think you should marry him.

For one thing, he doesn't have his own money, and, baby, you need someone who can afford to take care of you. I don't want to meddle in your business, but why don't you just wait awhile?" She wasn't the only person with reservations; several friends remarked that Pedro was just using me. Still, I knew him better than they did, and I loved him.

In August Jean, Lynda, and I opened at the southern California amusement park Magic Mountain. It was one of our best engagements ever. Knowing that Jean was quitting, and possibly Lynda too, made it a bittersweet occasion. The irony was that they didn't want to leave the Supremes so much as leave Motown. I knew from experience that once someone's mind was made up, that was it. Flo taught me that. All the disappointment and struggle had soured Jean and Lynda, and I couldn't change that.

Jean was finished with me. No matter what I said or did, she took it the wrong way. When I couldn't take any more rejection, we stopped talking. I wrote her a letter, which, though I never sent it, expressed my feelings:

August 26, 1973

Jean:

I can't for the life of me see why you are venting your frustration at me. I feel that we—you and I—could take the Supremes and put them back at the top where they belong. You have a tremendous talent that I admire, and to be very candid, I went to bat for you with Berry. I don't know what he promised you when he first signed you to Motown. Did he say he'd make you a star? I've heard that before.

It's Motown that is constantly causing the problems by not doing its part as a recording company. You should be angry at them, not me.

Please, let's stop these childish games and go about achieving success while we are still young.

—Mary

Bill Loeb kept quietly making calls to other labels, and I talked to accounting firms about auditing Motown's books on the Supremes. I'd been considering an audit for a while; it was something Jean felt very strongly about. She once said, "They're not even keeping an accurate accounting. Don't tell me you can give me two pennies just because I was only making one at first, and that I'm supposed to be happy with it." Coming into Motown as an adult, Jean asked more questions, and she was right.

I knew, though, that an audit wasn't something Motown would take lying down. Once you started it, you had better be prepared to finish. If I proceeded, I would be one of the first artists in the label's history to audit. So many people had been hurt by the Motown system, and I saw what might well happen to me if I didn't get in there before it was too late. Here I was, having made millions for Motown—but out of the tiny fraction of the profits it gave me, I was terrified to spend a penny.

Around this time several disc jockeys and radio-station music directors (who determine playlists) started revealing to me that they didn't always get our records, and that Motown no longer pressured them to play them or offered them promotional favors if they did. Fans organizing campaigns targeted at radio stations often heard the same thing: Motown wasn't providing the records.

Through it all, our fans were always there cheering us on. The Supremes have always had one of the largest, most active fan clubs in the world, and I was grateful that the membership stuck with us. Many of the fans who joined in their teens were now young adults. They formed a national network and undertook several massive letter-writing campaigns on our behalf. They phoned radio stations to request our records and contacted other media to ask for press coverage. Almost every major city had its dedicated Supremes fans, and occasionally they were quoted in stories about us. It helped to know somebody still cared. In a couple of cases, fans were single-handedly responsible for our records hitting big in major markets.

Their activities encouraged me but infuriated Motown. I heard that Motown was angry and blamed me for the rumors that we were leaving and the press stories denouncing Motown's mistreatment of the Supremes. I said, "Berry, the fans are angry because they aren't hearing us on the radio, they don't see us on TV like they used to, and they don't see any publicity about us." He disagreed, maintaining that I was behind it all, that it was my plan to embarrass him.

He was half correct, but the fans acted on their own, doing what they believed was right. The real source of Berry's anger was that nearly four years after he'd "washed his hands" of the Supremes, we hadn't died. He intended for us to fade out quietly, and instead we had four gold singles and piles of rave reviews. Now Berry didn't know what to do. He couldn't ignore the fact that even without hits or exposure, the public still loved us. The Supremes remained high on popularity polls around the world.

From our talks, I managed to get some concessions from Motown: promises of special promotion men to work our future releases and some important contract changes. It all looked fantastic on paper. I didn't know, however, that Motown would arrange things so the Supremes could not release another record for almost a year and a half.

CHAPTER 7

I clung more to Pedro as our romance became hot and furious. We were now together twenty-four hours a day. He and I had recently returned from Dionne Warwick's celebrity tennis tournament in Aspen, Colorado, when Ewart Abner called. "Mary," he said, "I have some bad news."

My mind racing, I thought, *Is it my mother? Flo? Diane? Is the label dropping us?*

"Paul Williams was just found shot to death in his car a few blocks from Hitsville."

"Oh my God." I felt my knees buckle. Not Paul. I thought back to the last time I'd seen him, at a 1970 taping of Smokey Robinson's first prime-time television special. It was like a wonderful family reunion performing again with Paul and the Temptations, Smokey and the Miracles, and Stevie Wonder. Just being around them all, especially the Tempts, brought back lots of great memories. Paul and Eddie

Kendricks had been in the Primes, and way back in 1959 they convinced our parents to let us become their sister group, the Primettes. Paul helped us choreograph our early act. Melvin Franklin, his cousin Richard Street, and Otis Williams were friends from those days too.

On Smokey's special the Temptations performed "The Impossible Dream," one of the rare songs that Paul sang lead on. Paul was the Tempts' true leader, creatively speaking. He'd been the group's guiding spirit and developed their trademark choreography. He was also a great singer, as you can hear on many of the Tempts' early records, like "I Want a Love I Can See" and "Don't Look Back." Because most of the later leads went to either David Ruffin or Eddie Kendricks, the public saw Paul as "only" a background singer. Motown turned the group's choreography over to Cholly Atkins, who, of course, was the best. It was typical of Motown to take ambitious, talented people and relegate them to the background, never acknowledging their contributions. Like Flo, Paul felt stifled and frustrated, and he quit the group not long after this taping. He had so much more to offer, but also, like Flo, he kept his pain inside.

Everyone around Motown knew that Paul had been drinking heavily for some time. As he sang the line, "To beat the unbeatable foe," he was shaking. It was sad to watch him struggle to put across the words; they held a lot of meaning to him. In that moment I recalled all the beautiful moments Diane, Flo, and I had shared with Paul. How dapper and suave he'd looked that day he came to my house to persuade my mom to let me be a Primette. His natural elegance and grace were really something back then.

Since I couldn't attend the funeral, I gave Abner a message to deliver from me.

I wrote in my diary:

I've been thinking an awful lot about Paul, the way I think about Flo. I've always had a love in my heart for both of them. Just mentioning the funeral on the phone, Abner and I had to hang up because we both started crying.

I've been asking for strength because I see it's so easy for a person to be bumped off, smothered, or just to end it all yourself. I tried to sleep tonight but I couldn't, so I placed a call to Eddie Kendricks. He and I talked for an hour and a half. It was very nice. We talked of Paul and Flo. Eddie sounded very optimistic about the future and how Paul's tragic ending has given us strength. I agree. It's funny how certain events can bring people closer. I've always known Paul and Eddie were special to me, just as Flo and Diane are. I am glad to know, as Eddie told me, he and Paul felt the same about me. I asked Eddie to say good-bye to Paul for me.

Paul's death was ruled a suicide, but in many minds there will always be a question as to the real cause.

On August 25 we appeared on the "Model of the Year." This was a TV special broadcast live from the old Ed Sullivan Theatre in New York, the site of Jean's television debut three and a half years before. I was pretty sure this might be Jean's last appearance, but I didn't know it would be Lynda's as well. We had a few more commitments before year's end, and Cindy had agreed to step in if we needed her. That way Lynda and I would share leads. Less than a year and a half away from the business, and Cindy was eager to come back. As always, I could depend on her, and I felt thankful.

No matter what happened, Bill Loeb had already decided that the act should be revamped around me. It was getting harder to keep a consistent lineup, and since I was the only original Supreme left and the only person *I* could count on, I agreed. Secretly, I wondered if I could do it. But I had to.

As we stood separately in the theater waiting to rehearse, Jean turned to our road manager and snapped, "I'm going to sing my solo." When he told me of Jean's remark, I was furious and stormed over to them.

"No," I replied, "that's not possible. Weeks ago I asked both you and Lynda what songs you wanted to do for this show, and all I got in reply were blank stares." Since we had no new single to promote, we ended up singing "Touch" and "Bad Weather."

While we were in New York, word leaked to the press that Lynda was pregnant and planning to leave. At the time, I blamed her lack of enthusiasm on what was happening with the Supremes. Now I realize that like any mother-to-be, she was understandably preoccupied with that, and it made her moody. I offered to throw her a baby shower, and she declined. I was so hurt. With Jean on her way out, not knowing what Lynda was going to do threw me off balance.

Lynda was trying to up her position in the group, demanding a larger percentage and special concessions like extra money for singing solos. Several Motown execs told me they didn't think Lynda was much of a team player. Between her pregnancy and the people at the company warning me "Mary, this Lynda is something else, you'd better watch her," I didn't know what to think. I was looking for a new girl to take Jean's place, without knowing if I should be trying to fill Lynda's spot too. The executive who criticized Jean and Lynda never owned up to how the business drove these woman to be that way. I understood where Jean and Lynda were coming from, perhaps too well. They were just rebelling. But I couldn't go on letting other people run my life.

The next week Pedro and I were going to Santo Domingo to meet his parents. As the date of departure drew nearer, Pedro became increasingly restless. The night before our trip he told me the truth about his parents' identity. Pedro confessed that Mr. Roig was indeed a banker, but *not* his real father. Apparently Roig had taken Pedro under his wing when he was a young man, and for whatever reason, Pedro contrived an extravagant fantasy about who he really was. In many ways he reminded me of the hero of F. Scott Fitzgerald's *The Great Gatsby*, a poor boy who recasts his life in the mold of a wealthy mentor.

In truth, Pedro was raised by his mother and stepfather, a politically powerful Dominican. The Dominican Republic occupies roughly two-thirds of an island, Hispaniola; Haiti makes up the other third. The country has a long history of colonial rule and dictatorship alternating with revolutions and democratic movements. In 1930 Generalissimo Rafael Leónidas Trujillo Molina took over and ruled the nation with absolute power until his assassination in 1961. Countless thousands who spoke out against him before his death were executed or died under mysterious circumstances.

Democracy eventually came to the Dominican Republic, but not without civil unrest and violence. Even now there are areas of shocking poverty. Pedro's family belonged to the professional class that worked to make possible the country's first free election in almost four decades, in 1962. They exerted a great deal of influence, which in the Dominican Republic was more valuable than money.

The few days we spent with his mother, stepfather, sister, and brother were pleasant but awkward. And in one sense, surprising. Pedro was so dark-skinned, I'd assumed he was black and expected his family to be as well. Imagine my shock when I saw that they were white! Pedro was not black, or at least not an Afro-American black person. He had black skin, but underneath it he was a true Latin. Boy, did I feel like a dummy, especially in view of how strongly I felt about marrying a black man. There went my perfect fairy-tale ending! Well, it was too late to worry about that now. We were in love.

Visiting Santo Domingo was fascinating. His family took me all over the small island. We swam in the crystal clear water of the Atlantic, strolled through the swank hotels and casinos. Pedro was the island boy who'd come home and made good. After all, I was a great catch: a wealthy singing star.

His mother prepared all the exotic Latin dishes of their region, one of which was a soup made of cow's intestines. I tried to eat it and found myself almost gagging. It was like our Southern dish chitlins. It was very funny because his mother, who doesn't speak a word of English, broke out laughing hysterically. That broke the ice, and they immediately considered me part of the family.

I liked Pedro's family very much. His little brother Rafael was a huge Supremes fan, and his sixteen-year-old sister Malvena and I hit it off from the start. His parents were initially taken aback by me—or, I should say, by Pedro's plans to marry me. They wanted him to marry within his own culture, preferably to a more traditional Latin type, not an entertainer, and probably not a black American Baptist, or, as I like to say, a BLAP (Black American Princess).

For the first time, I really got to see the man I was engaged to. I also saw how different Pedro and I were. In his society men and women observed strict social codes: the man was the undisputed leader, the boss, the provider, while the woman was the queen of the home. In public she always deferred to her husband. This struck me as backward and quaint, and yet some things about Pedro's way appealed to me. Some of my values were old-fashioned too, but American traditions are pretty progressive compared to what Pedro was used to. I was an independent single woman. As my career consumed more time and energy, I longed for a man to be strong, to fight for me. During these years there was nothing I liked better than to be in my home, cooking, entertaining, and taking care of Willie and our many pets. Pedro completed the picture.

En route to Santo Domingo we had stopped off in Puerto Rico, where I had met Pedro's friends. Most were well-to-do, handsome, and on the make. They hung around the San Juan casinos and hotels, providing "company" for rich, lonely women. I discovered that I wasn't the first famous woman whose path Pedro had crossed. Part of me couldn't believe it, but part of me did.

On the flight back to Los Angeles I had one last impulse to dump Pedro and save myself. On the plane, I wrote:

> Today at the airport I saw what I was afraid it would be. The young, boyish face. At first he did not accept anything from me. Slowly, he's taking. Boy, I let him reel me right in. A real con job. Willie and others saw it. I played into Pedro's hands so easily. I really thought we had a chance. Now the problem of discarding him; it'll be messy.
>
> When he's around I feel like I'm being smothered by a dark, heavy cloud, or a windbag. Now suppose I take him back and try it for a while? I'll be the loser. I need someone who's going to lighten my load. I don't care how often he has played the game. This is one he won't win.

After several months of waiting for promised jobs to come through friends, Pedro finally decided to finish his law education here in the United States. Willie and Pedro were at each other constantly. Willie, then fourteen years old, was trying to establish his own identity and rebelled; he didn't want me to marry Pedro. Having suffered a strict, unreasonable upbringing myself, I was sensitive to Willie. Although I firmly believe in discipline when appropriate, it has to be mixed with understanding and love. And Willie was not an average child. He was bright and caring but needed extra time and patience. I knew when I took him there would be special challenges ahead for us both, but I really believed in my heart that love would help us overcome them all. Now I wondered.

One evening my sister Cat, a friend, and I went out to the Candy Store. We got in late, and Willie and his brothers were still up. They playfully jumped on me, and Willie got too rough. Seeing that he was trying to hurt me, I lost my temper and hit him. He tried stabbing me with a ballpoint pen. My bodyguard Benny, who lived at the house, broke it up. I wasn't physically hurt, but emotionally I was devastated. How could this happen? I loved Willie so much, but I'd seen this day coming. He was a young man trying to flex his muscles. He was to begin attending military school that fall, and I prayed it would help.

When it came to Willie, Pedro's ideas were almost completely opposite to mine. He was raised in the old-fashioned Latin tradition where the father ruled. Pedro's family had explosive, often violent, arguments. I'd become very upset after witnessing one of these scenes, but an hour or so later Pedro and his family would go on as if nothing had happened. This he brought to our quiet little family.

Pedro was determined to control Willie and did not brook the smallest infraction of the rules he set down. Naturally, part of Willie's reaction to Pedro was simple jealousy over having to share me with someone else. Willie had always liked my other boyfriends, and they all liked him. I had never had a serious relationship with a man who didn't spend time with Willie or take him places. Freddy, whom I nearly married just before I met Pedro, flew Willie and his friend Brian to Mardi Gras in New Orleans one year.

Had I looked carefully, I'd have seen the first sign of Pedro's violent nature. Instead, all I could see was a man who needed my help, a man who I could love into becoming the person I thought he should and could be. I knew all the reasons why I shouldn't love him, yet I couldn't stop. By month's end Pedro and I were back in Hollywood, planning our engagement party.

Pedro loved the nightlife, and Hollywood certainly offered a surplus. Because of work, rehearsals, or simple exhaustion, there were times when I didn't go out. Pedro hung out and talked to other men, the way guys do. For all its glamour, Hollywood is basically a small town. I knew everybody, and when my name came up, guys I knew, however casually, usually said something to Pedro just to be polite. If a man said he thought I was nice or pretty, Pedro assumed I'd slept with him. What was actually said, I never knew. I only know what happened when Pedro got home.

After one evening out he stormed in with his brown eyes flashing, and I knew immediately someone had said something to set Pedro off. Still, there was no way I could be prepared for what happened next.

"You fucking whore!" he screamed.

"What?"

I trembled as he stepped closer. He flapped his arms as if he were about to strike me, but changed his mind at the last millisecond. He was right up in my face. "You lied to me! How many men did you sleep with?"

"But that was all before I met you!" I cried.

"I thought you were pure!"

Pure? I couldn't believe that in 1973 two adults were having this conversation. Suddenly Pedro slapped me several times hard across the face, as if he hated it. He tore off my clothes and then shoved me outside to the pool area and locked all the doors. It was fall, hot in the day, but very cold at night. I was crying so hard I could barely breathe. I looked out across the shimmering pool and down on the lights of Hollywood. How did this crazy man get into my life? Why couldn't I stop it? Maybe I could. As I sat on a cold lounge chair, hugging myself against the autumn breeze, I kept asking myself, *Why is this happening to me?* It was very hard, but we made up again.

A few weeks later I went to the Dorothy Chandler Pavilion to see my good friends the Pointer Sisters. Their act was fabulous, and their singing was great. I felt very happy for them but left the show feeling sad and a touch envious. It was like the Supremes were old and on the way out. The past couple of years had brought a modest girl-group revival. With acts such as Barry White's Love Unlimited, the Three Degrees, and the Emotions, there was competition. While I knew we couldn't copy anyone else's style, the Supremes needed something new and fresh. Unfortunately, we couldn't accomplish anything artistically until the most basic question—namely, Who was still in the Supremes?—was answered.

All my career crises faded into the background as Pedro and I prepared for our engagement party. We threw it at our house, and over two hundred people attended, including Flip Wilson, Lamont Dozier, Brian and Eddie Holland, Lola Falana, Jim Brown, Gail Fisher, Yvonne Fair, Robert and Fuller Gordy (Berry's brothers), Bob Jones, Raymond St. Jacques, Ron Townson, Sammy Strain of Little Anthony and the Imperials (now with the O'Jays), Johnny Taylor and his wife, Richard Roundtree and Cathy Lee Crosby, Herb and Mauna Loa Avery, Ruth Pointer, Chuck Jackson, Smokey and Claudette Robinson, Mike Roshkind, and Bill Loeb. Everything was beautiful. The tables were dressed in yellow, and there were large bouquets of daisies everywhere you looked. I cooked black beans, corn bread, ham hocks, and although I was tired by the day's end, I was very content.

Everyone was dancing and having a great time. Mauna Loa started acting kind of crazy and walked up to Cathy Lee Crosby and lifted up her top. Cathy had nothing on underneath! She swore she'd never talk to Mauna again. Meanwhile Benny and Willie entertained us with a karate demonstration in which they broke some bricks. It was a great party, and before it ended, I made a date to meet with Smokey.

During dinner a few days later, Smokey and I talked. "I want to sing lead now, Smokey," I said. "I know that I'm going to stick with the group, which is something I can never be sure of with anyone else. There has to be some consistency. It's getting to the point where people don't even know who we are."

"You're right, Mary," Smokey replied. "It's time you took that step."

Smokey discussed my idea with some Motown executives, but they didn't think I could carry the whole lead alone. They did, however, want me to assume part of the lead if we found a third girl who could carry the rest. That was pretty good news.

"I'll start recording an album with you," Smokey offered, "and then when you find your third girl, you'll share the leads."

I was so elated. I called Cholly in Detroit to tell him what I'd done.

"Well, Mary, you know it's about time you started speaking up for yourself, because nobody else will."

"Yeah, Cholly. I guess I had to find that out the hard way."

With just a few weeks before our next dates, the pressure to replace Jean intensified. I had auditioned many singers, but I liked Shelly Clark the best. A beautiful girl with a great personality, she'd been in the group Honey Cone, which had had a Number One record in 1971, "Want Ads." But Shelly declined due to other personal commitments.

I desperately called everyone I knew in the business to see if I'd missed any great singers. On a whim I called Lamont Dozier. "Hi, Lamont, it's Mary Wilson."

"Hey, girl. How are you doing?" It was typical Lamont, warm and friendly. "Lamont, do you know any great female singers?"

"For who?"

"For us." I sighed. "Jean is leaving, and probably Lynda too."

"Wow!" He laughed. "I know Scherrie Payne, and I think she would be good, because she grew up with the Supremes. She's pretty, and I know personally that she digs the group." Lamont went on to say that she was Freda Payne's younger sister and that, by the way, he and Scherrie were dating. That was enough recommendation for me. As one-third of the Holland-Dozier-Holland team, he'd produced hundreds of hit records. If he thought Scherrie was great, she must be.

Next I called Scherrie in Detroit. When I told her who I was and why I called, she was very excited. "Mama, it's Mary Wilson!" I heard her shout. I explained our predicament, and she seemed willing to help. When I asked if she'd like to come out to L.A. and audition, Scherrie said she'd be honored to. A few days later she was there, and I was sold. She was pretty, easy to get along with, and her voice was phenomenal. As far as I was concerned, she was in.

Scherrie and Freda Payne grew up in Detroit. We'd

worked the circuit with Freda in 1970, the year of her first hit, "Band of Gold," on Holland-Dozier-Holland's Invictus Records. Scherrie was asked to join the label as well, and she took over the lead spot in Glass House, a group that recorded only a few records.

My timing was perfect, as Scherrie was considering taking a regular job (she had studied medical technology and taught school) when I called. Her eagerness was refreshing, and she and Cindy hit it off. Like Jean and Lynda, Scherrie was opinionated and outspoken, but tactfully and with a sense of humor.

I'd hired Cindy assuming that Lynda too was leaving. Neither she nor Jean had come to my engagement party, and I heard from Lynda only through our manager, who kept me posted on her latest demands. She wanted a full one-third financial share of the group, which was unrealistic. I didn't see how it could be settled, and, besides, I figured to replace her in a few months anyway because of the baby.

Once we accepted Scherrie, Cindy and I began rehearsing right away in my living room. Cindy, as always, was a great help. Because she'd put on a little weight, though, her gowns had to be altered. We had only a handful of days to get ready, so it was going to be tough. But I was so hopeful and confident that I wrote my New Year's resolutions for 1974 in October:

1. Conserve money.
2. Check business.
3. Learn to sing and act.
4. Love Willie.

I decided to hire an outside lawyer. I needed someone good and strong, someone Motown couldn't intimidate or sway. For me or anyone with Motown, this was a big step.

One night at a show I ran into one of my favorite singers and close friends, Nancy Wilson. She introduced me to a tall, handsome black gentleman accompanying her and her husband. "This is my lawyer, David Williams."

David was one of the very few black attorneys coming up then. His father was a judge, and after talking with him, I felt that he was the right person for me and the Supremes. I could no longer ignore the ominous signs that Motown was abandoning us. I had to fight back.

A week after Scherrie joined the group, David and I met with Motown's lawyers, Abner, and Bill Loeb to review the Supremes' situation. When Abner heard that I had hired Scherrie on my own, boy, was he upset. He went through the ceiling. But Motown hadn't lifted a finger to replace Jean or Lynda. Why was the company mad at me for doing what had to be done?

"Mary," Abner said firmly, "you have overstepped your bounds. Besides, it's impossible for you to hire a new Supreme, when none of you are Supremes."

"Wait a minute, Abner," I said. "I *am* a Supreme."

"Well, Mary, you haven't even signed your new contract yet," Abner replied.

It was then that I knew I was right to instruct David Williams to have my new contract include a clause saying that I was a Supreme for life, unless I was disabled. How could Abner claim with a straight face that just because I hadn't signed a piece of paper I wasn't a Supreme? It was ridiculous. The stakes were suddenly clear. If I didn't start playing their games, I was going to lose.

On Halloween Cindy, Scherrie, and I played our first date together, at the Phoenix State Fair. The fans were thrilled to see Cindy back, and they loved Scherrie from the start. This was the first night I sang lead on most of the songs, and my performance was good, though I missed some notes on

"Somewhere." Between shows, some local reporters came for interviews. All the questions were directed to me, and all evening the promoter spoke only to me, as if Scherrie and Cindy weren't there. I hated this and told Bill Loeb to make sure that people knew there were three Supremes, not just me. Everyone was beginning to see me as "the boss," but in my heart I still wanted to be just one of the girls.

Two days later we did a Cincinnati show where only a few people came specifically to see the Supremes, with most of the audience there for Bloodstone and Donny Hathaway. I was thrilled to share the bill with Donny. His rendition of Leon Russell's "A Song for You" inspired me to perform a medley of it and "How Lucky Can You Get" a couple years later. Donny complained that the crowd was cold, but they certainly responded to us. When Cindy addressed the audience, fans screamed, "We're glad you're back, Cindy!" Tears came to my eyes. But that was about the only thing that went right.

We'd gone to Cincinnati thinking the promoter had sold five thousand tickets, only to find it was more like a few hundred. After the show the police tried to arrest him because he couldn't pay the acts. The sound was terrible, and we had to perform without a bass player, which the promoter was supposed to supply. These things never happened when Motown took care of us. No one was looking out for the Supremes. No one cared.

Afterward I went back to Detroit to visit Mom. Although she can neither read nor write, she is very wise. I respected her so much for her love and compassion, and I was happy to provide for her. She never asked me for anything, but on this day she said, "Mary, I would like you to get me a car."

"*What?*" Obviously she'd been talking to her friends, and one of them must have remarked that they thought I should buy her a car. I was a little annoyed, and without thinking snapped, "No. For one thing, you can't drive. And you can't read, Mom. How would you get around?"

"You could get someone to drive for me," she replied innocently. I felt so sorry for her. She was right; I should have had the money to give her a car and a driver, but money was getting very tight. I felt a twinge in my heart for having hurt her feelings.

I'd never thrown up her illiteracy to her before, but maybe I did on this day, because for years I feared that I might grow up to be just like her. I always secretly feared that ideas and information eluded me. And with the games Motown was playing, I was beginning to doubt my abilities to think and reason. I guess my Aunt I.V.'s constant harping when I was little about how sorry I'd be if I didn't learn had sunk in. To this day I regret lashing out at Mom. I was beginning to feel like a loser; I was beginning to unravel.

As usual, I went over to Flo's. She had lost a lot of weight and was looking better than she had in a while. In addition to her adorable daughters Michelle and Nicole, there was now a third child, sixteen-month-old Lisa. For several hours we talked about a little bit of everything. Flo was still very unhappy, though. Outside of lending a sympathetic ear, there was not much I could do.

In late 1973 the Supremes technically had no contract with Motown, but because I didn't own the name, we stopped shopping for a new label. I had told my attorney David Williams my whole story, starting from when Flo, Diane, and I signed with Motown in 1961. We were sixteen, and each signed a recording contract with Motown Records and a management contract with Berry Gordy, Jr. The day of the signing we still hadn't come up with a new name, hoping that would force Berry to accept the *Primettes*. Our mentors the Primes (Eddie Kendricks, Paul Williams, and Kell Osborne) had given us the name, and we didn't want to change. But

Berry stood firm, so we became the Supremes. Flo picked the name the Supremes, which we didn't think was as pretty as our former name, the Primettes. But Berry said, "Look, I don't like the name *Primettes*. Change it before you sign your contracts," and we did. Short of sleeping with him, we'd have done everything Berry wanted if it would get us a record deal.

When we signed our contracts, we didn't fully understand the clause stating that Motown owned the name the *Supremes*. Diane, Flo, and I *weren't* dummies. We *were* three enthusiastic, idealistic minors signing contracts without competent, independent legal counsel. God forbid if one of our parents—our only representatives there that day—decided not to sign for us. We lost our fourth member, Barbara Martin, when her mother refused, saying she didn't like the terms of the contract. From the beginning, our parents saw our signing as the best alternative to running the streets. In Motown they saw our Big Chance.

Meanwhile, no one at Motown said anything about a contract for Scherrie. They never indicated whether they liked her or thought she should be in the group. It was November; I decided that New Year's Day 1974 was my "deadline." We had to have a group, we had to know who was in it, and their contracts had to be in order. The Supremes had not recorded in almost a year, a period during which we'd normally have released two LPs and three or four singles. Remembering Smokey's promise to produce us, I started pushing Motown. We needed a new record out, and soon. Without contracts, Scherrie and I, along with Cindy, hit the road: another new group of Supremes.

December 1973

The shows here at Bachelors III in Fort Lauderdale have been going over very well. Scherrie and Cindy are doing an excellent job. Our reviews were great. Thank God for that. I know people are asking, "Just what are the Supremes trying to prove? Why don't they give up?" But if we did, what would I do? Could Pedro take care of me? Could I lean on his shoulder then? Would he stay with me? God, no, I must keep working.

December 13, 1973

5:30 A.M.—Well, I was lying down, trying to sleep, when the phone rang. Pedro sounded drunk or strange. He called me a prostitute, saying he was tired of hearing things about me, and no wonder no one liked me. He started talking about the photo of me on the couch. He said the next time I see him, it will be with someone else. I guess it's over. I was hoping so much that we could make it, but I've lost again.

11:00 A.M.—Pedro has called me three times already. At first I got the impression that we were finished, but when he called back he started asking if there were any other men. He brought up other names, some of whom I never had anything to do with, like Berry and Marvin Gaye. But trying to tell him now wouldn't matter because he has it in his head that I am a prostitute. Now he's even bringing up the fact that I went to bed with him the first week. I finally told him that he'd have to live with my past or get out.

While cleaning out some papers a few months earlier, Pedro had come across a photograph of me and Tom Jones. Tom had his arm across my chest so that although I was wearing a two-piece bathing suit, it looked like I was topless. Without a word, Pedro stalked into the kitchen and swatted a tray of food from my hands. He shoved the photo at me and screamed, "You fucking whore!"

I was beginning to see a pattern. Pedro always caught me off-guard, then made outrageous accusations and carried on so wildly I couldn't think fast enough to answer him. I knew he was wrong, but each time he came at me I became frightened little Mary, afraid of everything.

"Tell me everybody you've ever slept with, you fucking whore!"

Pedro yelled and waved the picture in the air. "I don't remember," I stammered, fearing for my life. His eyes looked like those of a madman.

"Tell me! Tell me who you slept with, you whore! I want you to write down their names on this piece of paper!"

When reason failed, I said, "Okay, okay," and he pushed me down into a chair by my shoulder. Suddenly I was a little girl again, being forced to recite my ABCs, or being reprimanded for wetting the bed. I started writing: Duke, Flip, Tom . . .

"Who else?" Pedro shouted, reading over my shoulder.

My mind raced to recall everyone. I knew that if I overlooked anyone, there would be hell to pay later. I listed my true loves, I listed some one-night stands. Tears streamed down my face, and sobs racked my body. Long ago, my mother told me, "Mary, never tell your husband everything; you'll live to regret it." Now I knew what she meant. I tried keeping my list to just those men whose names were well known.

When I finished, Pedro snatched the paper, read it, then said, "And you've got your fucking boyfriends' pictures all over the house." He was referring to some cocktail tables Willie and a few friends had helped me make. The tabletops were made of resin in which I had embedded dozens of mementos: photos, hotel-room keys from around the world, foreign coins, and other little tokens. Pedro tore through the house, shattering the tabletops and tearing up every photo he found as well as many of my diaries and scrapbooks.

"You think you're so great!" Pedro said derisively. "Who do you think you are? You never display your family's pictures. How do you think that makes them feel?" I was speechless with fear. When he finally calmed down, he left for Mexico. As he went out the door, he warned, "Mary, don't you dare leave this house!"

What was wrong with him? How could he accuse me of "hiding" my past when almost every man I'd dated was mentioned in the world press? He also knew that I was over Duke and Tom. Still, whenever I insisted on going to see the Four Tops perform, Pedro got moody and angry. He was the same way about Eddie Kendricks, although I told him many times that Eddie and I were only friends now. Nothing I said mattered.

Despite his hateful words, on his way to Mexico Pedro phoned from San Diego. He wanted to know, would I still marry him? Days later, he was back.

November 22, 1973

When I returned from acting class, Pedro poured champagne and said that he wanted to talk. He said he had read my diaries and now understands me. That was really a shock, because, as you know, I write everything. Well, he said that he found out that I had been very right in everything and that people just didn't understand me. As he was talking, I thought, *Wow, if my diary was that explanatory, then I must really have been writing well. Maybe I should write a book.* We talked for hours. I couldn't believe that just by reading my diaries he would really understand me. When he first said he had read them, I was ready for him to go into a tantrum and call me all kinds of names. Also, he said he had torn out the pages where there was something with a man. That hurt, because now I'll never know what I wrote. He said he was sorry about that and asked if I would forgive him. Plus, he said he will keep those photos so that he can control me and possibly use them . . .

Instead of seeing what was wrong with Pedro or with our relationship, I found myself more often looking for what was wrong with me. Instead of thinking about how to get away from Pedro, I blamed myself for falling in love with him in the first place. Pedro was stronger than me, and before long I was writing in my diary about how I should change, how I should improve, and how I should be more of a real woman, one who sacrificed for her man. In other words, be more like what Pedro wanted me to be. It was easier for me to stand up for the Supremes than for Mary Wilson. I'd opened myself up to Pedro, and in return he was destroying my self-respect.

I was really looking forward to Christmas this year, my first in my adult life I'd be spending with my own family. Having everyone together and the group's suddenly brighter prospects combined to lift my spirits. I'd usually been on the road during the holidays, so I rarely got to celebrate the way I wanted. I remembered how as a teenager all I wanted at Christmastime was a big, fat, beautiful tree flocked in pink artificial snow. It wasn't traditional, but to me that was how the other half lived.

On a day off I decided I'd surprise everyone. I went out and found *my* tree, then I unpacked boxes and boxes of angel hair, tinsel, glass balls, electric lights, and other ornaments I'd collected over the years. While trimming, I flashed back to when I was a kid in Detroit, and we would put anything we could find on the tree, including earrings and ornaments we'd made in school. When it was done, I stood back and admired my tree—which looked like the one I remembered from Hudson's Department Store—happily thinking how surprised Pedro and Willie would be. Oh, how beautiful it looked to me. This would be the best Christmas ever.

Pedro walked into the living room, and I stood there, waiting for him to smile or reach to hold me. Instead he began screaming, "What is this? This isn't a Christmas tree! It's cheap and trashy! Like everything here in Hollywood!"

As I watched silently, Pedro pulled down the tree. The

glass ornaments and lights made muffled tinkling sounds as they shattered on the floor. As Pedro clawed at the branches and threw the tree around, tufts of pink flocking settled on the carpet like little clouds.

Pedro had made his point. Christmas in my house—now *his* house—was to be celebrated not with the gaiety of the southern black holiday traditions I knew, but with the solemnity of his Latin, Catholic upbringing. More disturbing, the object of Pedro's rage wasn't just his perception of my pink-flocked tree, it was me. That tree symbolized everything about me and my life. I saw that who I was, what I was, threatened him.

I promised myself I would change.

CHAPTER 8

*E*ven today I still believe that of all the Supremes' seventies lineups, Jean, Cindy, and I had the most potential to make it. But this new lineup with Scherrie and Cindy had the most glamour and pizzazz, an opinion shared by fans. Visually we were perfect, and vocally, fresh and dynamic. Scherrie was more than a terrific singer; she had that indescribable something that makes audiences sit up and listen. Scherrie and Freda were vocally similar, like Dionne Warwick, Dionne's aunt Cissy Houston, and her cousin Whitney Houston. You know that their talent was genetic, honey!

Although she was only a petite five feet one, Scherrie was very sexy, and several writers dubbed her "the devil in the red dress." With her unique, powerful blues-and-jazz-inflected style, Scherrie, like Jean, was a great singer. No one would ever compare her to Diane, for which I was grateful. Scherrie had a fire, a spark, that the Supremes had been missing.

For the first time in a couple years, writers were taking a renewed interest in the Supremes. Local critics unimpressed by our latter-day appearances with Jean and Lynda noticed us now and raved. We could not have asked for better, more encouraging reviews, but we still had no new record out.

We spent New Year's Eve performing at the Contemporary Hotel in Disney World, ringing in 1974 after singing the O'Jays' "Love Train." Following the show, Scherrie invited us to go with her to a party at a nearby cabaret. When Scherrie came out wearing a simple cotton pants set, I told her tactfully that we just couldn't go around looking however we wanted.

"I don't care what people think," Scherrie replied. "I hadn't planned on going out tonight; this is what I'm wearing."

"People don't care if you planned to go out or not, Scherrie," I said shortly. "All they know is that we are the Supremes, and we have to look like it—all the time."

"Yes," Cindy chimed in. "We do have to be sure we look our best wherever we go."

Scherrie changed into something more appropriate. *Not this again*, I thought. Every group had one person who always swam against the tide. First Flo, then Jean. Right or wrong, the image mattered and had to be maintained. Cindy promised me she would keep an eye on Scherrie.

The cabaret was a lot like the little places we used to go to in Greenville, Mississippi, where my mother and cousins came from. Everything was very informal, and everyone was so friendly and "real down-home," as I wrote in my diary. Pedro enjoyed it because it reminded him of his homeland. It was the first good New Year's Eve I'd had in years, with my husband-to-be, my son, and Scherrie and Cindy.

In the past few years, I'd been approached by a number of people either connected to or part of what I think of as the record industry's underworld. Often, these were not even face-to-face meetings with the alleged Mr. Big, but cryptic messages passed to me orally by someone who *knew someone* who *had heard that someone* was interested in "helping" the Supremes. One time I got the "word" while flying to a date with a very prominent entertainer. He advised me that it might be "better" for me and the Supremes if I was on the "right side." *The right side of what?* I wondered.

A casual acquaintance familiar with the music industry once outlined for me an elaborate and incredible scenario about who controlled the business. Most of it was so blatantly outrageous, I couldn't believe it. But then this person said things that only someone with connections could know, things I won't even talk about today. Some things he said about the Supremes were plausible: that our records weren't being played because "someone didn't want them played," a situation that could be "rectified" if I would align myself with the right "important people" and stop fighting. But who? No one was about to answer me unless I first agreed to go along with the secret agenda, whatever it was, whoever it involved. In the past couple of years, I'd heard through the grapevine that "someone" wanted the Supremes and could get me the name. As far as I knew, no one had the name. I ignored these offers of "help."

Shortly after one of these encounters, I went to see a famous psychic, something I did now and then in those wild days of the seventies. The psychic said that my father was my guardian angel and was looking after me. I wouldn't make the wrong move, and I would succeed eventually. I was warned not to let anyone stop me or pull me down. He also said that I would have very bad times, and fifteen years of bad luck. That turned out to be true.

Over the past few years, I had gradually set up and controlled a separate corporation that handled all the Supremes' business. Motown had no objection; if anything, it was probably relieved. Before, the company handled every business and financial detail of our lives, professional and personal. Every expense—meals, gowns, car rental, salaries for musicians, conductors, road managers, assistants and the required payroll taxes, dry cleaning, storage, wigs, makeup, recording sessions, *everything*—was managed and paid for through Motown but out of our pockets. When I started going over the books, I was amazed to see just how much it cost us to work.

One big expense was our stage wardrobe. Our designers included Mike Travis (who also designed for Dionne Warwick and Liberace), Bob Mackie, Mike Nicola, and Pat Campano. We spent hours reviewing designs, picking out colors, fabrics, and other materials. Our outfits were some of the most lavish in show business. Many of the sequins and beads were imported, and all were applied by hand. Diane once remarked to Johnny Carson, "Little old ladies have gone blind trying to sew on all those beads." Some costumes contained tens of thousands of them. The red-beaded jumpsuit we wore for our first appearance on Ed Sullivan's show cost over $1,000 in 1970, and it was one of the cheaper ones.

Before long, each costume had its own name, and audiences had their favorites, such as a thirty-five-pound, bead-and-rhinestone-covered "Pink Chiffon," the green, lime-green, and white "Swirl" gowns from "T.C.B."; or the beige, beaded "Chandelier" gowns. Each fit us so snugly that a pound gained spelled disaster. If any of us got the least bit out of shape, costumes were returned to designers for painstaking, complicated alterations and whatever rebeading was needed.

Certain parts of the outfits required special care, and there was a perpetual stream of costumes on their way to and from designers so that seats, underarms, crotches, and other well-worn areas could be rebeaded. Because of all the handwork, the delicacy of some fabrics, and the unique dyes used, cleaning and storing them was yet another expense. Some outfits cost over $100 each just to clean. The cost of shipping trunks of thirty- to forty-pound gowns and suits all over the world was exorbitant. We probably worked several weeks each year just to keep our costumes alive!

Years before I'd never given a second thought to what it cost to put together a show. Just making changes each year to incorporate new songs (which required new arrangements, new choreography, new costumes, maybe new musicians, and weeks of rehearsal time) cost a minimum of $40,000 and as much as $100,000. Every date meant at least a dozen round-trip airfares for us, staff, musicians, and whoever else we needed, a dozen hotel rooms, three dozen meals a day, and other incidentals. On some dates, the "miscellaneous" unforeseen expense was a local hairdresser or a series of long-distance calls; other times, it was renting several cars or sound equipment, flying in and paying last-minute replacement musicians, or something even more costly.

In the sixties and early seventies we traveled with our own hairdresser, for example. Now we couldn't afford more than a skeleton staff: five musicians and three assistants. Meanwhile, back at home, we had people on staff, such as Hazel, Benny, and maids, drawing salaries whether the Supremes worked or not.

Retaining top musicians, however, was one major expense I never regretted. No matter how small the venue or how little the pay, I was determined to sound great. Cutting corners with second-rate players would only hurt us in the long run.

I'd decided that each Supreme receive a percentage of the corporation's income after all expenses were paid. I learned more than I ever wanted to know about unscrupulous or undercapitalized promoters, contract breaching, and the natural tendency for money to mysteriously disappear on its way from the box office to the Supremes, Inc., bank account. I found falsified receipts—a $60 piano-tuning bill with a suspiciously placed extra zero added, making it $600—and evidence of countless other ruses. It was impossible to keep on top of every single detail, and this is where Hazel proved a godsend. She examined, checked, and questioned every bill, check, statement, and contract that crossed my desk. She found countless errors and oversights, and, now and then, outright stealing.

Motown still had not finished our contracts or reached a settlement with the Hollands on Scherrie's contract, or so it claimed. Technically, she still "belonged" to Invictus, but the label wasn't doing much with her, so it's hard to figure out why Motown was having so much trouble getting her released. When I questioned one executive about why we weren't in the studio, he said the company couldn't record us without a contract. What a joke: in the early days, Berry recorded most of us without contracts. Something else was going on. Why weren't we recording?

After not hearing one word from Smokey about his promise to record us, I knew I was on my own. Not that I had really expected all that much from him. I love Smokey dearly, but his first loyalty will always be to Motown and Berry.

Because I still felt so close to the Motown clan in those days, I thought nothing about asking my few friends in the business to produce us. Marvin Gaye was one I approached over the years. When we got together, I described to Marvin what was happening, and he promised to stop by. When I told my housekeeper Ethel to expect Marvin Gaye, she looked as if she were going to faint. "Mary, should I make lunch for Mr. Gaye? Do you think he'd like some of my sweet-potato pie?" I told her I was sure he would. I had to laugh. Marvin was the sweetheart of every woman in the world, young or old.

It was a couple hours after Ethel's regular quitting time when Marvin arrived, and he didn't let her down. First he hugged me warmly, then after I introduced Ethel, he hugged her too. I know she will never forget that.

As we sat in the living room, Marvin ate a piece of Ethel's pie and drank a glass of milk. One of my cats climbed onto his lap, and we sat for quite a while in front of the fireplace.

"How do you feel about what's happening for Diane?" Marvin asked me. Because Marvin was Berry's brother-in-law and had fought so bitterly for his creative freedom, I knew that he—like most Motowners—had mixed feelings about her. Marvin was always Hitsville's rebel, and always, in his way, an outsider.

"I don't even think about it," I said. "I don't think she's the cause of my problems with Motown. I'm so busy trying to get my own life together, I hardly have time to think about anything."

"Well, baby," Marvin said softly, "you'd better slow down. Don't let anybody drive you crazy."

He promised he would write for us and produce us. I believe he really meant it, as he would mention it several more times over the years. None of these plans was realized, though, because Marvin had enough problems of his own.

Scherrie, Cindy, and I were up at Motown, finally picking songs for our next record, when we heard there would be yet another delay with the contracts. Berry was in his office, so I decided to stop in with Scherrie. The minute I saw him I felt like an old shoe he had tossed away.

"Hey, Mary, how are you doing? Scherrie, what's happening? Have you two signed your contracts?"

"No, Berry, we haven't," I said. "There are still all kinds of legal problems, and we are getting nowhere. We have to record, and this is really holding us up."

"Okay, okay," Berry said. "Let me call Abner and see what's going on."

He called Abner, and after speaking briefly, Berry hung up. "I've given Suzanne dePasse a lot more authority," he said, "and you can work with her when the contracts are all signed.

"You know," he added, "Diane's opening in Las Vegas."

"Yeah," I replied. "Tell her I said hello and good luck."

Scherrie and I were partway out the door when Berry suddenly remarked, "Mary, you know you're the one responsible for all the other girls leaving the group. You're always giving all the other girls too much power, like Diane and Jean. You really did it with Jean. That's why she left."

"It wasn't me, Berry. Especially not with Jean. It was you giving her all those lines, promising her the moon, and then letting things drop."

Berry said nothing.

"Berry, we're going to sign our contracts. I just want you to know that this time I'm going to be sure to read mine. *Very carefully.*"

"Well, Mary," he replied in all seriousness, "you know, if it weren't for me, you never would have had a contract."

So that's what Berry truly believed: everything that I was—everything that everyone there was—was only because of him. Sometimes I wanted to point out to him that everything he was, was because of *us*. I wanted to say, "You stole our name, and now I want it back!" Or, better yet, "Kiss my you know what," and walk away. But I didn't. I was caught in an invisible web.

In the meantime we got the go-ahead to sign our contracts. Mike Roshkind called me to say that, yes, Motown would delete the clause saying I waived all rights to the name. Within an hour of phoning Scherrie and Cindy with the good news, I got another call from Mike. This time he said, no, they could not do it.

When Bill Loeb, David Williams, and I met Mike at his office, he seemed surprisingly grim. "I have just spoken with . . ." he said, naming some other attorneys, "and they advised us not to let you sign the contract unless you waive all rights to the name."

Mike and I went back and forth, firmly but politely, for a while. Mike saw that I wasn't about to capitulate, so he went into what I called his hatchet-man bag. David Williams became so agitated that Mike asked him to leave.

"Mike, I am not signing under those terms," I said. "That's it."

"Fine," he replied evenly. *"We'll just have to get three other girls."*

The velvet glove was off, just like Flo had said it would be. But I wasn't going to be beaten down.

"You just try," I said, rising to leave. "Good-bye!"

Not long after *Dreamgirl* was published, I found myself on a plane sitting across from Mike and Smokey Robinson (whom he now manages) in first-class. Smokey was on a promotional tour of England. Between my first book and the "Motown 25" debacle, my relationship with Motown was nonexistent, so at first things were a bit awkward. After a while we got to talking, and I was surprised when Mike said he liked my book but felt I'd been too kind to many of the people in the story. "Mary," he said, as we sipped champagne, "you should have been harder. No one likes to hear all nice things." I smiled to myself, knowing my second book was in the works.

We talked some more. It was Mike who'd negotiated Florence's departure from the Supremes and presented her with the outrageous terms of settlement, including that she could never use the name *Supremes* again. "Mike," I asked, "how could you have done some of the things you did at Motown, those horrible things that really hurt people?"

"I was younger then," he replied. "But that was my job. One of the reasons I'm managing now is that I want to do something positive."

I was surprised at his frankness, but it did little to dull the memory of what he and other Motown executives had put me and the Supremes through in the seventies. I guess it goes to show that business, money, and power can make people do strange things.

This day in 1974, however, I saw Mike in a much less charitable light. I drove home nearly blinded by tears. As I turned off Sunset Boulevard and onto my street, my neighbor Johnny Mathis waved to me; I waved back, hoping he didn't see my face. I was a mess. My hands were shaking. All I could think was, *How can Mike do this to me?* By the time I pulled up my long driveway, I was weeping uncontrollably.

"What's wrong?" Pedro asked. I didn't answer as I ran down the mirrored hallway and into my red-velvet bedroom.

It was over. *Over.* Everything I'd worked for was gone. The one thing that had given Diane, Flo, and me the chance to make something of ourselves, to have something more than what our parents had, was gone, dead.

When I calmed down I told Pedro everything. Despite his persistence, I'd never let him see any of my business papers, until now. He read the contract Motown was offering and pointed out that it was essentially the same as the old one. I depended on Pedro's judgment. In fact, I began to feel that I could trust no one except him. Now I see that it was so simple; I was running from Motown and into my lover's protective arms.

I had no choice but to leave Motown. But then what? At moments like this a paralyzing fear crept over me. I could study all the facts, put together all that I knew, and know what was right for me to do. Still I was so afraid. Poor Flo's face loomed in front of me. *Oh God—don't let this happen to me,* I thought to myself, *I've never done anything to hurt a soul, I just want to sing, and be happy.* I felt so small and frightened. Somewhere deep inside me, though, was a powerful belief that I would do the right thing, that my life would eventually turn out all right, one way or the other. God would come to my rescue. There wasn't any real reason for me to believe this, but I did. That's the supreme faith that always seems to pull me through, even when all around me seems lost.

Early the next morning Berry called. "I spoke with Mike Roshkind and heard about the problems," he said quietly. Berry didn't sound like himself. He actually seemed concerned. "Mary, just what is it you want?"

Without thinking, I blurted out, "Fifty percent of the name *Supremes.*"

There was a second of silence, then Berry said, "You

got it. I'll have my people get right on drawing up those papers."

Was it that easy? I'd expected a hard time. As he spoke, I said a silent prayer of thanks to God for saving me and my family. *At least now*, I thought, *I won't end up destitute like Flo.*

In late February 1974 we went to Mexico City to appear at the Casino Real. We were all looking forward to working, because we needed the practice, the exposure—and the money. We attended a charity concert given by the Fifth Dimension.

Our trip to Mexico started out nicely enough, but soon we could only conclude that there was a hex on us. First we had trouble getting our luggage to the plane on time, then Cindy lost her passport. A week later our dressing room burned down, destroying tens of thousands of dollars' worth of gowns. The club owner signed a statement claiming that the full extent of the damages amounted to $250. Two hundred fifty dollars! We had costume jewelry that cost more than that. We lost nine sets of gowns, so the actual loss was more like $30,000. I phoned Hazel back in Los Angeles, and four more sets of gowns were shipped, but only one set fit all three of us. A few days later we were making a publicity appearance at a club. Suddenly the police broke in and, for some mysterious reason, arrested everyone. After being detained for three hours, we were set free. When we finally finished the engagement, we were glad to be home.

While we were gone, our manager and attorney tried to quietly interest another record company in us. ABC Records, which had done so well by the Four Tops, expressed the strongest interest, but later declined. I heard that the label got cold feet because Motown threatened legal action over the name the *Supremes*.

While all this madness was going on, I was still touring, mothering Willie, cooking meals, and planning for my wedding. Against my better judgment, several months earlier our manager had booked us to coheadline with Joel Grey at the Riviera Hotel in Vegas. So Pedro and I thought, *Why not get married there?* Vegas was still very glamorous. I became very excited about this great event. For a while I got so caught up in the happiness of picking out fabric for the wedding gown, finding the right wedding chapel in Vegas, making up the guest list, and so forth that all fears were forgotten. Now that I had decided to marry Pedro, it was just all too exciting.

During this time Pedro and I were just like two lovebirds. Plus, since I had allowed him to become more involved in my business affairs, he was happier, but I noticed that the more I allowed him, the more he took. The wedding was on, the cake ordered, the gown and the guest list were ready. I couldn't stop the wedding now.

Scherrie, Cindy, and I had to work our tails off to get ready for Vegas. We had to be a hit there. Since the Supremes now earned most of our income from performances, we needed to be in the top venues. For two days in mid-April we tried out our show at the Sahara in Lake Tahoe. It was a last-minute booking, so we weren't fully prepared, and it showed. The only bright spot came when, during her show at Harrah's, Liza Minnelli introduced us from the stage as "three entertainers I have admired and respected." She was one of those stars, like Cher and Dionne Warwick, who were always friendly toward me and never passed by without stopping to say hello and chat.

We got very bad reviews, all driving home the point that we could not take this same old show to Vegas. We needed the money and the exposure, true, but why embarrass ourselves? The constant pressure to be out working, even to our reputation's detriment, was a sore point between me on one side, and our manager and Motown on the other. They couldn't have cared less what happened to the Supremes, as long as they got their cuts. We should have been reworking the show or recording a hit. Couldn't they see that they were running the Supremes into the ground?

With just six days before the Vegas opening, we brought in Cholly Atkins and some other professionals to put together a new production. It was an impossible task, but we had to try. New songs, new steps, new group, new everything. We rehearsed every day until we couldn't stand up.

Phil Moore, an arranger, conductor, and pianist who had worked on Broadway and with such stars as Dorothy Dandridge, Marilyn Monroe, and Lena Horne, came in. He told us which songs we'd be doing, but when Cindy realized she had no solos, she became upset. She ended up getting a solo part in one number, which was fine, and fair. What bothered me, though, was her saying, "If I don't look out for myself, no one else will."

It never dawned on me that she wanted to sing lead; we'd never discussed it. If she had said something about it, I wouldn't have objected. I was crushed and, for a moment, quite angry. *After all,* I thought, *no one told her to leave the group the first time.* Now she was back, and all that time off showed. She still hadn't lost the weight. I begged her to take classes with my voice teacher, and she did for a while. More than anything, though, I was deeply hurt that my efforts on her behalf went unnoticed. I knew she wasn't that kind of person, but it made me think how things had changed.

It felt strange to do a thirty-five-minute opening set instead of our usual hour. Richard Roundtree, Cher, and Lamont Dozier came to see us. Everyone was complimentary and kind, but I knew we weren't as good as we should have been, and it was sad.

The important people at Motown knew that Pedro and I were getting married in Vegas. I still didn't know what the label was up to; it seemed a strange coincidence that Motown chose this time to send out Abner to work on me about the contract.

Abner had the agreement stating that I owned 50 percent of the Supremes' name ready for me to sign. The same day that Pedro and I got our marriage license, David Williams gave me the bad news: he'd heard from the Trademark Office that Motown owned the name. It was odd that it had taken him months to find that out. I was beginning to lose my grasp of all the legal intricacies. I did know, though, that I needed the name. Since getting 50 percent was better than getting nothing, I signed, against Pedro's advice. He told me that I would regret signing this deal, and he was right. The ink had barely dried on the new five-year contract when Abner said, "Look, Mar-ry, Motown should be managing the Supremes. Why don't you let us take over?"

"For nearly four years now I've held it together while Motown's done nothing," I answered. "There's no record out, and we are an opening act."

Motown's "giving" me 50 percent ownership of the name came with so many restrictions that it was essentially worthless *except* in one case: if Motown ever sold the rights to the Supremes' name, I would be entitled to half the proceeds. I'm sure Motown thought this "fine-print" restriction was quite clever. And it was. At that time, I'm sure it never occurred to Berry or anyone else that he would ever sell the name, or Motown. However, in 1988 he did.

Although I felt something was fishy about all of this, I couldn't figure out what. I had doubts and questions, but I wasn't an attorney. Short of getting a law degree myself, all I could do was listen to and trust my advisers. I'd tried my best. But besides my suspicions about the deal itself, I had questions about how it all came down. For one thing, Motown had been taking its sweet time with the contracts and hadn't recorded us for months. Suddenly, the day of my wedding, there was a big rush. What had made it so urgent that Motown flew in people from Los Angeles to get me to sign the paper? Why couldn't it have waited a few days? I was crushed at these new developments on the eve of my wedding.

Most of my family had flown in for the wedding, and many of our friends were there, too. Pedro and I were getting on each others' nerves, but that was normal. The morning of my wedding, my mother, my sister Cat, and my Aunt I.V. helped me get dressed. We were to be at the chapel at three o'clock, but by two my gown still had not arrived from Los Angeles. I was beginning to get nervous, wondering if Pedro really wanted to marry me, wondering where my dress was.

"I think I'm about to cry," my mother said.

"Mommy, please don't." I knew that if she did, I would too, and I'd already cried enough that day. I'd just finished applying my makeup, and I had to look gorgeous. After all, this was the day I'd waited for since I was a little girl, with the whole works: the church, the white gown, the handsome prince. But was I happy? At that moment, Mom and I *both* started crying, probably for the same reason.

At two-thirty my gown finally arrived. It was made from a Spanish-style pattern and trimmed in white lace and pearls. I put it on, and when I turned to look in the mirror, I began crying again. I didn't know why. The gown was perfect, and there I was, finally a bride. Maybe they were tears of happiness.

I arrived at the chapel before Pedro in "Grace," my Rolls-Royce. I had to wait in the back until he came, as the bride is not supposed to arrive before the groom. Then it was time.

I was taken to the front of the chapel. Pat Campano, my dress designer, pulled my veil over my face, telling Willie how to pull it back. I could feel the sun beating down on my head, and I could see the few remaining people hurrying inside the chapel. As Willie and I started down the aisle, I felt spaced. Our rhythm-section guys were playing my wedding march, "I Hear a Symphony." Cat walked in front of me, a beautiful bridesmaid. Pedro's sister Malvena, a flower girl, looked radiant, and Joey and Dax, Pedro's friends from Puerto Rico, were best men. Willie (who'd stepped on my gown coming down the aisle) pulled back my veil. He and I laughed as he squeezed my hand.

Pedro and I stood side by side. The lady nondenominational minister spoke to us. I felt like I was in a movie: the beautiful girl marrying the handsome man. I noticed Pedro had shaved off his mustache, which I despised because it made him look like a hard black militant. His eyes looked big and warm, his face as soft as a baby's. We held hands. His was shaking and a little cold, but firm. As I listened to the minister, I felt very happy. Pedro started repeating after her in his heavy Spanish accent. Most of the words he didn't say correctly. I started repeating after her and didn't say them correctly either. My voice was so quiet, it seemed to be coming from someone else. Pedro couldn't get the ring on. I laughed. The minister started reading from Gibran on marriage . . .

Then we kissed. I couldn't believe it: Man and Wife. As we turned to leave, my eyes brimmed with tears. Everyone kissed us and wished us well. We went outside to take photos and throw the bouquet. My sister caught it. Now on to the reception. It was nice. However, I had to paint the miniature couple on top of the cake brown with Hazel's eyeliner.

In addition to our relatives, other guests included Jim Brown, Joel Grey, Berry Gordy's mother, Cindy and Charles, Scherrie, Hazel, Bill Loeb, David Williams, and Ewart Abner and Bob Jones from Motown. Pedro and I left the reception around four-thirty and went up to our room, where we opened our gifts and jumped into bed. At eight that evening we were awakened by the phone. Our show started in fifteen minutes! Pedro and I ran around like crazy trying to get ready. When I got to the stage, everyone was waiting, and I was so embarrassed, holding up the show for ten minutes.

Our honeymoon was spent on the road with the Supremes. From the end of May through June we toured Hawaii, Hong Kong, Australia, and Japan. While in the last country, we taped a television program that aired there as a prime-time special and received great reviews. We planned to release the soundtrack here as a live album, and our manager sold the tape to ABC Television, which was going to broadcast it as part of the network's *Wide World of Entertainment* series. Somehow, the tape "disappeared." The soundtrack album was released in Japan, then suddenly and inexplicably withdrawn.

The weeks of work and travel took their toll on everyone, but especially on my marriage. I had been pretty much alone since leaving home at seventeen. Now I had a constant, domineering companion, my husband. The honeymoon was over almost as soon as it began.

A lot of problems started because, now that Pedro was my husband, he became the boss not only of me, but of the group as well. We were three women alone out there, and he took over. The one thing that bothered me was that he

Flo, Diane, and I at Big Bear Mountain in 1965, taping a Dick Clark TV show. We used a photo like this for the Supremes' Merry Christmas *album. (Photo: Mary Wilson Collection)*

*T*he Supremes in Holland in 1965.
(Photo: Paul Hux/Mary Wilson Collection)

*F*lorence Ballard, who was
the heart and soul of the
Supremes. (Photo: Mary
Wilson Collection)

*B*elting out a song with *Ethel Merman on* The Ed Sullivan Show *in 1968. We were performing an Irving Berlin medley with Ethel on that particular show. (Photo: Jeffrey Wilson's Hot Wax Music Archives)*

*C*indy and I in our "farewell" show with Diane, at the Frontier in Las Vegas, January 14, 1970. (Photo: Mary Wilson Collection)

My early-seventies "Black Pride" look. Photo sessions paid for by an admirer who prefers to remain anonymous. (Photo: Mary Wilson Collection)

We recorded three albums with the Four Tops in the early 1970s and had a ball. They called us "The Magnificent Seven," and we also toured together. In this photo I'm standing next to the main love of my life, Duke Fakir (far left). *(Photo: Hendin/Mary Wilson Collection)*

With Willie and the Jackson 5, giving out Christmas gifts to needy children. *(Photo: Mary Wilson Collection)*

This photograph was taken for the cover of our album New Ways but Love Stays, *and I always thought that it was the most dramatic portrait we ever had taken of the Supremes. (Photo: Mary Wilson Collection)*

In 1972 Lynda Laurence replaced Cindy in the group. I'll never forget these dresses: bugle beads for days! (Photo: Mary Wilson Collection)

*S*eated between Lynda and Jean on the cover of my favorite Supremes album, **Floy Joy**, which Smokey Robinson produced. Although Lynda (left) appeared on the cover, it was Cindy who was singing on every cut. (Photo: Mary Wilson Collection)

*O*nstage with Lynda and Jean in Los Angeles, 1973. (Photo: Allen Poe)

Mrs. Johnnie
requests the honour of
at the marriage
of her
Mary
to
Mr. Pedro
Saturday, May 11,
1820 Rising Glen
R.S.V.P. (213) 273-

He turned on the charm, and the rest is history. (Photo: Mary Wilson Collection)

In 1973 Jean and Lynda left the group, and I reformed the Supremes with Scherrie Payne (left) and Cindy Birdsong. (Photo: Harry Langdon/ Mary Wilson Collection)

The family wedding shot: Dax Diaz, best man; Malvena, Pedro's sister; Rafaela, Pedro's mom; Pedro; me; Johnnie Mae, my mom; Cathy, my sister; I.V. Pippin, the aunt who raised me; and my adopted son, Willie. (Photo: Mary Wilson Collection)

*C*utting the cake.
(Photo: Mary
Wilson Collection)

*S*cherrie Payne (left), Susaye Green (center), and I formed the
final Supremes incarnation from 1976 to 1977. (Photo: Sam
Emerson/Mary Wilson Collection)

The poster for my solo debut, in August 1979, at the Manhattan nightclub New York New York. This poster was done by the famed artist Eula, who painted the well-known Supremes poster from our Lincoln Center concert in 1965. The Supremes poster from 1965 is reprised at the bottom of this caricature, by my feet. (Poster: John Christe collection)

A truly rare shot: me singing a duet with Diane at my New York New York solo debut, August 28, 1979. She told the audience that night that we were still the best of friends. (Photo: Charles Moniz)

*F*lashing a supremely triumphant smile after my opening night at New York New York. (Photo: Robin Platzer)

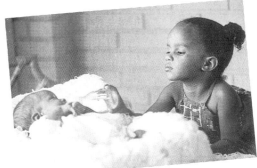

Turkessa feeding her baby brother, Pedro, Jr. (Photo: Mary Wilson Collection)

My children and my mother in 1983. (Photo: Mary Wilson Collection)

With Diane's father, Fred Ross, in Las Vegas in 1984, before joining him and Diane for dinner at Dionne Warwick's club. (Photo: Mary Wilson Collection)

The infamous Mercedes-Benz limousine that I bought from George Harrison, which was once owned by John Lennon. A Supreme and two Beatles . . . Honey, if this car could talk!!! (Photo: Steve Wood)

At Dionne Warwick's all-star AIDS fund-raiser, held at Lincoln Center, June 10, 1989. Left to right: Cyndi Lauper, me, Leslie Uggams, Dionne Warwick, Patti LaBelle, Gladys Knight, Whitney Houston, Blair Underwood, and Rita Coolidge. (Photo: Robin Platzer)

Starring in the play Beehive *was a big thrill for me. (Photo: Mary Wilson Collection)*

This is the real Mary Wilson—always looking forward to the next adventure and ready to pack my bags at a moment's notice! (Photo: Greg Gorman/courtesy of Thomas Smallwood at Rich's)

spent money as if it were his own—paying for everyone's dinner and buying "drinks on Pedro." He was the big shot, at least in his mind. Then, he began openly ordering me around. I was so tired of fighting now, after losing to Motown, that I just went along with this outlandish behavior.

I resigned myself to my situation. Whereas before I promised myself that I would try harder to make everything in my life better, now I accepted that I was different from the person I had been before. One night in Australia, I was lying in bed when suddenly I felt the sensation that another woman was taking over my body. She was all those things I fought so long to not be: negative, frightened, suspicious. All my courage and confidence disappeared. When I tried to picture myself now, I saw someone very small and cowardly.

I felt ashamed. But why? I tried to reason with myself. I promised I would stop being suspicious of people, although many of my problems stemmed from not being suspicious enough before. I wondered if other married women also felt they were being absorbed by their husbands, washed away. For a minute I thought I should see a psychiatrist.

In Hollywood, nightlife still retained a certain stylish cachet, and Pedro and I went out on the town like other people did. We partied hard. I had grown accustomed to "behaving" in public so as not to arouse Pedro's jealousy. We frequented private clubs where we saw many friends. I stopped dancing with men, even such old, close friends as Billy Davis. Billy didn't care for women, but that didn't prevent Pedro from acting insanely jealous toward him. The tension of having to monitor my every move was too much. Around this time I pretty much stopped going out at all. Unless I was on a stage, I was at home.

One of the few close friends I had was Teddy Pendergrass. He was still singing with Harold Melvin and the Blue

Notes, and Pedro knew them from their days playing clubs in Puerto Rico. The Blue Notes had been together since 1956, but their big hits began after Teddy became their lead singer in 1970. By 1976 or so, the Blue Notes had a solid string of hits ("If You Don't Know Me by Now," "The Love I Lost," "Wake Up Everybody"), and Teddy began to consider going solo. He and Pedro were running buddies from way back, so he often came to our house, and we'd talk.

That day Teddy said, "I really need to talk to you. I'm thinking about getting out of the group and going on my own. But I like the guys, and they gave me my start. Still, I feel like I can do other things too. I just don't know what to do."

"Teddy, if you truly feel that you have done all you can with the group and that you can do more on your own, you should go," I said. "But if you do leave, be honest and forthright about it." I must have been thinking about Diane and the Supremes. "Do it the right way, so there won't be any bad feelings."

"Do you think I could really make it alone?" he asked.

"I'm sure you can, Teddy. But remember: you've got to do it the right way."

"Thanks, Mary. There weren't many people I could talk to who would understand this."

Of course, Teddy went solo and became a sex symbol known to his female fans as "Teddy Bear." In 1982 he was paralyzed from the neck down in a freak car accident. We'd kept in touch, and I visited him at his home. One day he said to me, "You know, Mary, of all the people I've known, you're one of the few who's come to see me. It really means a lot to me."

Nine months after Scherrie and Cindy joined the group, they were still technically without contracts. These delays caused a lot of friction, because Cindy and Scherrie were essentially working for Supremes, Inc.; in other words, me. Despite my efforts to reignite the group spirit, I was the boss, and that made it hard.

I didn't like the fact that our husbands were suddenly so active in the business, either. Charles and Cindy's baby, David, traveled with us, so it made sense to find something for Charles to do for the group. Pedro had already pressured me into naming him road manager; we created a similar position for Charles. Even though I had reluctantly let Pedro work with us, I still felt that I could keep him out of my professional life. Before long, though, both were asking our manager about our business. The meddling husband is an occupational hazard for any female entertainer. I admit that while Pedro did push his way in, I wanted him there because he was strong, and I needed him. Cindy probably felt the same way about her man. Shutting out Charles would only have caused hard feelings, and besides, he and Pedro got along well and kept each other company on the road.

I loved Cindy and loved having her in the group, but her personal problems were affecting her performance. At times Cindy appeared quite happy to be back; then there were moments when she seemed ambivalent. "I want you to take some time and get yourself together, mentally and physically," I told her. Cindy cried a little bit, and my heart went out to her. Like me, she had marriage problems. Neither of us could accept not being able to give everything to both our careers and our marriages. I was beginning to see, though, that the only way many men can deal with successful women is to stifle their ambition and undermine their confidence. That's what Pedro was doing to me, and from what I saw, I believed that's what Charles was doing to Cindy. When I suggested to Cindy that she indulge herself and make herself as beautiful as possible, she gave me a sad, blank stare. There was nothing else I could do; the rest was up to her.

Diane was appearing in Los Angeles, and I really wanted to go see her. Even though we didn't talk very much anymore, I still enjoyed her concerts. When I asked Mike Roshkind for tickets, he said there were none. Funny: in all my years with the label, I'd never been denied tickets to see another Motown act; it was one of the perks. Later in the day, however, I got two tickets through Abner.

As I watched Diane sing, I thought of how far she'd come. Her inconsistent chart showings (only one of eight singles released since 1971 had made the Top 10, and her latest, "Sleepin'," had struggled to Number 70) did nothing to tarnish her stardom. She was far beyond all that, it seemed. The following year she starred in her second film, *Mahogany*.

Whatever exasperation I'd felt toward her had dissipated. As a grown woman, it was easy for me to see that many of the original Supremes' problems simply grew out of our youth and the pressures of our careers. Flo, Diane, and I responded as best we could. Not to say that I didn't think each of us could have handled certain situations differently; there's no one alive who couldn't be a better person. But through my recent dealings with Motown, I was coming to see that much of what I'd believed was Diane's doing back then was really Berry's. Ultimately, Diane was just like the rest of us working for Berry—only she didn't know it.

I'd never seen Diane give a better show. Once the curtain fell, I hurried backstage to compliment her. As I walked toward the dressing rooms, a guard stopped me and refused to let me pass. Several fans were standing nearby, and one said, "But she's one of the Supremes! You've got to let her go back!" The guard laughed in my face. Abner walked right past me with Stevie Wonder, making no effort to intervene on my behalf. I was speechless.

When I finally got back to her dressing room, Diane seemed happy to see me, but surprised. "Hello, Mary, how are you?" We embraced, talked about our families, and that was it.

Berry said, "Hi, Mary. You sure look good." And then he and Diane turned away. After having lied about the tickets, Mike was obviously embarrassed to see me there. I held my head high, but inside I felt like nothing. I wished Pedro were there with me. I felt so alone. It goes to show, you're only as hot as your latest project.

We began an eventful run at Magic Mountain, one of my favorite places to play because it always attracted lots of fans. This was our third year back, and tickets sold out so quickly that several shows were added. We had several special guests the first few nights: Freda Payne, Johnny Taylor, Berry's mother and sister Gwen, and Stevie Wonder. Stevie came onstage and did a song with us, which the crowd loved, and then afterward came backstage to visit.

I always remember this night, because it was the first time I really felt that Stevie was my friend. While guests and visitors poured into the small dressing room, Stevie and I sat back in a quiet corner and had our first—and last—deep conversation. He seemed concerned about what was happening with the Supremes and Motown's other groups. With the possible exception of Diane or Smokey, no one was happy with what Motown had become.

Stevie asked why I thought Lynda had left the Supremes, how I felt about the possibility of the Holland brothers producing the Supremes again (he thought it was a bad idea), and remarked that in his opinion Cindy lacked something onstage. I found this last point interesting, considering Stevie couldn't *see* her. He just heard something in our show and suggested that we might think about replacing her. He added that he'd written some new songs for us. Although he was very upset about what had happened with "Bad Weather," he said it didn't bother him that much anymore.

A couple days later Flo arrived from Detroit. We'd talked on the phone several times over the past months, and somewhere in the back of my mind I entertained the idea that she might rejoin us. Realistically, I knew it was a long shot. As I wrote in my first book, Flo drank quite heavily during this visit. We talked about her problems, and I was surprised to hear her say that most of the things that had happened to her were her own fault. She said she would stop listening to her family, and that now that she was broke, they wanted nothing to do with her anyway. All this time I'd been concerned about Flo because of her all-consuming anger over what her life had become. But now she seemed to have accepted her fate, and that killed me. I didn't know which was worse: to fight a losing battle or to never fight at all.

The first night, we agreed it might be better if she stayed home instead of coming with us to Magic Mountain. Flo said she looked forward to having some time alone. When I returned home, she was already asleep, and my house was a mess: liquor stained the rug, a statue lay broken on the floor. I cleaned up, and before I went to bed wrote in my diary, "If only I could save the world. But I can't even find the solutions for my own problems."

We talked for hours and hours, but never resolved anything. The trip's one bright spot was the night she joined Cindy, Scherrie, and me onstage at Magic Mountain. The fans cried out, "We love you, Flo!" She seemed happy for that moment, but a few days later she returned to Detroit, and I knew she was lost forever.

Having seen both Diane and Florence within a few weeks of each other, I thought about how different their lives were and how much we had all changed. I believed that deep inside, we were still the same girls we'd been back in high school, that all the changes everyone else saw in us were just external. *If we ever sat down together and really talked*, I thought, *it would be all right.* In their own ways, though, Diane and Flo said something else. Flo all but told me to give up on her. And Diane seemed so preoccupied with her stardom that I might as well not have existed. There didn't seem to be room in either of their lives for what we had been or for me. For very different reasons, Diane and Flo wanted to leave the Supremes far behind. But I couldn't, and it hurt.

After Magic Mountain, there were no live dates, no recording sessions, nothing. I entertained friends, went to parties, tried catching up on things around the house. Even though I was relaxing, I felt very, very tired. I couldn't even imagine going to Las Vegas with Pedro for a weekend, something I'd always loved to do. Was I depressed, physically exhausted, or what? Then one day my doctor called and said, "You'd better start knitting baby booties." I hung up the phone and cried for an hour. It didn't seem real to me. I was finally going to have a baby!

Pedro was thrilled, and I was walking on clouds. But the reality of having a baby soon hit me. I had to start planning for time off, and this gave our unresolved problems with Motown a new urgency. Now we had to get some work to pay the bills, and Pedro and I had to find a new, larger house.

Besides Willie, we had Pedro's younger brother and sister, Rafi and Malvena, living with us. Pedro worked, but as our road manager; he'd quit law school. Still, in his mind he was boss. While he felt no compunction about reprimanding and even disciplining Willie, I was not to raise my voice to either of his siblings, even though I supported, fed, and clothed them, and paid their tuitions. Our different ideas about how the kids should behave was a constant source of conflict.

September 1974

Well, it finally happened: Pedro beat me up. It all started when I wouldn't take Rafi with me to see Al Green in concert. Boy, Pedro looked like he hated everything about me. He said I wasn't going unless I took Rafi. Of course I said no, because Rafi had been bugging me all afternoon. When I refused, Pedro went off. I took a good look at him. His eyes became like steel. He was like a stranger, very unreasonable. He kept repeating that Rafi was his brother. He slapped me around, onto the floor. At one point, I couldn't believe this was happening. Why can't we be happy? I thought of the baby, especially when I fell to the floor. I didn't want him to hurt me, so I fought back. The times before, when Pedro broke the windows, threw me in the pool, I was very afraid, because I've never been around someone who completely lost control. But this time, with the physical beating, I felt it was too much for me to handle. I mean, is love worth all this?

October 1974

A Married Woman's Poem of Sadness

Love comes in many varied shapes, forms, and degrees. I have had many different kinds since my childhood, but I have never had one as confusing as this one. Most of the love I have experienced brought me varied degrees of joy and pain, but never this complete numbness.

It smothers me. It's like being in a room with no windows, like what I'd imagine solitary confinement to be. It's like being under a heavy

blanket. I can neither see nor breathe. I have
no freedom. Love shouldn't be so restricting.
One should still have the freedom of being one's
self, maintaining one's own beliefs. It's hard
being completely blanketed by someone. It makes
you want to fly away.

CHAPTER 9

The early months of my pregnancy were wonderful. I enjoyed being pregnant, finally having my own baby to dream about. If anything, I was tired all the time because of the constant travel. The postshow parties and dinners went on, and Pedro went out, while I stayed in my room. I wished that I could just stop and rest for a while.

In October the Supremes went to Japan at the invitation of Princess Shimazu and her husband to host an international celebrity tennis tournament. Also with us were actresses Janet Leigh, Claudine Longet, and Barbara Anderson, composer Burt Bacharach, Peter Lawford, and Davy Jones and Mickey Dolenz of the Monkees. We paired off in different combinations to play tennis. I was pitted against the top Japanese tennis pro. Of course I lost, but I was awarded a kimono for being the most enthusiastic player.

We gave a dinner concert for over five hundred politicians, entertainers, other VIPs, and the princess. The concert raised $20,000 for UNICEF and was a huge success. During our extended version of "Love Train," I invited the princess's husband to "come up on stage, honey, and join my love train." He politely declined, and later I learned that this wasn't exactly proper protocol. The Japanese are far more reserved than Americans. Still, I think everyone had a good time, and the show was later broadcast as a prime-time television special in Japan. The Supremes were still stars everywhere—everywhere but America.

When I got home I called Florence, who was living with my mother for a few days. She'd lost her house to foreclosure. Unfortunately, none of her brothers and sisters could take her and the three little girls in. There was even talk among people who knew Flo that her family wanted to put her in a sanitarium.

Despite all the misfortune that had befallen Flo, I was surprised that she sounded better than she had in years. She was relieved to be staying with Mom, and Mom was happy to have her. Flo and I spoke very honestly to each other. "I told you years ago, Flo, that you gave your family too much," I said. "It's a sad thing to realize, but when it comes right down to it, family is just like other people. They're there for you when things are good, but when things get rough they may or may not be able to hang around." There wasn't very much I or anyone could do for Flo. While I was advising Flo about spending too much money on her family, I should have listened to some of my own advice. I now barely had enough money to support my husband, his siblings, Willie, my mother, and the Supremes; in fact, I was in debt.

We remained on the road almost constantly through November. Pedro wasn't always with us, so his paranoia increased. All through the night, he would call to carry on about some "rumor" he claimed to have heard about me. After a night of this I'd wake up feeling like a zombie. This couldn't have been good for my baby, and now, three months pregnant, I worried more and more about my health.

One evening I came into the dressing room crying my eyes out. By now Cindy and Scherrie knew that Pedro often beat me. Like most battered women, I said nothing about it. Cindy held me as I cried on her shoulder. "Everything will be all right, Mary," she said softly. "Don't cry." Neither of them mentioned Pedro's cruelty; they just made me feel cared for. After this, their problems with Pedro escalated, and Scherrie seemed to disagree with him on almost everything.

Pedro was determined to become someone important and powerful in Hollywood, just as he had in Puerto Rico and in his homeland. Besides a failed film company he'd launched with Jim Brown, Pedro always seemed to be "making deals." Pedro was nothing if not charming and smart, and he knew how to get things going. Unlike me, he wasn't afraid to meet new people or try new things.

For example, he gave a luncheon at our home for a young Muslim leader named Louis Farrakhan. Mr. Farrakhan espoused black financial independence and wanted to meet all the black entertainers in Hollywood. In exchange for Pedro setting up introductions, Mr. Farrakhan promised to see that Supremes records were played on the Muslim radio stations in New York and Chicago. Many people dropped by to meet him, including Stevie Wonder, Lola Falana, football-star-turned-actor Bernie Casey, and Paula Kelly, the first black *Playboy* playmate. I felt it was important to publicly support black causes and blacks who were making positive contributions. This is one reason I had so many qualms about saying anything against Motown, a black-owned company.

In the last decade the civil rights movement had brought so many changes, but there was still a long way to go. Yes, there were more successful blacks than ever, but racism was something we all contended with daily. Pedro and I went to Las Vegas with our friends Herb and Mauna Loa Avery for the weekend. One morning Mauna Loa and I got word that our husbands had been arrested. Pedro and Herb had stopped by a local club off the main strip and were just talking. Or so they told us. Because they didn't buy any drinks, the owner called the police and had them arrested for trespassing. We bailed them out, and they had to stand trial at a later date.

It was outrageous and unjust. Even though black performers brought millions of dollars into Las Vegas, if you were a black man walking around town too late at night or happened across someone who didn't like you, you were suspect. The whole episode was upsetting for everyone, but especially for Pedro and Herb. Both very proud men, they were angry about their treatment. This wouldn't be the last time the two of them got into a scrape because of their color.

After a period of relative calm, Willie began having trouble in school. He was now fifteen and a half, and I suspected that he was smoking cigarettes behind my back. Hollywood wasn't a great place to raise a kid, and in our neighborhood there were few children to play with. I tried talking to him but sometimes felt I couldn't reach him. If I'd raised him from birth, maybe things might have been easier. It broke my heart to see how hard things were for Willie, despite all the time spent tutoring and helping him.

Around this time, my brother Roosevelt briefly reentered my life. We really didn't have that much to say to each other. He was very easygoing and seemed to take life as it came. He also smoked what I considered far too much pot, but I said nothing. Who was I to lecture him? Back then everyone still thought of marijuana as safer than alcohol. From our few conversations on the subject, I knew that Roosevelt's experiences in Vietnam were never totally out of his mind. In Willie and my brother I saw two proud young black men whose futures were dimming, through no fault of their own.

Pedro was still talking to Marvin Gaye about working with us, but things never came together. We visited Marvin in his studio once. He was singing in the control room instead of the vocal booth, because it made him more comfortable.

When he saw me, he said, "Hey, baby," and kissed me on the cheek, carefully leaning toward me so he wouldn't crush my swollen stomach. I was alarmed at how exhausted and run-down he appeared. I don't think he'd slept in days. After this meeting we stopped pursuing the idea of working with Marvin.

In December we finally started recording with Terry Woodford and Clayton Ivey, two writer-producers from Muscle Shoals. The songs included "Give Out, but Don't Give Up," "You Turn Me Around," "Color My World Blue," and "You Can't Stop a Girl in Love." These appeared on our next album, *The Supremes;* its other tracks were produced by a number of producers: Brian Holland, Greg Wright, Mark Davis, Michael Lloyd, and Hal Davis. I sang lead on four of the nine songs and shared a lead with Scherrie on the first single, "He's My Man."

Pedro insisted that I be given more leads, which created a degree of tension. Some people saw this as me just flexing my ego, but it was a matter of survival. I finally accepted the responsibility to prepare myself for future personnel changes and possibly the end of the group. After all my years in the Supremes, I was still the least known of the originals. Record buyers and club-goers assumed there were no original Supremes left. That hurt.

As I prepared to sing my leads, Scherrie grew very quiet, and Cindy acted strangely. We'd rehearsed for days, but wouldn't you know it, once in the studio I lost my voice! It was totally psychological; I was scared to death and felt guilty taking leads meant for Scherrie. I wasn't ready to really step out as a full lead singer.

Pedro and I met with Cindy and Charles and pleaded with her to apply herself. She had started taking voice lessons, then dropped out. Now that we were officially signed and recording again, Motown took a keener interest in our internal affairs. I heard that Motown was secretly looking to replace Cindy. I hated them for that, but I was angry at Cindy for giving them an excuse. Scherrie and I felt that Cindy could make herself great again and told her so often, but nothing worked.

January 1975

Pedro said I should realize by now that my career has gone downhill. I've known it's been slipping, but I keep assuring myself I'll make it to the top again. Each night I cringe as we walk onstage. The audience is all young kids. Plus, this place is out in the dumps, and it's wintertime, to make it worse. My gowns are getting too short in front as my baby gets bigger, and I am finding it very difficult to move as rapidly on stage. I must admit, though, I look very pretty being pregnant. In fact, I feel beautiful.

Pedro said he feels hurt when he touches me and I reject him. Of course I don't openly reject him. I know he's speaking of those fears I have that creep up on me. I don't know why I still walk around like a frightened kid. But Pedro feels it. He thinks of them as something personal against him, but it's more than that. It's the fear within me of losing everything. I've tried to rid myself of it by working hard, but it's still there.

When not working, I was getting things ready for the baby and trying to salvage our working relationship with Motown. Not long after Diane and Berry returned from Rome, where they were filming *Mahogany*, she called me. We had an interesting chat. I was surprised to hear from her. But, typically, she just rang me up as if we talked on the phone all the time.

She asked me what was happening, and I told her that I thought Motown could be doing more for us. This wasn't any secret; I had been widely quoted in the industry trade papers as saying the same thing months before. It was the talk of Motown for some time. Diane was surprised. "Well, Mary, you just have to go to Berry and tell him. You can do it, I know you can. You just get them to do what you want."

"Diane," I replied, "you don't understand. Motown is doing nothing for us. I've done all that I can do alone."

Diane knew that my baby was due soon, and she promised she would come by the house to visit, but she never did. I could never figure out what prompted these calls. I sometimes wondered if she felt the way I did, like there was some unfinished business we should address, like she missed me. But I never knew.

I treasured my happy moments and could separate the good parts of my life from the bad. Whenever I had cause to feel happy or blessed, I accepted it. I am the same way about people. For better or worse, I tried to love those around me as they were and help them. I could not write them off or turn them away.

As my birthday approached I began to feel forgotten. Here it was just weeks before my baby was due and still no baby shower. The weekend of my birthday Pedro and I went out to dinner, although Peter Lawford had invited us to a party. I couldn't understand why we weren't going to the party, but Pedro was very insistent about this dinner. We had a wonderful meal at La Scala, then headed over to Peter's party at the Candy Store.

When we got to the private club, a woman at the door checked a list and then said haughtily that she wouldn't admit us. I felt my temper rise and began to say, "Of course our name is on the list—" Suddenly I heard yells of "Surprise!" There were all my friends, including Peter, Cindy, Herb and Mauna Loa, Richard Roundtree, and the Fifth Dimension. Even Lynda Laurence and Jean Terrell were there. I received so many beautiful gifts, and after the club closed the party moved to our house.

That Sunday I went to a luncheon at Scherrie's house, and there was another surprise: a baby shower. Cindy, Hazel, Jayne Kennedy, Dionne Warwick, Natalie Cole, Freda Payne, and some other friends were there. More beautiful gifts and happiness. Not long after, we attended a party that Berry's sister Gwen gave for our mutual friend Billy Davis. Earlier that day I had felt my first labor contractions. Berry hugged me warmly. He seemed a little awkward, but it was nice to be together. All night people came over to rub my stomach and wish me good luck. For a short time everything seemed so wonderful.

A couple days later, though, I was back in a blue funk. Pedro and I were fighting. My mother was there, waiting for her grandchild to arrive, and when she wasn't looking, I cried. This was supposed to be the happiest time of my life.

That day Herb instructed me to go to the hospital; the baby was coming. I was so thrilled. My elation lasted until I got to the hospital room, where the real nitty-gritty of childbirth hit me right between the eyes. Two nurses came into my room arguing.

"I'll do the shaving," said one, brandishing a razor.

"No, you do the enema," replied the other.

Then a laboring woman in the next bed screamed out, cursing her unborn baby's father. Well, that turned me around. My contractions started slowly, but I made steady progress, with Pedro at my side. We weathered six hours of labor, and even though Pedro had attended only a few of the natural-childbirth classes, he was supportive. Unfortunately, he'd missed the classes about when things go wrong, so he didn't fully comprehend what was happening when Herb said, "Your baby's heart rate is a little funny. We may have to take it."

"What do you mean, 'take it'? " Pedro asked, turning pale.

"It may have to be caesarean," Herb explained, trying not to alarm us. "That means we cut the abdomen and take out the baby."

"What? Okay, Herb," I said, "whatever it takes."

Pedro sat beside me, trying to put up a brave front, but I could see his fear when they began to cut. It seemed like no time at all before Herb peered over the sheet and announced, "It's a girl!" A few more seconds, and I think Pedro would have fainted right there. Herb laid my baby across my chest, and I knew what being blessed truly felt like.

My next thought was, *What will Pedro say?* I knew he wanted a boy. In fact, I had been afraid to even pick a girl's name. But suddenly it didn't matter. I had my baby. While I lay in the recovery room, Pedro and Herb drank champagne, and when I saw them several hours later, they were in fine shape.

Pedro brought me a beautiful plant. I asked him was it was called. *"Turquesa,"* he replied, "Spanish for *turquoise."* So we named our daughter Turkessa. She was the most beautiful baby. I spent hours looking at and holding her. She was an angel to me, a gift. My mother was so excited, she stayed over in my room, sleeping in a chair. Everyone visited, and by the time we received all the flowers and fruit baskets, my room looked like a florist's shop. Diane and her husband Bob tried to visit one evening but arrived too late; they promised to come by the next day, but never made it. Lola Falana and Mira Waters also dropped by, along with Scherrie, Cindy, and Hazel. Herb, Jim Brown, and journalist Walter Burrell were Turkessa's godfathers.

With all the euphoria came the physical reality of having a baby, which every mother knows. After major surgery I needed plenty of bed rest, but sitting around the house wasn't for me. I had to save my energy, though, because Motown planned to release *The Supremes* next month, and in three weeks we were to tour Japan again.

Having a baby brings many couples closer together; that wasn't the case for us. I'd be breast-feeding Turkessa, and Pedro would dash in and dash out, going here and there, never stopping to talk. When we did talk, we fought. I'd become more worried about money. Our commitments to our employees and Cindy and Scherrie continued, even without money coming in. We had to stop spending, but Pedro would not. Even though he brought in little money, he'd long ago gotten into the habit of spending as much as he wanted.

Pedro was now our manager. He'd been pushing me for months, and I gave in reluctantly. When I told Berry, he didn't say much, but I could tell by his expression that he didn't think it was a great idea. "I'll be here to guide him," I said. "I can tell him what to do."

"Mary, you can't," Berry replied. "And it won't be the way you want it to be."

Needless to say, I didn't listen. I needed Pedro because I felt he was the only person I could trust, so I overlooked everything: the flashy clothes, the fast talking, the bravado. Berry, and everyone else at Motown, saw right through it.

Could Pedro do a worse job managing the group than

anyone else had? The answer was no. At least he could offer the one thing no one else could, and that was concern for what happened to me.

Cindy and Scherrie were opposed to this change. When Pedro told them that he was taking over, they said nothing, and that said it all. I knew what they were thinking: the same things Flo and I used to think about Diane and Berry.

It was very obvious that Pedro had a lot to learn, but he refused my help, and his flaws as a manager were soon apparent. We went to Las Vegas in May 1975 to sing the National Anthem before the Muhammad Ali–Ron Lyle heavyweight title fight. The live national broadcast began, and Cindy, Scherrie, and I stood in the ring, waiting for the music. After a few interminable seconds, I spotted Pedro outside the ring.

"Where's the music?" I mouthed to him.

"There is no music."

Oh, no, I thought. Scherrie hummed a note, and we sang "The Star-Spangled Banner" a cappella. Happily, we rose to the occasion, and Howard Cosell even commented on how good we sounded.

Three weeks after Turkessa's birth we arrived in Tokyo to kick off our two-week tour. Hardly any fans were waiting for us at the airport. Every year it seemed that fewer people came to greet us; even the number of reporters at the press conference dwindled. My mother and mother-in-law came along to help with the baby, and Herb and Mauna Loa were there too. The crowds were okay, and most of the shows were fine, but some of the clubs we played, like one in Manila, were small and dirty. It was demeaning to be in places like that, especially when people would say, "Oh, you're at *that* club? You really should be at . . ." As if I didn't know that.

Pedro was out almost every night. He insulted me when

we were together in public. He made me hate myself. I began thinking that if all I could have was my career, and Pedro could help me put that together, fine. Sometimes I saw my situation very objectively: I'd made a mistake, and it was my job to fix it. At other times, though, my insecurities overwhelmed me. Then all I wanted was for Pedro to love me and care for me. It was almost schizophrenic. Because Pedro could be like two different people, I began to think like two different people just to deal with him.

In June Motown finally released the Supremes' first single in two years, "He's My Man," a sexy disco number. Scherrie and I traded off leads, and although I was never fond of disco, I loved this song. The single and the album got very positive reviews, and the renewed interest in the Supremes garnered us lots of press and many television appearances on such shows as *Soul Train, American Bandstand,* and Dinah Shore's program.

The industry treated *The Supremes* as a comeback album. Working with so many different producers kept the LP from achieving the kind of cohesiveness our albums with Frank and Smokey had, but maybe that wasn't so bad. There was a little something for everybody, as they say. In the year and a half the Supremes hadn't recorded, times had changed, and several girl groups came on very strongly, particularly the Three Degrees (especially in England) and Labelle.

Labelle was Cindy's old group and the Supremes' former cohorts, Patti LaBelle and the Bluebelles, but totally revamped with futuristic costumes and a sassy style. Their recent Number One "comeback" hit, "Lady Marmalade," was fresh and daring. Interestingly, the song's writer-producer, Allen Toussaint, had dated Jean Terrell years before. At the time, Jean didn't think it was important that he produce us, even though I suggested she ask him. I'm not one to speculate, but in this case it is tempting. Labelle took a drastic step, and it worked. Now if we could just find the right person with the right ideas for us, the Supremes could be on top again.

That August we attended the first annual Rock Music Awards show, Don Kirshner's answer to the Grammys. Diane and Elton John cohosted the nationally televised event, and performers included Kiki Dee, Chuck Berry, and Labelle, who won best r&b single for "Lady Marmalade." After the show, we went backstage to visit Diane and Labelle. When we got to Diane's dressing room, she was leaving with her two daughters and Mike Roshkind. She seemed very distracted and only waved as she walked right past me. I made a silent vow not to visit her backstage again. It wasn't worth the humiliation.

Next we went with Cindy to visit Labelle. She had stayed in touch with Sarah Dash, Nona Hendryx, and Patti LaBelle, and was understandably proud of their great success. Like me, she was hoping to rekindle some kind of warmth among them, but when we got there, the three of them acted coolly toward us. Cindy was her usual friendly, outgoing self, but it wasn't being taken the way she meant it. An unspoken rivalry between our two groups seemed to color the conversation.

Show business is hard, and sometimes performers struggle for so long that it makes them hard too. I realized that the reason I didn't regard other groups as competition was because the Supremes had been on top for so long. Once some of those performers who'd been second, third, fourth, or fiftieth to us made it, they let me know it. Now that the Supremes had fallen on lean times, the tables were turned.

In interviews I spoke frankly about where we stood with Motown. I've been accused of being foolishly optimistic about the group; if only I could have been. By summer all signs indicated that we weren't going to have a hit. "He's My Man" wasn't out more than a couple of weeks before we could tell it wasn't receiving adequate promotion. Despite all the promises to promote us, many key radio stations across the country didn't receive the record, much less get pushed to play it. I took heart, though, because without any help from Motown, the album and the single made respectable showings. "He's My Man" was a Number One disco hit and reached Number 69 on the black singles chart. Our other 45s, "Where Do I Go from Here" and "Early Morning Love," were picked up on by club DJs, spurring more record sales.

Motown's ideas about what our problems were and how they could be solved differed radically from mine. In one of the Supremes' monthly fan club letters, an upper-level company staffer was quoted (anonymously, of course) as saying, "The Supremes' troubles started when they went independent . . . We at Motown are a family and we, as any family does, like to deal with members of our family. We work well together. When someone brings an outsider in and tries to force him into our family, the family is apt to rebel. Now, I'm not saying we rebelled against the Supremes, but the fact that we did not like their independent management was to the disadvantage of the Supremes. We could not communicate.

"I'd be the first to admit," the mystery spokesman continued, "that Motown hasn't always been fair with the group. But by the same token, the group has not always been fair with us."

I'm still trying to figure out just what we did to Motown that was so "unfair." I could only take perverse pleasure in noting the label's problems: the Jackson 5 had just split to go to Epic, Diane and Marvin were having trouble with their singles, and Stevie Wonder was beginning another lengthy holdout for a better contract.

That summer we hired Phil Moore and Geoffrey Holder to redo our act. Phil did the music, and Geoffrey choreographed our routines. Geoffrey, who was responsible for the Broadway hit *The Wiz* (and who had become a familiar face as the man in the 7-Up TV commercials extolling the virtues of the "un-cola nut"), had a million ideas. They wanted to give us a good repertoire as well as an exciting, new visual image. It was a huge expense, over $60,000 coming out of our pockets, but it was now or never.

Phil and Geoffrey spent a lot of time talking to us, explaining how they saw our personalities and how we presented ourselves onstage. We felt they had the right ideas. The syncopated choreography we'd done for so many years was changed. One new number, "Body Heat," was very suggestive, with us caressing ourselves—tastefully, of course. For another bit, a fantasy sequence, a genie granted us wishes to be anyone we wanted. Scherrie played Bessie Smith; Cindy, Marilyn Monroe; and I chose Josephine Baker, the legendary black diva. Growing up, I had idolized Baker. She was beautiful, sophisticated, exotic, and sexy, scandalizing Parisian audiences in 1926 by coming onstage wearing only a single pink flamingo feather.

Before we started doing this routine, Geoffrey said to me in his resonant Jamaican accent, "Mary, you *are* Josephine Baker. I think you should play her in a movie." He later introduced me to Miss Baker, in Hollywood on her last U.S. tour. It was such a thrill for me.

"Jo," Geoffrey said to her, "this is Mary Wilson of the Supremes."

Miss Baker studied me carefully for a moment, then said to Geoffrey, "You were right. She does look like me."

That made my day.

Opening night in San Francisco basically went well, but I was tired and at points lost my voice. Still, we got very nice reviews, and the new show and new gowns gave us a lift. While we were there, *Billboard* was holding a convention, and

Flip Wilson invited us to his cocktail party. I declined, fearing what Pedro would do. He'd already torn up all my pictures of Flip and destroyed all my diary entries containing his name.

Scherrie, Cindy, and I were outdoors in a nearby garden, posing for a magazine cover, when someone told me that my son and Pedro's sister were at Flip's party. I ran up to the suite, grabbed Willie and Malvena, and told them they had to leave immediately. The whole time I looked over my shoulder, hoping Flip didn't see me.

We were almost out the door when Flip approached us. He was very happy to see me, but all I could think about was getting out before Pedro showed up or someone there saw us. I knew Pedro would go crazy if he found out I'd seen Flip. Flip didn't understand why I acted so strangely; I think his feelings were hurt.

That night Pedro came home and gave me the third degree, asking over and over where I'd been that day, what I'd done. I'm a poor liar, and Pedro knew this. He questioned Malvena, and she told him the truth, so he immediately assumed that I'd gone up there to see Flip, to sleep with him. Pedro went out, came in late, and the next morning announced, "Now you and Flip can be together. I'm filing for divorce, and I'll get custody of Turkessa too."

Silly as it sounds now, I took his threats seriously. Although my mother had raised me with many old-fashioned ideas about sex and men, I had disregarded much of her advice. After all, this was a new era. I was never ashamed of how I conducted my life or my relationships, but some deep-seated, residual guilt left over from my upbringing seeped into my consciousness. Furthermore, I believed that when you married and had a family, you stayed together for eternity and worked out whatever problems you encountered. Whenever Pedro harped on how I was trying to attract men,

I reviewed my every word and gesture, wondering, *Did I really do that? Did it really look like that?* At first I easily dismissed his accusations as silly. But soon the guilt about sex my mother had passed on to me mixed with Pedro's archaic ideas, and I began to believe I'd done something wrong. I didn't even bother arguing with Pedro. He acted like an irate, powerful parent, and I reacted as the child I had been so many years ago.

Pedro's paranoid obsession with my (nonexistent) affairs escalated over the years, so that before long I was afraid to look any man in the eye. I rarely left the house alone, and if I did I had to report my every move. My baby and my work were the only escapes from my prison of fear. I had lost most of my friends; either Pedro had scared them away, or they felt uncomfortable witnessing the abuse. Many of my women friends called and tried to be helpful by hinting at Pedro's infidelities, but I didn't listen to them. Almost all my male buddies were either out of my life completely or, like Herb, Jim Brown, and Marvin Gaye, had become Pedro's friends too. No one ever called me anymore. I felt truly alone.

I see now that the main reason I continued fighting the losing battle for the Supremes was that I felt alive only when I was with my daughter or singing. Performing was like therapy to me, the stage my home away from home. At least there I knew who I was and that people loved me. Having my career and Turkessa gave me faith that my life would eventually work out. My heart breaks for women who are totally alone in an abusive marriage. It's a hell you cannot emerge from unless you have some hope, no matter how slight. I thank God I had that.

Like most abused women, I protected myself by learning to deal with my husband's insults and outbursts. I knew what upset him, so I did all I could to prevent those things from happening. With each abusive act or cruel word I lost another bit of myself. Only after reflecting on the awful experience years later did it become clear what had happened to me and how it had happened.

Pedro's power over me was complete. You can be presumed guilty for only so long before you begin to act and feel guilty. I walked around full of shame for nothing. In my heart I truly believed that if Pedro went before a judge, I would lose Turkessa. My husband could be so convincing, so smooth. In my worst dreams, he would produce that photograph he'd found of me and Tom Jones; then everyone would see what a bad person I was. I remembered when Pedro forced me to write that list of men I'd slept with. Those names now haunted me like ghosts.

Turkessa meant everything to me; I couldn't lose her. To prevent that, I'd do anything, including staying with Pedro.

CHAPTER 10

*B*y late summer Pedro had made headway with some of Motown's top people, especially Suzanne dePasse, who then headed the creative division. Of everyone, she put forth the most effort on the Supremes' behalf. Suzanne saw to it that we got good material, the best photographers, and so on, and she and Pedro worked well together.

Pedro tried to ingratiate himself with the label's higher-ups, sending flowers to their secretaries, for example. He began believing he'd turned Motown around. Pedro thought it would be great to throw a dinner for Suzanne and Abner. He invited other guests, rented tables, and got me to cook a lavish buffet-style dinner. I knew these people were just playing with him; they weren't going to show up, and I told him so. Sadly, I was right.

The company line—one that many Motown historians and journalists have accepted unquestioningly—is that Pedro caused the Supremes' downfall. In truth, Motown had ruined the group before he came on the scene. If nothing else, Pedro made it possible for us to continue. Though making many mistakes, we recorded some great music during that time. He got us the best booking agents, publicists, accountants, and attorneys.

I saw through Pedro's games, but I also knew his other side. No one had ever believed in him. I felt that if Pedro accomplished something real, like making the Supremes a success, he would stop all the make-believe and settle down.

Part of Pedro's campaign to get around Motown included asking Mike Roshkind to be a godfather of one of our kids. I vetoed that one right off. Then one day he asked, "What do you think about asking Diane to be Turkessa's godmother?"

Growing up, I'd always thought that each of my children would have two godmothers, Diane and Flo. But so much had changed. Asking someone to be your child's godmother is a very personal thing. "I don't think it's a good idea," I said. "We aren't close anymore." I felt Diane would think I was using her because she was a star.

Pedro badgered me until I relented. Patching up things between Diane and me was important to him. Frankly, I was surprised and very touched when she accepted the invitation to be Turkessa's godmother. In 1979, when Turkessa was four years old, she was baptized at St. Patrick's Cathedral in New York City. Diane stood as her godmother and Herb Avery became her godfather.

In early September we took our new act to England, where the press roundly criticized us for being "too slick." The British had tired of us too, it seemed, and "He's My Man" did not even chart there. Making this all the more frustrating was that even our sharpest critics made a point of mentioning how much better we looked and sounded. There was something about our presentation, our approach, *us*, I guess, that missed the mark. We were not the *Supremes*.

Soon after arriving in England, I had to undergo painful surgery for a chronic health problem. While I could work, I was miserable with pain and should have been home resting in bed. Then someone connected with the Irish Republican Army set off a bomb in our hotel lobby, killing two people and injuring sixty-three. We were all up in our rooms, getting ready to go out sight-seeing with some record-company representatives, when we got a call saying they would be about half an hour late. Had it not been for that call, we might have been down in the London Hilton lobby at the moment the blast occurred.

Pedro awoke me from a nap. The elevators were out, so we rushed down twenty-five flights of stairs with Turkessa bundled in our arms. In the lobby bells rang and sirens screamed. Every window was blown into a million fragments, injured people lay everywhere, and blood splattered the floor.

As we stood across the street in Hyde Park, I took a head count and discovered Scherrie missing. She turned up later that evening. Because she'd gone back upstairs for some personal things, the police held her for questioning. Since no one was permitted back in the hotel, she stayed at another nearby hotel. We all worried about her as we spent the day wandering around the park.

It was an off day for us, so I hadn't dressed too well. Still, people were coming up to me and asking if I was Mary Wilson of the Supremes and would I please give them an autograph. One person said, "I've been a fan since you started. By the way, where's Diana?"

"Where have you been?" I said, laughing. "She's been gone since 1970." It was a strange day.

Cindy walked up to me and, grinning, said, "Mary, come here."

She had on a brown trench coat wrapped tightly around her. "You have to come *real* close," she added mischievously, "I have something to show you." Cindy opened her coat and closed it quickly, revealing that she had on nothing under it. We all laughed. It was the one bright spot in an otherwise miserable day.

Later we found out that our assistant, Gill Trodd, just missed being in the blast, and that she and Hazel had seen the woman suspected of planting the bomb minutes before the explosion. By the time we were let back into our rooms at around seven, we were all exhausted.

It was during this trip that we purchased ex-Beatle John Lennon's custom-made stretch Mercedes limousine from George Harrison. Pedro was very sociable, striking up fast friendships with people I had known for years and yet never been close to. In England Pedro went out a lot with Peter Lawford, Ringo Starr, and George Harrison, who invited Pedro and me to visit him and his girlfriend (now wife) Olivia at their home.

It was one of the most beautiful places I'd ever seen. George's grounds were like a huge park. I recall one especially beautiful swan-filled lake. The house resembled a small palace, decorated with precious objects from all over the world. Except for George's extensive guitar collection, everything reminded me of a scene out of a fairy tale. George had just finished building a recording studio in the house, and he proudly gave us a tour of it.

While Olivia prepared dinner, he asked me countless questions about Motown and how we made our records, how we got that sound. It was a very relaxing day. What struck me about George was how happy he seemed. It made me realize how few people I knew, especially performers, who were content and at peace. After this I became a great fan of George's music, especially its spiritual aspect.

George showed us the Mercedes limousine that had been custom-built for John Lennon. The moment Pedro saw it he had to have it. That it had belonged to John Lennon meant nothing to me or Pedro. It was a beautiful, rare car, that's all. Although we got it for a very, very low price—cheap, actually—it was still more than we could afford. I tried persuading him not to buy it. We already had the Rolls. What did we need with two luxury cars?

As fate would have it, the Mercedes limousine later assumed a life of its own too. We brought it back to the States, but after a year returned it to England because we were there so often and could use it for touring. Following John's assassination in 1980, anything connected with him skyrocketed in value. I stored the limo in a garage, from which it was stolen in 1984. Next thing I heard, it was up for auction. After retrieving it from the selling block, the British High Court ruled that I was the rightful owner, and I had it auctioned off at Christie's in London in 1989. I can honestly say I wasn't all that sad to see it go.

Just as we were leaving for the States, our European Motown affiliate asked that we stay an extra week to do more radio and television shows. Everyone's nerves were shot, and some of our musicians got angry and left. Cindy and Scherrie complained bitterly that Pedro was disorganized and never told them anything until the last minute. For example, we were scheduled to perform at the Shubert Theatre in Los Angeles toward the end of the month, and Pedro hadn't bothered to tell Cindy and Scherrie that we were giving a benefit performance, for which none of us would be paid. They were upset, and understandably so. Everything was coming apart. When I mentioned these problems to Pedro, he always snapped, "Sing, and don't worry about the business."

"But I have to work with these people. You cannot do things behind everyone's backs, including mine."

Pedro ignored me unless he was lecturing me on what I was doing wrong. During this trip he complained a lot about our love life. I had a typical new mother's responsibilities and then some. Pedro couldn't fathom why after performing sometimes two shows a night, taking care of Turkessa, and overseeing the group's business, I had neither the energy nor the interest in a wild, romantic sex life. I was failing at everything except being a mother.

After stopping off in Santo Domingo to visit Pedro's family for a few days, we returned home and immediately went to work publicizing the upcoming Shubert date, a benefit for the Citizens Action to Help Youth and the University Community Health Services. Herb Avery was actively involved in these organizations, and he and I appeared together on many local talk shows to promote the work these groups did in the community. I've always felt that performers have an obligation to devote time and energy to worthwhile causes such as these.

This was our first performance in Los Angeles in nearly three years, so we were psyched. When we walked onstage to a half-filled house, my heart sank. We made a few minor mistakes here and there, but the audience loved us. We did the basic show Geoffrey Holder and Phil Moore had developed for us, including the Josephine Baker/Marilyn Monroe/Bessie Smith number we'd just broken in, in England.

Moments before we went on, Pedro informed me that Diane was in the audience and that I should introduce her, which I did. She received a thunderous ovation. I still hadn't fully recuperated my energy, and the show really knocked me out. Before going into my dressing room, I specifically instructed my assistant not to allow anyone backstage until the three of us caught our breaths and freshened up. No sooner did I sit down than I heard a knock, and in walked Diane. She was friendly, but that didn't make up for such a breach of courtesy, especially after she hadn't said more than a handful of words to me the last two times I'd visited her backstage. I was growing weary of constantly turning the other cheek.

Pedro insisted that I go straight home and skip the after-show party, which, of course, he attended with Cindy, Scherrie, and assorted other guests, including Gladys Knight, Natalie Cole, Sarah Dash, Lola Falana, Freda Payne, and a group of Motown VIPs.

The next morning we left Los Angeles for Miami, our first stop on the way to London and our final destination, South Africa. Once word had gotten out that we were going to South Africa, the Supremes became the focus of a national controversy. I admit, I wasn't surprised that our going there provoked such a heated reaction. Cindy, Scherrie, and I were keenly aware of how South Africa's black majority lived separate, impoverished lives under the nation's racist apartheid laws. After careful consideration, however, I decided we should go; Scherrie and Cindy, while voicing reservations, agreed.

One provision of our appearing in South Africa was that all our audiences be fully integrated. In South Africa it was customary to present shows for either all-black or all-white audiences. While in America we are especially aware of the conflict there between blacks and whites, South Africa is home to other ethnic groups, such as Indians and Orientals, and also maintains a very strict caste system that groups people of mixed blood in a clearly defined hierarchy. Our promoters promised to secure the required permits for mixed audiences and to sell tickets on a "no-barriers" basis, so that anyone could see us.

I can speak only for myself, but I felt very strongly that as a black I should witness firsthand what was happening. I was opposed to apartheid before I went there, and my experiences only reinforced my belief that the system must be abolished.

After reading the hundreds of letters and telegrams imploring us to cancel our trip, I understood our critics' arguments. They advocated a full cultural boycott of South Africa, of all its people, both white and black. The parallels between the black struggles for freedom in South Africa and in the United States are obvious, although the repression in South Africa is much more extreme and brutal. When considering all these facts, I kept recalling the racism I experienced during the fifties and sixties in the South. While we blacks who lived in the North didn't agree with what went on down South, we didn't boycott those places or those people. We went there by busloads and carloads. Just because the South African blacks are across the ocean doesn't mean we can't help them.

I always believed that by confounding racist expectations and being a source of pride to blacks, in some small way I had helped in that struggle. My brother Roosevelt criticized me in the early seventies for not using the Supremes as a platform for political comment. I reminded him that I wasn't a marcher or a speech-maker, and that we each contribute to change in our own way.

This argument didn't cut it with our antiapartheid critics. In 1985 Artists United Against Apartheid brought the issue to national consciousness with the hit "Sun City." Many people don't know that American black entertainers and prominent people were organized against South Africa and apartheid as early as 1975. We received letters from organizations who had the support of some of our friends—Bill Cosby, Sammy Davis, Jr., Richard Roundtree, Diahann Carroll, Brock Peters, Wilt Chamberlain, and others—begging us not to go. Interestingly, once we returned to the States, none of those I knew personally whose names appeared on the antiapartheid organizations' letterhead and petitions ever rebuked me publicly about our trip. The wire services picked up the story and it ran for several days all over the country. I think it probably goes without saying that, careerwise, going to South Africa was not the most prudent decision.

As soon as the plane landed in Johannesburg, we were swamped by reporters. On the car ride from the airport, a black South African journalist interviewed us. We were so exhausted from the long trip and the jet lag, all we wanted to do was sleep. But the first night, after a brief nap, Pedro and I were guests of honor at a dinner given by our promoter and Motown's affiliate there.

The next day we gave at least fifteen interviews, with an hour off for lunch. Our publicity people there were white, and from the beginning I detected a dismissive, rude attitude toward their black journalists. Our press person wanted the writers to avoid political issues and stick to the same old topics, such as how the Supremes started in Detroit, etc., etc. As this was my opportunity to learn something, I always ended up asking more questions of the black reporters than they asked of us.

One PR woman got very perturbed with me and reprimanded a black reporter for "wasting time" with questions she didn't believe were "pertinent"; namely, those concerning oppression of South African blacks. Her attitude toward him was unacceptable, and I called her on it. She replied that the blacks were "ridiculous people," then left the room and sent her partner in to deal with me. That was it.

I recounted this incident to Pedro, who didn't seem to understand my outrage. I tried explaining to him that while I hadn't been born into a world as repressively racist as that of my parents or grandparents, they had passed on to us their feelings of inferiority, their fears, their insecurities. No matter how successful any black of my generation might be, these "messages" we'd received all our lives about how the world was and where we fit in it affected us, whether we knew it or not. Pedro, coming from a Latin background, never understood American blacks' problems.

In Johannesburg we canceled some interviews so that we could visit a black school. Our promoters, the Quibell brothers, were very polite; in fact, almost all the South African whites we encountered were. This was in stark contrast to how they regarded the native blacks. We were taken to see a number of sites, but they pretty much took us to all the tourist traps, steering us away from seeing too many black South Africans. Finally, through a black connection, we were able to arrange a trip to Soweto, the all-black township outside Johannesburg.

As we drove into the township, it was as I imagined it would be: dirt roads and poverty everywhere. It was very hot, but still hundreds lined the streets to see us. At the school a crowd of youngsters, the principal, and the teachers greeted us in the courtyard. The children ranged in age from five or so to eighteen and wore clean, crisply pressed uniforms. A little program had been prepared in our honor, at which the students sang songs in English and in Zulu. One little boy recited a very beautiful, moving poem. Following the children's presentation, Cindy, Scherrie, and I talked to them about education, hygiene, anything we thought might be helpful. Many times when we bent down to speak to the children they touched our faces and exclaimed with awe, "You are so beautiful!"

We took lots of pictures, and many of the children talked into a tape recorder we'd brought. When I asked "What do you think about your black American brothers and sisters?" the children cried out in unison, "We love our black American brothers and sisters!"

During our run in Johannesburg, we did a benefit concert for an organization called TEACH (Teach Every African Child), and with the proceeds three badly needed classrooms were built. It was a multiracial audience, and we were honored by the white mayor of Johannesburg and the black mayor of Soweto. The Coliseum where we performed didn't sell out, so only $6,000 of an expected $10,000 was raised through ticket sales; Pedro suggested we donate the balance. I too was determined to make our visit to South Africa yield positive results. By helping to build the three classrooms, I felt we'd accomplished something constructive.

It was a moving, gratifying experience. This was not discussed with the girls, and when they heard, they were furious. Then Pedro got into an argument with them. Scherrie and Cindy were upset to learn I'd turned over my share of the group to my husband, giving him full control of the Supremes.

"If you have control over the group, and you are managing us, isn't that a conflict of interest?" Scherrie asked. "Couldn't you be sued?"

I don't think Scherrie meant this in a hostile way, but Cindy, who had been pretty unhappy throughout most of the trip, jumped right in.

"I should be told who the boss is around here!" she said angrily.

"How soon people forget," Pedro sneered, obviously directing his comment to Cindy. He'd been after me to let her go for almost a year, but I couldn't do it. The meeting ended with Scherrie and Cindy threatening that we'd hear from their lawyers. I sat in the corner, watching it all and saying nothing. I was wrong to have given control of my ownership in the group to Pedro without telling them, and I understood that they deserved to know where they stood.

In Johannesburg we made an appearance at a new department store. From the moment we pulled up we could see it wasn't well organized. Many black people gathered to see us, and as we sat up on a platform, the emcee kept pleading with people to stop pushing. But no one was trying to form orderly lines or help the situation. Outside were policemen with vicious dogs, which they threatened to turn loose on the crowd if it didn't settle down. One organizer only exacerbated things by tossing out records and photographs. This caused people to push and shove one another, resulting in an ugly riot.

By the time Pedro finally took charge and established some semblance or order, it was too late. I'll never forget the hateful expressions on the white people's faces. They really didn't care what happened to our black fans and were on the brink of violence to stop the noisy surge. When it seemed that the platform might collapse, we left, reluctantly. Most of the whites blamed the blacks because of the way they behaved. I saw it as the responsibility of the people in charge—black or white—to make things run smoothly. That the black people were in danger of being injured or crushed didn't seem to enter anyone's mind. It was as if all blacks were invisible.

During our stay a black South African woman named Susan took care of Turkessa, now six months old and beginning to crawl. Susan was very kind and intelligent, in her early thirties, and she was wonderful with Turkessa. From the moment we met, I insisted that she address me by my first name. A look of fear crossed her face, and she politely explained that she could not do that, even though I was black too. Even among blacks, the South Africans drew distinctions. We discovered that the reason we could go places and do things that black citizens could not was our "honorary white" status. This did not come to our attention until toward the end of the tour, and it upset all of us. I didn't see why Susan and I could not relate to each other as equals, not as a boss and a slave. It hurt me to see how living in South Africa had stripped Susan of her pride and self-worth, and brainwashed her into believing that she had no right to such things. In the weeks we spent together, I tried to change some of that.

Susan was in the room during one of my many heated discussions with our PR people. When I spoke up to the white publicist, she became visibly shaken. Later she confided timidly that she was worried about what would happen to me, how I might be punished for addressing a *white woman* that way. I explained that the white woman worked for *me* and that she'd done something I disagreed with. There was no reason why I should be afraid to address anyone—regardless of color—as I chose. Susan understood my words, but her experience was so different from mine, she really didn't know what they meant.

The full extent of the constant fear blacks live with there became clear one evening when Scherrie, our conductor Teddy Harris, and some others from our entourage dined in Cape Town. Now, Cape Town was one of the more "liberal" areas, or so we'd heard. One of our party asked his black waiter to find out from the chef when his meal might be ready. The waiter went into the kitchen, and the white chef slapped him simply for *addressing* him. When the waiter returned to the table, everyone was furious about what had occurred. Naturally, everyone's first reaction was to do something about it, but the frightened waiter pleaded, "Please, please, do not say anything, because I will lose my job."

Another time I was in a beauty salon getting my hair done, and a white beautician chattered on about how it was such a shame the way black South Africans were treated in her country and how wrong it was. Not a moment later, a black hair washer politely asked her if she might use the telephone; she was ordered to use the phone in back. Racism was everywhere.

The tour was plagued by mix-ups about what type of

audiences our promoters had permits for. In Johannesburg the shows were mixed, although this had not been officially sanctioned. During the part of our show where we invited people on stage to dance with us, integrated couples seemed to come from everywhere. It was a beautiful thing to see, and something many Johannesburg newspapers commented on favorably.

In Durban, however, reporters tipped us off that, despite what we might have been promised, the shows planned there were not for mixed audiences. The promoter swore he'd applied for the permits over two months ago but that the bureaucracy was stalling, which I believed. The situation became front-page news for several days running. Our white promoter gave out free passes to blacks, who could not buy tickets at the box office. He assured us he was doing everything possible, and Pedro kept reminding him of our contract's stipulations that we play only for mixed audiences.

Finally, the day before our first show, things appeared to have been worked out. The local paper heralded it as "a major breach in the apartheid barrier," and I felt certain everything was settled.

I was walking through the hotel lobby when a group that included Indians and blacks approached me. They begged me not to let the Supremes go on that night. Whatever integration was reflected in our audience was token at best, they claimed. I was very embarrassed and told them to purchase tickets at the box office. If they couldn't, I promised we would not go on. It was sad to see their resignation. I guess they didn't think it was worthwhile to even bother.

Each night before the shows, we made sure the audience was integrated. In addition to the preshow feature stories and postshow concert reviews, our tour there prompted many antiapartheid, pro-integration editorials. Despite our efforts to ensure that our audiences were mixed, it came to our attention toward the end of the tour that not all the audiences we had believed were integrated really were. In some cases, just enough blacks and other nonwhites were put in the audience so that when we looked out from the stage, it appeared fully integrated. For having performed before one such audience in Durban, the Supremes were roundly criticized by local black leaders.

This upset all of us. But Cindy and Scherrie, obviously very angry, went public with their feelings. Scherrie said that the country was beautiful but that some of its people were "bigoted and ugly." Cindy said that she was insulted to be considered an honorary white. Both vowed that once they returned to the States they would tell everyone what they saw and discourage other black performers from coming over. I shared their basic belief that the government and the promoters of South Africa could not be trusted, but did not go to the press.

The story was picked up by papers all over South Africa, and almost immediately the government there demanded that the Supremes leave the country, which we did. Before we left I gave Susan a wig, which looked very pretty on her, and a dress, which she said she would give to her daughter for Christmas.

As I looked into Susan's eyes, I saw a spark of hope. I prayed that one day soon the bonds of apartheid would be broken.

CHAPTER 11

The South African tour drew Cindy and Scherrie closer. Once again I was the outsider. I needed the Supremes to be a group again, but everything was working against that, namely, lack of money. Everyone knew that whatever monies we earned first went into the corporation, and that's how we paid ourselves weekly salaries, as well as musicians, assistants, travel expenses, stage wear, public relations, photographs, and various professionals, like choreographers, to work with us. Whatever remained at year's end was divided among us by contractually set percentages. The real cream—the only way any of us would make Big Money—was to have a hit record. As that possibility slipped away, everyone started to become edgy.

Scherrie and Cindy had very different reasons for sticking with the Supremes. Scherrie and I were splitting our solos pretty evenly, and while Scherrie was a stunning, gifted singer, I was getting progressively better notices. Cindy, though, had changed since the last time she was in the group.

She seemed unhappy; things had come to a head with Charles, and her divorce from him was finalized the day of our Shubert Theatre show, but I think she still loved him. As a mother, she had to feel torn between her career and her child, as I did.

Cindy couldn't seem to lose the weight she'd gained, and on stage she appeared to be just going through the motions, occasionally flubbing cues. I kept encouraging her to change, for her own good. Cindy took any comment I made defensively. She kept missing a certain step, and when I mentioned it, she replied, "I didn't know that's what we were supposed to do."

"This is how Geoffrey had us do it, Cindy," Scherrie chimed in.

Cindy felt we were ganging up on her. Staring at me, she snapped, "All right, Boss!" It hit me right between the eyes. *Diane.* How I'd hated feeling pushed aside by her ambition. Now the shoe was on the other foot—my foot—but it didn't fit. Scherrie always tried to come to the rescue, imploring us not to fight, and not to go onstage mad at each other. But she too snapped whenever Pedro was around.

It was getting harder for me to disguise my impatience with Cindy. I thought back to all the years I had gone out of my way to make excuses for other people. They had probably laughed at me behind my back then, thinking I was such a soft touch. Those same girls would probably someday go around saying they had been one of the Supremes.

I started admitting to myself what I had known in my heart all along: no one would ever care about the Supremes more than I did. I started looking at everything with a colder eye. Rather than accepting things at face value, I became more skeptical. Before, I would have silently hoped Cindy would lose the weight; now I said something to her about it.

We had put off the decision to ask Cindy to leave long

enough. Pedro wanted to replace her with Thelma Houston, who had enjoyed moderate success with "Save the Country." Her big break would be 1977's Number One "Don't Leave Me This Way." I often caught Thelma's show in Vegas and thought she was a great singer, with an incredible gospel voice. But I knew that she would never want to be part of a group.

Turkessa and I spent two weeks in Detroit, and I could see that she was beginning to resemble my mother. As always, all my friends dropped by, and I went around visiting. I looked into selling the houses I owned there because we needed a bigger place in Los Angeles, and I didn't have the money to buy one. It was so distressing to learn how little my properties were worth. When I'd moved onto Buena Vista in 1965, it was a beautiful area; now I was told I'd be lucky to get what I paid for those homes. Detroit had really changed.

I went to our old hangout, the Twenty Grand, with a bunch of friends. Stepping into the nightclub was like entering a time warp. It was there that Diane, Flo, and I had decided to pursue a record deal. This night the Four Tops were performing, and they had people out of their seats, dancing. People kept coming up to me, asking, "Hey, girl, when did you get back in town?" I couldn't really relax or really enjoy myself, though, because I kept glancing at the door, expecting Pedro any moment. He was in Los Angeles taking care of business but planned to fly in for Thanksgiving. When I got to my mother's later, he was there, obviously peeved that I hadn't met him at the airport.

Flo came over, and she looked so different. She had put on a lot of weight again and after only a few beers was very high. During dinner she asked, "Mary, can you help me? I want to get back in the business."

As Flo spoke, I realized that my whole attitude toward her had changed in the past year. Things had gone wrong for her; things were going wrong for me too. Life is unfair, but there comes a point where you have to face where you are and do something about it. Diane had made a statement that she wanted to shake Florence. She'd been widely criticized for saying that, but I understood how she felt. Eight years after she'd left the group, Flo still couldn't get on with her life.

I told Pedro that I'd seen the Four Tops, and as I expected, he took it badly. He was perfectly charming at Thanksgiving dinner, then without a word went upstairs and packed. I followed him up the stairs, trying to reason with him. When I told Flo that I had to take Pedro to the airport, I could see that she was hurt.

After I got home from the airport, Flo called, sounding tipsy.

"You're a good girl," she said. Then, after a long pause, she added. "You're very nasty . . . and I'm listening to the Jackson 5. . . . I'm sorry if I hurt your feelings."

"Hurt my feelings about what?" I asked.

"I'm confused, Mary. I can't talk to you now." The line went dead.

There was always something left to say.

November 30, 1975

We are playing a Hotel Executive Inn in Evansville, Indiana. The first night there was no one in the audience. The next five nights there was close to no one. It's such a letdown. Scherrie fell off the stage one night. It was one of those little portable stages they roll out for the show, then roll back later so people can dance. One minute she was there, the next minute she was gone! But she pulled it off beautifully, like a pro.

Now when I go onstage, I don't think we're good. I know that Scherrie is a wonderful singer, but I feel like I am not good. I sound awful. I don't have any soul or technique.

I can't even look people in the eyes without feeling fear and uneasiness. Oh God, where am I? I never used to be this negative.

In late January 1976 Scherrie, Cindy, and I played at a small club in Toronto, to wonderful reviews. This turned out to be Cindy's last show with us, and soon after we got home her departure was announced. Animosity between her and Pedro had worsened since South Africa, and he asked her to leave. Once again, another singer; the fifth new lineup since Flo had left.

Earlier, Pedro and I had discussed the idea of me going solo, but I felt that I owed the Supremes one more chance. And, besides, I was scared to death. When Pedro said bluntly, "The Supremes are dead," I hated him. He was only trying to do what was best for both of us, but I didn't see that; I felt like everyone was trying to take the group away from me.

Cindy, Scherrie, and I had already begun work on our next album, *High Energy,* for which Motown teamed us up with Brian and Eddie Holland. The brothers now collaborated with Harold Beatty in place of Lamont Dozier. They cowrote and produced the entire LP except for "I Don't Want to Lose You," by Thom Bell and Linda Creed.

Pedro and I were driving through Beverly Hills, and he was excitedly telling me about a great new singer he'd found, Susaye Green. A meeting was arranged with me, Pedro, Brian and Eddie Holland, Scherrie, and Susaye. I was surprised by how short she was, even shorter than Scherrie; at five feet four and a half inches, I still towered over them. My first thought was, *All Cindy's gowns will have to be cut down.*

Susaye had been in show business most of her life, attending the Professional Children's School and the High

School for the Performing Arts (the real-life setting for *Fame*) in New York City. Her mother taught voice, and so Susaye was exposed to all manner of formal training from a very early age. She first worked as a singer with Harry Belafonte and for a number of years toured with Ray Charles as a Raelette. She and Ray also dated during that time. More recently, she'd been a member of Stevie Wonder's Wonderlove (like Lynda Laurence).

It's interesting to note that as time went on and our records became less successful for a variety of reasons, one thing the Supremes never wanted for was talent. Ironically, as time passed and fewer people got to know the group, we were better than ever technically and talentwise. Susaye, who composed music as well, was a very good singer, with a five-octave range. We took her on the spot.

Although *High Energy* was already completed, we over-dubbed Susaye's voice on two tracks: "High Energy" and the first single, "I'm Gonna Let My Heart Do the Walking," which made respectable showings on the pop (Number 40) and black (Number 25) charts.

I was at Hazel's home with Scherrie and Susaye, trying on some gowns that needed to be altered, when Hazel told me that Flo had just died. Her last year had not been a happy one. At one point she'd checked into a hospital, apparently on the verge of a nervous breakdown. Flo's nerves, weight problems, and high blood pressure were all being treated with different prescription drugs. On Saturday, February, 21, 1976, she was admitted to Mt. Carmel Mercy Hospital, complaining of numbness in her arms and legs. She'd been drinking while on medication. The next day a blood clot blocked a major artery, and her heart stopped.

I left immediately for Detroit, where I went straight to Flo's house to see her family and children. Flo was laid out at Stinson's Funeral Home, and over the next couple days thousands stood in line to pay their last respects. All Detroit seemed to mourn Flo's death. The *Detroit Free Press* reported that the funeral would be held the following Saturday, under such headlines as EX-SUPREMES TO ATTEND BALLARD RITES and DIANA EXPECTED. The ceremony threatened to become a media circus, so at the last minute it was decided to have the funeral a day early.

Shortly before noon that Friday Flo's body was moved from the funeral home to the New Bethel Baptist Church, where Aretha Franklin's father, the Reverend C. L. Franklin, presided. Despite all attempts to keep the funeral plans secret, word leaked, and even before the flowers were arranged around Flo's coffin, a thick line of fans wound around the corner and down the block. Within the next two hours over 2,200 fans, mourners, family, and friends filled the church to capacity.

The police presence outside was doubled, and inside a dozen uniformed nurses stood by to help the overwrought. It began to seem more like a show than a funeral. Around two-thirty someone announced from the altar, "The stars have asked you not to take pictures of them in the church," which only fueled the crowd's anticipation. When Stevie Wonder was led up the aisle to the front of the church, a wild round of applause erupted.

"Clear the center aisle!" Reverend Franklin ordered, and suddenly Diane appeared, surrounded by bodyguards. She started down the aisle, then let out a loud sob, dramatically swooning and stumbling until her bodyguards swept her to her seat. Now the crowd was on its feet, hundreds of flashbulbs popping.

"Would you please clear the aisle so that we can get the family in!" someone pleaded over the public-address system. Flo's family quietly entered and took their places in the front pews. Her six sisters, four brothers, mother, husband Tommy, and three daughters were in the church, so that by the time my mother and I arrived, all the seats down front were taken, and we had to sit farther back.

Finally, around three o'clock the choir began singing, and Reverend Franklin delivered the eulogy. "We have experiences that are not always good and true," he said. "Sometimes they are frustrating and crushing, but positive good comes out of negative situations. . . . Even though some of you were not as orderly as you could be, I know that you are here in a gesture of respect for this deceased young lady, Florence Ballard."

After nearly an hour of song, prayer, and sermon, Reverend Franklin was bringing the funeral to an end when Diane got up and asked for his microphone. She said, "Mary and I would like to have a silent prayer." I hadn't spoken to her in months and had no idea that she had prearranged a tribute to Flo. My grief was personal and private; I didn't want to get up. She said, "I believe nothing disappears, and Flo will always be with us." As I stood beside her, stunned, she passed me the microphone. All I could muster through my tears was, "I loved her very much."

I looked down at Florence one last time. They closed her coffin, and the procession slowly headed for the door while "Someday We'll Be Together" poured from the huge pipe organ. We proceeded to Detroit Memorial Park, and I was surprised to see that Diane didn't come to the grave site, as I'd assumed she would. Flo's death is another subject we have never talked about.

Now, years later, when I think about Flo's death, I think most about the promise I made to her at her grave: "Don't worry, Flo; I'll take care of it." I don't concentrate on the events that struck me so deeply that day: the packed church, the people tearing at the floral arrangements, Diane's grand entrance and her "incorporating" me into her tribute to Flo,

Berry's conspicuous absence, the sight of her three little girls, Michelle, Nicole, and Lisa, so young, not really comprehending the awful fate their mother had met.

All those things remind me that Flo actually died, and they become harder for me to focus on these days, because Flo's spirit is not dead for me. I can still feel her now as I did when we were young together, and that's how she will always remain in my heart. When I'm down, all I do is think of her hearty laugh, or imagine her rolling her eyes, planting her hands firmly on her hips, and saying, "Honey . . ." like she's about to let me in on the greatest secret in the world, and I get shivers. Her spirit is so alive for me now, I know that all the things we deal with every day that seem so urgent are external things. The *real* us is our spirit, and this non-physical part that so many consider "unreal" is probably the only real thing we have.

Flo had more soul in one little finger than anyone I ever knew. I see her spirit especially in a familiar Supremes film clip of us singing "Back in My Arms Again." Flo's sassy expression as she watches Diane sing, ". . . And Flo, she don't know, that the boy she loves is a Romeo," is priceless and uniquely Flo.

Unlike Diane and me, Flo couldn't slip between the black world we grew up in and the white world we later seemed to have conquered. She was honest and direct, and not always when it was the wisest thing to be. But Flo didn't think things out that way; she didn't connive or have ulterior motives. She was what she was, and she stuck to her principles, even when it wasn't to her advantage. She had so much pride—probably too much for the likes of people like Berry and those who wanted to manipulate her.

To this day I'm totally mystified by the claims of some people, including several members of Flo's family, that Diane or I could have done something to save Flo. Would money (assuming I had it to give) have saved her? What Flo needed more than anything, I now realize, was serious psychological therapy for the lingering aftereffects of her rape at age seventeen. Today this is such an obvious solution, but it wasn't then. The alcohol, I have contended all along, was to ease the emotional pain of that rape.

Pedro and I moved into our new home, a beautiful mansion in Hollywood's exclusive Hancock Park district. The classic Tudor was designed and owned by the preeminent architect of this old Hollywood style. To give you an idea of how things change, when Nat "King" Cole moved into a home across the street back in the fifties, he was threatened by bigots.

This was my dream house, and although we probably shouldn't have bought it when we did, Pedro and I fell in love with it. It had twenty-two rooms, seven bedrooms, ebony wood paneling throughout, a large library, an office, a magnificent winding staircase that looked like something out of *Gone with the Wind,* and a built-in, three-story-tall pipe organ. Because the chief architect built this house for himself, it had all sorts of little features and improvements (pool, tennis court, full basement) that made it very special. Whenever in England and Europe, Pedro and I shopped for antique furnishings and paintings with which to decorate our new home. It made me feel the star people thought I was. Yes, Pedro and I were living high on the hog, but to keep all the staff, such as Hazel and two servants—including a driver—I had to work constantly. As soon as the money came in, it went out.

This new home was more than a house to me. Like the first houses Diane, Flo, and I bought in Detroit, this one symbolized something. Inside the walls I felt safe and secure, and I remember seeing it and thinking that this would be the house I'd raise my children in, the house where I hoped Pedro and I would settle our problems and grow old together.

Pedro continued to come and go as he pleased, while I stayed home decorating, cooking, planting a garden, and playing with the baby. I'd seen so many other women get themselves into this situation; I remembered looking at some of them and knowing what everyone was saying about their husbands, thinking it could never happen to me. But it had.

One of the things that attracted me to Pedro was his need to control: his single-minded determination to get what he wanted. The first few times I'd seen his more dangerous side—when he pushed me outside in the cold, when he beat me while I was carrying Turkessa—I made myself deal with it. Wives who are in this situation are very misunderstood. People think that one day you fall in love with a man, the next day he beats you, and then leaving him is the obvious choice. When I was young, I heard pimps beat up on whores right down the street from where I lived in the projects. But that seemed so removed from my life, and I'd never seen it for myself. I had too much pride to let that happen to me. Or so I thought.

Instead of helping to build me up emotionally and showing me how to love myself, Pedro exploited my insecurities. It was this part of him that I found very strange and confusing, because at tender moments he was so kind and concerned. These were the times I was sure of his love, and I let it eclipse the pain that he caused. Long before he ever raised a hand to me, I sensed he was dangerous. Why didn't I walk away then, or at any time along the way?

Obvious question; difficult—maybe impossible—answer. I still don't know, except to say that the subtle, almost imperceptible steps toward that living hell were far behind me when I finally realized where I was. A part of me needed to see firsthand how people who needed power operated. I felt by staying with Pedro I could learn.

I decided to have one more go with this new group of the Supremes. If this didn't work, I would take Pedro's advice and go solo. Susaye made her debut with us in April at the Royal Hawaiian Hotel in Falls Church, Virginia. Vocally the act was very exciting. Nearly half the solos were mine, and Susaye and Scherrie both had featured solo numbers as well. Finally the Supremes were back to three lead singers like on the *Meet the Supremes* album in 1963. I was determined to give this new group 150 percent of my time and energy.

The reviews for our initial shows were very positive, and it looked like we'd made the right choice. We appeared on several national television programs during this time—*The Dinah Shore Show, Soul Train, American Bandstand, The Merv Griffin Show*—and "I'm Gonna Let My Heart Do the Walking" went Top 10 in discos across the country. We also appeared (but with Cindy, not Susaye) in a series of commercials for the American Heart Association, of which we'd been named ambassadors. None of this could counteract the effects of Motown's lack of support. There was again evidence that the label had not supplied review copies of the album and the single to the industry trade magazines.

In May we toured England, then went on to Germany, Italy, and France. English fans and critics who'd found our last tour too Vegas-y loved the new show. Susaye drew notice for her voice, and during a performance in London her rendition of "He Ain't Heavy, He's My Brother" got a five-minute ovation.

One of our shows was taped at the Jazz Festival in Montreaux, Switzerland. Right before the taping, I decided to change dresses. The one I put on was a sexy, see-through, covered in all the strategic areas—nothing outrageous. When Pedro saw it, he exploded, beating me up and blackening my eye before we went onstage. Hazel and I tried to cover it with makeup, and I pretended nothing had happened. But everyone knew.

The European tour was a success. However, when we got to Bachelors III in Fort Lauderdale, Florida, ticket sales were so slow that some nights we did only one show instead of two. I hadn't wanted to come back here to begin with, but I knew we had to. It was the old story: we needed money. About the only thing that cheered me up was Turkessa, who was beginning to talk. Fortunately, she was a very easy child to be around, and Scherrie and Susaye really liked her. Willie too was with us, working as assistant road manager.

The summer was uneventful; then in August we had a great engagement at the Roostertail in Detroit.

It's nice coming back to Detroit to perform. Everyone here seems to genuinely like the Supremes, even though we are not the same hometown girls. The name *Supremes* really carries a lot of weight. I've been having dinner over at Aunt I.V.'s house every day. It feels nice to spend time in my hometown without being rushed. I even went to see Daddy [J. L. Pippin] in the old neighborhood where I grew up. All the houses looked so small. As a child, everything looked so big. Even some of the same people were still living there. The family I stole fifty cents from still lived on Bassett Street. I brought it up to them so I could get it off my conscience. All these years I had been ashamed of that.

Well, the show was a success, and everyone loved us. I was getting standing ovations every night. It really made me feel great. Scherrie was her usual great self, and Susaye also got standing ovations. She has been the catalyst in making Scherrie and me free with our singing, especially me.

Supreme Faith

I've really been getting a great response to my tribute to Flo. I am glad. Sometimes I feel guilt, using her for my own gain. But everyone has loved it. Many people have told me they were close to tears because of it, so I think it's good. At least her name is out there.

One guy gave me a standing ovation after "How Lucky" and shouted, "Thanks for Flo, Mary." It's amazing how many people know Flo. I've been with the group eight years more than (or after) her, and they're just starting to know me. But they all knew Flo.

One evening Pedro was up at Motown and happened to run into Berry. They went into the studio, and Berry listened to some tracks from our new LP, *Mary, Scherrie & Susaye*, our second with the Hollands. He seemed very pleased and told Pedro it was the high quality we needed. The signs seemed encouraging, but it was so hard to know what Berry really thought. Berry had recently told us that Motown wanted to manage the group again. Pedro was very hurt; I didn't know what to do.

The album, our last, came out in early fall. Initially it got more of a push than the others; we were on the cover of the trade magazine *Billboard*, for example. But after a promising start—the single "You're My Driving Wheel" bowed on the national disco chart at Number 29—sales fell off.

August 1976

Susaye, Scherrie, and I arrived in San Francisco to perform at the Fairmont Hotel for two weeks. Lucky for us it's the middle of the convention season, so it has been packed every night. In fact, we went into percentage (earning a part of the take at the door) the first week. Anyway, nice to be on the plus side instead of always being in the red.

Hazel told us that the bank will not honor any more checks unless the money is there. We have been operating on pennies, always behind, these past three years. It's finally catching up with us. I am glad I never really let it get me down. However, we've got to start making that big money again, because we are too far in the hole. The Supremes have to repay me the $30,000 I lent them. The bank's screaming about bouncing checks. All our employees want raises. Several of them have threatened to quit. But fortunately, we are at a time when maybe the cards are in our favor. So it always seems to be its darkest just before the dawn. I'll get it together. I'll give myself and the Supremes another chance.

I firmly believe we'll be greater than ever, even though somewhere in my mind there are doubts. But I am going to do what I believe is right and face the future when it gets here. As Pedro said the other night, we can only go so far wrong because it's in us to be big. We are big. We'll always find a way.

After a lot of thought, Pedro and I decided to move the Supremes' booking to the William Morris Agency, something we'd considered for quite some time. One of our new agents there mentioned that there was a December opening in Las Vegas on a bill with the comedian Alan King. It was a great break; it was also just two weeks away.

At Pedro's insistence, Motown finally came across with money for a new stage act, and we rehearsed furiously in our new home. Gil Askey worked out arrangements in the basement, while George Faison, a popular Broadway choreographer in charge of staging, had his secretary and various assistants and technicians running in and out all day. For a full week it was utter chaos from noon until night, but we were excited and happy to be working.

George suggested, "Since everyone always mimics the Supremes' choreography, like the 'Stop! In the Name of Love' hand gestures, maybe you should do something like that." We talked about the Broadway play *Hair*, which had a sequence that parodied the original Supremes. Three girls sang together à la the Supremes, but at the end of the number you saw that they were wearing a single gown. In the early seventies one of my girlfriends had appeared in the L.A. production, so I'd seen it countless times and thought the takeoff was cute.

"Look, Mary," George said. He stood up, all six feet one of him, and sashayed across the room in a perfect imitation of how the Supremes moved. Scherrie, Susaye, and I laughed out loud. "Now, wouldn't it be funny to see you guys mimic the three black girls in *Hair* mimicking you?"

"Great!" I said. We all thought this was a wonderful idea, a good chance to show that while we loved the Supremes image, we also knew that it was extreme. I was always looking for something new and were sure that this routine was a winner. We worked up an arrangement of greatest hits to sing with it. Who wouldn't like that?

In the middle of rehearsals Mike Roshkind called, demanding that Pedro and I attend a meeting at Motown that afternoon. Besides being logistically inconvenient, it was insulting to be ordered around like that. When we arrived, Mike was there with Suzanne dePasse, chief publicist Bob Jones, company lawyer Lee Young, Jr., and Susaye's mother, who was also her manager. The gist of the meeting concerned Scherrie and Susaye's dissatisfaction with Pedro's management, which annoyed me. This had all been planned behind my back. I'd brought those girls in, and now they were conspiring against me. Joining the Supremes is like going into a job in a department store. You follow their rules or you leave. They didn't come into the Supremes as owners, but as employees. They knew that. I felt that someone there wanted Pedro *and* me out of the way. As I learned later, Motown was promising Susaye and Scherrie that it would give them creative freedom and label support if only it weren't for Pedro and me.

Our opening in Las Vegas, which should have been fabulous, was another all-time low. There was no talk about "coheadlining"; we were clearly the opening act, with a meager thirty minutes to perform. However, I was very excited that we were playing Caesars Palace, one of the top hotels. Mike Roshkind, Suzanne dePasse, Thelma Houston, and Bob Jones were all there, along with dozens of industry friends.

From the minute the curtain rose, we knew the set wasn't right. George had had to make so many changes in so little time, we looked and felt like amateurs. Then came the medley of Supremes hits, with the three of us in one dress. It was an unmitigated disaster. People in the audience just didn't get it, or if they did, they didn't think it was funny. Where there should have been laughter, there was stony silence. Once the number ended, we struggled to get out of the one big dress, but we couldn't get it off before the lights came back on. What an embarrassment!

At our opening-night party, I ran into Mike Roshkind and Bob Jones. Mike barely said hello; his expression was so cold I shuddered. Bob was pleasant enough, but I could read his mind. No one would say what we all knew was the truth: we were awful.

Over the next several days, we spent every free minute with George, revamping the show. Everyone had a very negative attitude. Conductor Teddy Harris was annoyed that we'd brought in other arrangers to work out certain numbers, Susaye was behaving like a petulant child, and Scherrie was joining her. Every time George made a suggestion, those two shot him down. As I sat there, watching this, I thought despairingly, *This is it.* At one point, George approached me and apologized for Scherrie and Susaye's attitude. That was very kind of him, but I knew that it should have been me apologizing to him.

Pedro decided right then to notify Motown that I was going solo. I'd been fighting it for a long time, though not for sentimental reasons, as many people thought. I wanted to leave the Supremes with a hit record. To top it all off, over the years I'd lent the group tens of thousands of dollars from my personal account. If I left now, or if the Supremes were dissolved, I could kiss that money good-bye.

One night our show was so bad that people got up and walked out in the middle. We had rearranged the hits medley, but it was worse than ever. "Baby Love" went by so fast, we literally missed it, or so we thought. We started singing the next song, "Where Did Our Love Go," before we all realized the band was still playing "Baby Love."

Pedro came into the dressing room before the second show and announced, "Mary is leaving the group. This is it."

Scherrie and Susaye seemed genuinely shocked. "Mary, is that what you want to do?" Scherrie asked. I think she was trying to see if this was my idea or Pedro's.

"Yes, Scherrie, I am leaving." I was tired of the constant bickering, the pettiness, the embarrassment of failing. From our dressing room we could hear the crowd roaring with laughter at Alan King's jokes, so the audience wasn't the problem; it was us.

The rest of the run, cut short because of poor attendance, just dragged on and on. One bright spot was a show when, no matter what we did, we received a very loud, enthusiastic response from one corner of the room. Onstage, you can't see more than a few rows into the crowd, so we had no idea who these rabid fans were until after the show, when the Pointer Sisters came backstage to visit. It turned out that they were the ones. Now, that's what I call true friends. We spent hours talking, playing cards, and being real crazy.

With Pedro and me on our way out of the picture, Scherrie and Susaye must have wondered what Motown had in store for them. Surprisingly, they seemed to believe everything the company said. They were promised an album deal and Motown's full support. Pedro and I pointed out how the label hadn't adequately promoted the Supremes since Diane left. We warned them to be careful. Naturally, Susaye and Scherrie were suspicious of everything we said; nothing penetrated. They were two very headstrong women, determined to carve out their own careers from the Supremes.

Since having Turkessa, I'd tired of the whole party scene, but on occasion I missed it. Hollywood was no longer a truly glamorous place; there didn't seem to be the same magic. Even the private clubs, like the Candy Store, weren't what they used to be. Everything I'd loved about Hollywood in the late sixties and early seventies was dying.

Also, the music scene had changed. All the clubs played only disco. Whereas the music of the O'Jays, the Temptations, and the Four Tops made me want to jump up and dance, disco's soulless, mechanical thumping made me want to cover my ears and run.

Almost every time Pedro and I went out, there was trouble. One evening we were at a club, and I was speaking to a television producer, thanking him for how well the Supremes had been treated at a recent taping. As far as I was concerned, this was simply good business. But Pedro became upset, so we left a few minutes later, and at home it was a familiar scene. As I wrote in my diary:

December 1976

We silently got in bed, then he started talking about it. What could I say? He had his own point of view. Then when he wanted to make love to make up, I wasn't ready for that. It takes me a long while to get over a quarrel. He became very strong, and that turns me off even more. Those are the moments when I know I am closer to hating him. When I wouldn't return his advances, he slapped me and slapped me. Why does he think his strength will make me love him more? I need tenderness and understanding. He told me a friend of ours has found a girlfriend because he is tired of how his wife has become. Somehow I feel that Pedro is talking about us, although he said if he ever did that, he would tell me in some way. Maybe that was a hint.

CHAPTER 12

I had all but accepted that Pedro and I would divorce eventually, and, to be honest, I'd stopped loving him. My career was another question. Anything might happen: we could get that hit record and be on top again, or we could continue our slide downhill. Our financial situation was bleak, my confidence was shaken, but I still had faith.

My diaries from these years are filled with entries that alternate between utter despair and soaring optimism. As always, there were two—or three or four—sides to every story, and I saw them all. Instead of becoming embittered and cynical, I kept looking for and believing in what was good about people and life. Despite all that had gone wrong, I had my family, my baby, my talent, and my friends. I didn't need to have everything; I didn't even want everything, just happiness.

The idea of going out alone during the coming year was exciting and frightening. I felt like both a mother leaving her child, and a little bird leaving the nest. It was agreed that the

Supremes would continue with Scherrie, Susaye, and a third girl. I had mixed feelings about that. On one hand, I felt I owed it to Scherrie to let her continue. She'd given the Supremes so much. In my heart, though, I knew it was time for the Supremes to end, with or without me. Susaye was another story; she'd been in the group such a short time and had caused so much dissension. I also wondered whether the fans would accept a group with no original members, and I worried about Motown. Would it offer me a solo contract? Would it kill the Supremes, but openly this time? What was going to happen?

The main thing I can credit Pedro with is pushing me. Left to my own devices, I wonder if I'd have made the decision to go off on my own then. But he was right: I could not go on fighting like this.

It's funny how Pedro was so supportive of me professionally and yet treated me so badly in our marriage. I think he saw me as two different people: his client and his wife. When it came to my career, he showed all the characteristics that I loved. He was smart, strong, shrewd, and reasonable. I believe that he truly wanted to do what was best for me.

But at home or in social situations, I was just his wife, and he treated me like even less than that. His obsession about me cheating on him was out of hand. He told me he was having an affair with one of my best friends, a famous star. I didn't believe him, but I had to know, so I called her. When I told her what Pedro said, she replied, "Mary, that is a lie." I was so relieved. At one point, he told me that he was going to start dating other women. My first reaction was to say that I wouldn't stand for it, but then I looked at my situation: the baby, the career, the house, the image, the future. A famous advice columnist says to ask yourself, "Am I better off with him or without him?" In many ways I still needed Pedro.

Two people who felt they did not need Pedro were Scherrie and Susaye. The tension among us broke into open hostility. Both women hated Pedro and showed it at every opportunity. Susaye and her manager mother had their own ideas about the Supremes, and while Scherrie wasn't as bad as Susaye, she became her partner in crime. Soon Scherrie was as rebellious as Susaye.

While I was not happy with the way Susaye and Scherrie treated us, I understood. And to be fair, their futures were as uncertain as mine, despite Motown's assertions to the contrary. I tried not to take the cold glares and heated words personally, but it hurt nonetheless. I couldn't wait to leave, but there were still concert dates to fulfill.

We spent most of early 1977 overseas. By late March we had played Germany, El Salvador, San Juan, Mexico, and England. Ironically, our shows were getting better all the time. At last the contracts were signed for the Supremes' final "farewell" show: Sunday, June 12, 1977.

Motherhood was the most rewarding thing in my life. Even today I consider my children my real gold records. But as every mother knows, there are limits to how much mothering a mother can give. I was beginning to realize that society's double standards applied to parenthood too. Before it was fashionable, I was a working mother, and, in a sense, my daughter was a working child. She came with me wherever I went, and even amid all the chaos Pedro and I tried to keep our family intact. Even with all the help I had on the road, there was still only one "Mommy" as far as Turkessa was concerned. Others could hold her, change her, put her to sleep, but only I could nurse her. Of course there were alternatives, but I'd waited all my life for my baby, and I was determined to do everything right.

One night we were getting ready to go onstage in England at the Hammersmith Odeon. Turkessa was almost two years old, but because it was so much trouble carrying formula and bottles on the road, she still nursed. My usual routine was to dress, make up, then feed Turkessa right before the show. This way she'd stay calm until the show was over. As I stood in the wings, I held Turkessa in my arms, pulled down one side of my gown, and nursed her. Just then we heard the announcer introduce our band, and Teddy start our opening number. Gill Trodd, who also assisted with Turkessa, ran up, agitated. "What's going on here?" she asked.

I started toward the stage, gently pulling Turkessa away, only to find that she wouldn't let go. Gill took the baby in her arms and tried to coax her off while I kept walking, but no go. Turkessa was there to stay. The emcee was introducing the Supremes now, and there I stood, my bronze-sequined dress down to my waist and a baby stuck to me like glue. Finally, Gill and I gave Turkessa one strong (and, for me, painful) yank, and I was freed. Milk splattered up in my face, but I managed to get my dress up a split second before the curtain rose, and we began singing "Everybody Gets to Go to the Moon."

Returning stateside we had a successful run at Bachelors III in Fort Lauderdale, where just the year before we'd played to half-empty houses. One evening Pedro and I were invited to dinner by Bobby Van, one of the club's owners. We were having a wonderful evening until he received a phone call, and then the whole restaurant started buzzing: *Tom Jones was on his way over.* Everyone knew that Tom was in town to open a new theater, and I suspected that Pedro had brought me here because Tom might show up. In the next minutes, Pedro gave me an in-depth lecture on how I should behave: I should not approach Tom or seem too eager to talk with him.

I was in the ladies' room when two of Tom's backup singers, the Blossoms, came in. We had known one another for a long time, and we spent about fifteen minutes chatting. They both told me they were so proud of me, that Tom talked about me often and always with great respect.

When I finally emerged from the restroom, the restaurant fell silent, and it seemed like all eyes turned to me. Not everyone there knew about our relationship, but many of the same people in his entourage had been there in the sixties, and the affair had been reported in newspapers around the world. Tom walked toward me, extended his hand, and said, "You all right?" I felt my knees go weak.

"Sure, I am fine," I replied shakily. "Is your son Mark with you?"

What was wrong with me? My love for him was a thing of the past, so that wasn't it. I guess it was my guilt. Everyone was looking at us, at me, at Tom, at Pedro. They all knew what I'd done.

We sat at a long table, drinking champagne, ostensibly having a good time. I was a nervous wreck. Every time Tom tried making casual conversation, I could feel the heat of Pedro's searing jealousy.

The Blossoms attended one of our shows that week and told me that they knew Tom planned to come see us. One evening as I started "A Song for You," I looked out from the stage, and there he was, sitting in the first balcony, right in front of me. The line "I've made some bad rhymes" took on a whole new meaning. I glanced at Tom and thought to myself, *Clean up your wicked ways, girl.* Tom came backstage later, and we all stood around, awkwardly making small talk. When we left Fort Lauderdale for Nassau a few days later, I was relieved.

Months after our breakup and as I'd started maturing more, in the back of my mind I always feared that I would have to pay for that affair. Still, until now, I believed I'd been forgiven. Not Pedro, though. He said that I was a sinner who'd done something terrible, and I believed it. Pedro used guilt to control me, and because he always made me feel so wrong, I began seeing myself as a hypocrite who'd been fooling herself. Now I was being punished. I started reading the Bible, which only reinforced my feelings and made me feel dirty.

I began to feel tired all the time; the least little bit of excitement, and I'd have to sit down. I'd also noticed that my stomach was getting bigger. At first I just figured I was eating too much and sleeping too little. I vowed to take better care of myself.

Earlier in the year we had announced in our fan club's monthly newsletter that we would be appearing at one of Richard Nader's "oldies" shows at New York City's Madison Square Garden on March 4, 1977. Almost immediately we heard from fans who thought this was a terrible idea. The format of the Rock and Roll Spectaculars was old-fashioned, like the shows we used to do at the Apollo or the Brooklyn Fox; a three-and-a-half-hour parade of acts, each doing a handful of numbers. That evening was a typical Nader bill, with Ben E. King, the Duprees, Jay Black and the Americans, Johnny Maestro and the Brooklyn Bridge, and Dion DiMucci (of Dion and the Belmonts) all preceding us, the headliners.

When first offered the date, I seriously considered what our appearing on an oldies-but-goodies show would mean. I respected and admired the performers on the bill, particularly Ben E. King, whom the original Supremes performed with countless times in the early sixties, but there were many good reasons not to play the Garden. The audience generally viewed these events as opportunities to stroll down Memory Lane. The years of trying to put the Supremes back on top taught me a thing or two about what the American public expected from performers. In concert, our seventies hits, like

"Nathan Jones" and "Floy Joy," rarely got the same wild response as the older stuff. I had no problem with that; I was proud of all our records. Yet it hurt to know that in some people's eyes we might never do anything as good. As I once replied when asked about the public's taste, "What they had yesterday, they want today."

Almost anywhere else in the world, a performer is respected for his talent and accomplishments; in America, your past accomplishments can kill you. Here we see no middle ground between superstar and has-been. You're either one or the other, regardless of the artistic merits of what you're doing today. If your face is not on television once a week, if every one of your records is not in heavy rotation on radio and MTV, you simply do not exist.

At that point the Supremes were in a sort of netherworld. We weren't really an oldies act, but the general public had lost track of us. Where many acts on the bill had not been on the charts in several years, the Supremes were still a contemporary presence, if not a strong one. The deciding factor to accept the booking was Madison Square Garden itself, and the lure of its capacity. The average audience for one of Nader's shows was around fifteen thousand to eighteen thousand. It was irresistible.

The afternoon of the show we met with Richard Nader and ran down our set. He became very upset that we were doing too many new songs and not enough of the old hits. But we had a relatively new album out, and I wasn't about to pass up this opportunity to promote it.

"Everything will be just fine," I assured Nader. "We know our fans."

He looked at me like I was crazy, and I left the rehearsal hall furious.

When we got backstage at the Garden that night, we could hear the thousands upstairs screaming as Dion finished his set. We were confident they would love us. One of our more devoted fans whispered in my ear, "Mary, girl, I don't think you should go out there. This isn't a Copacabana audience."

"Don't worry," I answered. "We're going to go out there and sing our wigs off for them. And they're going to love it. We're doing 'Tossin' and Turnin' ' and all sorts of old songs and—"

"You don't understand, girl. These are a bunch of bikers from New Jersey. They hate disco songs like your new hits."

I thanked him for his concern, but my mind was made up. There were more than fifteen thousand people out there expecting the Supremes, and we were going to give them a show. We opened with our current disco hit, "You're My Driving Wheel," teamed with another song from *Mary, Scherrie & Susaye*, "Let Yourself Go." The crowd was on its feet, cheering and hollering. I believed we had won them over.

"Hello, New York!" I shouted.

"Yeahhh!" the crowd cheered back.

"We're the Supremes!"

"Yeahhh!"

"We want you to sit back, relax, and enjoy yourselves. We want you all to know that it ain't nothin' but a party—"

"Yeahhh!"

"And we want you to get on down and party!"

Next I introduced Susaye, and she began singing her slow version of the Hollies' "He Ain't Heavy, He's My Brother," which always elicited a standing ovation. The crowd cheered at first, but by the end some people were booing. It was bizarre. For the next twenty minutes the boos just got louder and meaner. What we didn't know until later was that while half the crowd was booing, the other half was applauding and shouting in support. Fights broke out around the arena between the Supremes fans who loved what we were doing and "old rock and roll" fans who disapproved. We tried to redeem ourselves with the greatest-hits medley, but it was too late. Finally, Susaye, Scherrie, and I looked at one another and realized we had to get off the stage before a riot erupted. A group of security men and a few diehard fans accompanied us back to our dressing rooms.

On the way backstage I started laughing just to keep from crying. Scherrie and Susaye were dumbstruck, and Scherrie was particularly unnerved. Her mother was in the last stages of a terminal illness, and Scherrie was feeling very down. Neither of them had wanted to play the Garden, and they were proved right. Their glares and the fans' looks that said, "I told you so," were more than I could bear. In all the years I'd performed, I had never, ever been booed. A scene like that was every performer's nightmare, but I never imagined that it would cut so deeply. Scherrie and Susaye blamed Pedro; however, the fault was really mine. I should have known better.

Pedro and I went with some friends to Regine's disco. I started drinking champagne and was pretty tipsy before long. I couldn't stop talking about what happened; I was dying inside, but Pedro didn't want to hear about it. Out on the dance floor, I started dancing alone with a drink in my hand. When a waiter asked me to put it down, Pedro angrily told me that I was "acting like a nigger, not a star." I was stunned. I'd never felt so rejected in my life.

A few days later *Variety*'s critic wrote: "The Supremes, unfortunately, provided the low point of the evening. The audience, which had been receptive until then, became rude, with much booing, and many leaving the arena in response to the Supremes' slick act, with their coordinated wardrobes and choreography. Fans who remained applauded the closing medley of their hits."

Two days later it was my thirty-third birthday.

Here I was, three months pregnant with my second baby, unhappily married, and setting out on the biggest challenge of my life. My leaving the group brought me head to head with Motown. Pedro was planning most of my legal strategy and hired Mark Turk, the attorney who just the year before had helped the Temptations get out of their Motown contract with their name and move to Atlantic Records. He was confident he could handle Motown, probably get me back more or maybe all of the name, and persuade the label to give me either a generous settlement, a solo contract, or even both.

I gladly let Pedro take over the legal business too. From then on, most of the information I got about how my legal situation was progressing came to me through my husband. The positive aspect was that Pedro had studied and understood the law; he made the complexities of the business comprehensible to me, and that was a big help. The negative side became clear to me nearly a decade later, when I realized that there might have been different approaches to take. It's impossible to know what might have been done that wasn't—especially since no attorney will criticize the actions of the attorney who preceded him on your case. The wheels that Pedro and this attorney set into motion in the spring of 1977 have created consequences that I am still dealing with today.

Back then, I was cautiously optimistic about the situation at home. Then came the Supremes' last tour of Europe, which was dismal and depressing in almost every way. Many times during this tour I wished that after Pedro announced I was leaving, I'd just left. Scherrie and Susaye were not comfortable with me, and since I was on my way out, they became more critical of Pedro. Scherrie, basically a very warm person, was at her worst; the stress of her mother's recent death wore her down. Despite Scherrie's occasional outbursts, we still remained friendly. I could see that had there not been so much adversity, Scherrie would have proved to be the best person of all the Supremes, in terms of talent and personality, to carry on with.

Susaye, on the other hand, had clearly come into the group with her own agenda. She was an ambitious girl, and it showed. She was increasingly difficult to work with, because she refused to sing the background parts we had rehearsed and often stepped out of the choreography, keeping Scherrie and me guessing where she'd be, in the song and on the stage. Scherrie and I always pulled back vocally so that it wouldn't sound like all of us were trying to sing lead at once. I respected Scherrie for being so professional and gracious; many lead singers would have thrown a fit.

After a gig in Austria the subject of Motown's plans for Scherrie and Susaye came up. Pedro wasn't on this trip, so we were a little more relaxed. I said, "Scherrie, when Diane left, Motown stopped doing anything for the Supremes. With me out of the way, they'll do nothing for you."

"Well, Mary," Scherrie said, "they've promised us a lot. They're even allowing both Susaye and me to write our own songs."

"Believe me, Scherrie, they have no intention of pushing another group of Supremes. If they had, they would have done it by now, and we wouldn't be in this position."

No one listened.

This European tour preceded my final dates with the group. I had known it was approaching as we toured through Austria, Germany, and Sweden—ending up in England. Before I knew it, we had landed in the British Isles, and the big night rapidly grew nearer and nearer.

Our last shows were on June 12 at the Drury Lane Theatre in London, an old-style legitimate theater. With its heavy red-velvet curtains and gold-leaf decor, it had a wonderful, dignified atmosphere. Unlike in the States, where the Supremes were all but forgotten, the English treated this final farewell performance as every bit the event the 1970 farewell had been. We had flowers, champagne, and our closest friends and fans all there to bid the Supremes good-bye. It was heavily covered by the media, and the BBC broadcast the show live.

I felt so many different emotions. I decided to just go with the experience; it was going to happen only once. That afternoon I told Scherrie and Susaye that I would like to sing "The Way We Were," a number we hadn't done for a while.

"Do we *have* to?" Susaye whined, obviously feeling put out.

"Yes. It's my last appearance, and that's my last request of the group. I think I deserve at least that, don't you?"

The two of them more or less agreed that I should get to do the song. We ran down the choreography and our parts, but it wasn't really all together. It wasn't until then that it really dawned on me: *This is it.* More than half my life I'd been a Supreme, and in a few moments, it would be over.

Billy Ocean, not as famous then as he'd become in the eighties, opened our show. I stood in the wings and listened to him; he was soulful all right, but the crowd just wasn't very receptive. They were waiting for us.

During the first show I started my solo, "How Lucky Can You Get," and suddenly started crying. I was so choked up with emotion that when I opened my mouth to sing, nothing came out. I stood there silently through the first verse, afraid that I'd sob all the way through it. I came in on the second verse, and sang my heart out. I got one of the most wonderful ovations ever. When we got offstage, Susaye sequestered herself in her dressing room.

Right before the second and last show, the whole backstage area got as quiet as a funeral. Herb and Mauna Loa

Avery had flown over to wish me luck. Gill and Hazel were crying as they carried in more telegrams, flowers, and bottles of champagne. I tried to cheer everyone up, but inside I was sad too. Then it was time to go on. Hazel helped me into my dress. Five months pregnant, I was radiant.

We opened our last show with a frenetic version of "Everybody Gets to Go to the Moon." English audiences were usually put off by our Vegas-type numbers, and one reviewer called this a "manic" and "improbable" opener. "Stoned Love," "Baby Love," and "Stop! In the Name of Love" followed, then an excellent slow rendition of "My World Is Empty Without You," which was Scherrie's showstopper.

This time I was able to sing "A Song for You" and "How Lucky Can You Get" without crying. Everything seemed perfect. I felt it happen. Suddenly, it was just me. I did all kinds of things on stage I had never dared try before. It was like I was a new person up there. Every number seemed to hit, and after our conductor Teddy Harris made a little speech about me, I felt like I was in a dream. Before I went into my next solo, I called for Turkessa, who toddled onstage in a beautiful white dress Pedro's mother had given her. As I sang, she sat beside me and hugged and kissed me. I felt like there were only the two of us there, in our own world. The big difference was that this wasn't the same old tired Mary Wilson. I was someone else, someone I knew deep down all along I could be.

Next we did several songs from *High Energy* and *Mary, Scherrie & Susaye*, including "I'm Gonna Let My Heart Do the Walking," "You're My Driving Wheel," and "You're What's Missing in My Life." We teased the crowd with a playful performance of "He's My Man," then closed with "Someday We'll Be Together." We did three encores, each to standing ovations, and flowers carpeted the stage as the crowd pressed to the front. Teddy handed me a beautiful bouquet, then made another little speech, calling this "the end of an era." I embraced Scherrie and Susaye, for the last time, I hoped. My bass player kissed me on the cheek, and I could see Teddy had tears in his eyes. It was beautiful and sad too. When it was all over I felt relieved.

It was three months after the Madison Square Garden disaster, and suddenly here I was, the toast of London. Everywhere I went people congratulated me and wished me well on my solo career. I was approached by lords and ladies, barkeeps at Annabol's and Tramps, cashiers at Boots and Harrod's. After the last show, Motown's EMI affiliate threw us a party at the swank London disco Maunkberry's. Pedro, Gill, Turkessa, Hazel, Herb, Mauna Loa, and the guys in the band had a ball. Despite my pregnancy, I partied late into the night. This was really it: my grand farewell was over, the Supremes were gone.

We spent the next few days in London, where Pedro and I bought some antiques for the house in Hancock Park, including a French armoire, some eighteenth-century paintings, a twelve-foot sideboard with matching dining-room chairs, and many other fabulous items. Herb and Mauna Loa came with Turkessa, Pedro's mother, and us as we began a long European vacation. We drove a rented green Mercedes to San Remo, Paris, the French Riviera, and Rome, dining and drinking fine wines everywhere. It was wonderful. There's nothing like stopping in the ancient French vineyards, or visiting small villas and opulent palaces, like Versailles. Taking a trip like this had been my lifelong dream, so I treasured every precious moment.

When we arrived on the French Riviera, we got in touch with Barry Sinco, a friend of Pedro's from Puerto Rico. Barry then managed a hotel in Monte Carlo. We planned to stay in the city a few days before heading for Rome. There we drove the winding roads that make up the Grand Prix race course, looked for nude beaches, and ate fabulous pasta at outdoor cafés. Even at six months pregnant, I looked gorgeous. Being the only black foursome just about everywhere we went, we turned heads. Even Turkessa; she was so cute.

Each night Mauna and I changed into exquisite gowns and emerged looking like two bronze Folies Bergère girls. Stepping out with Herb and Pedro, we headed for the fine restaurants, Regine's original disco, Jimmy's, and the Grand Casino. We stayed out in Monte Carlo's great casinos. Ringo Starr hung around with us, and between his wry sense of humor and Mauna Loa's natural outrageousness, I was laughing every minute.

Barry Sinco arranged for us to be treated to the most sumptuous, decadent meal of our lives at the Hotel de Paris, a classic, old-style European grand hotel. We were served caviars, soufflés, and the finest wines. The rarest china, crystal, and silver were laid out for us. We were dressed in the best clothes, having the time of our lives. Between bites of caviar, Mauna Loa said, "You guys are so great for giving us this fabulous trip."

We strolled out of the Hotel de Paris and stood in the square, right across from the palace where Prince Rainier and Princess Grace resided. Looking up at the clear, star-filled sky, I thought, *Will I ever experience this kind of life again?*

Suddenly several trucks pulled to a screeching halt in the square. Dozens of gendarmes, each armed with a semi-automatic machine gun, jumped out and surrounded us. None of them spoke English, but we gathered that we were under arrest. They took us to the police station, where for almost an hour no one told us why we'd been arrested. Pedro and Herb finally couldn't stand it and reverted to what I call their street ways. "Just because we're black," Herb shouted, "you're harassing us!"

Pedro added, "Wait till we get out of here! I'm calling Prince Rainier!"

"Yeah, me too," a cop replied, laughing. So some of them did speak English after all! They were still pointing their machine guns at us, so none of us was laughing.

Finally, after a couple hours, someone came from one of the hotels to identify us—and our car. It turned out that the police were on the lookout for a famous fugitive who happened to speak Spanish, drive a green Mercedes, and look like Pedro. Apparently, someone in a casino overheard Pedro's accent, saw the car, and figured he was one of Europe's ten most wanted. It was a simple case of mistaken identity, but for a while the situation was pretty tense.

We drove on to Rome and tried to enjoy the rest of the trip, partying at exclusive clubs and savoring the last moments of my grand vacation. Before I knew it, it was over, and I was back in Los Angeles, getting ready for my new baby and my new career.

CHAPTER 13

July 1977

You won't believe this, but I am rehearsing Cindy Birdsong and Debbie Sharpe to replace Susaye and Scherrie as the Supremes! Actually, the show is called "the Mary Wilson of the Supremes Show." We are to leave for South America in one day. The tour is three weeks long. How is that, you ask? Well, it's a long story.

As far as I knew, Motown was proceeding with Scherrie and Susaye's plan to find a third singer. I wasn't surprised to read the numerous stories on Scherrie and Susaye where they talked about how "their" new Supremes would be different. They boasted about Motown letting them write their own songs and all the plans they had in store.

I don't think they meant anything they said maliciously, but it seemed like the Supremes were being tossed in the trash. "We'll be adding another girl," Susaye told one reporter, "then we shall be setting about forming a totally new concept for the Supremes. . . . Instead of just being singers, we'll have some measure of creative control."

We did not talk about their plans after I officially left the group, although they did keep in touch with Hazel. That entire year represented a major coup for Susaye. She and her mother were so happy; they saw my leaving as their first step toward a great future. I think they really believed they would succeed where I had failed. Because of her mother's death, Scherrie still wasn't herself and, I was told, basically let Susaye and her mother call the shots.

I left the Supremes assured that all the business was taken care of. Tours, which are booked months in advance, were to be handled by Motown and the William Morris Agency. I felt that if Motown wanted the Supremes to fulfill these previously arranged commitments, it should send the "new" Supremes—Scherrie, Susaye, and a third girl—or come up with another solution.

However, when our agent informed Pedro and me that some dates in South America had not been canceled, and the "new" Supremes weren't doing them, we panicked. If we didn't fulfill the contracts, we would be sued, I was told. The Supremes had to do it, but how? We had given our "farewell" performance! Against my wishes, Pedro called Scherrie and asked her to come back; both she and Susaye refused. They were upset by the short notice, but it was short notice for me too. Frankly, we all needed the money from this tour desperately, so I decided to find two background singers and get ready to go. I had two days.

We called Lynda Laurence, but she wanted far too much money. Cindy was happy to go, bringing her son David along. Through Reggie Wiggins, a former employee, we found our third member, Debbie Sharpe. She had sung professionally with the Oral Roberts World Action Singers, so she had concert and television experience. When we called her, she was working a temporary job. She auditioned on her lunch hour, and by the time she got off work that day, she was in.

We were ready—almost. Visas, passports, papers, plans, wardrobe fittings, and musicians still had to be taken care of. While Cindy, Debbie, and I rehearsed all day, Hazel worked out the myriad details. It would take a miracle to put it all together, but good ol' "Red Haze," as we called her, came through. We flew to Caracas, Venezuela, the next morning, dead on our feet, but all during the flight Debbie rehearsed the songs. Cindy, Debbie, and I went over choreography in the airplane's aisles.

We arrived in Caracas to find that our gowns hadn't made it and that the musicians' charts and music sheets had vanished. Fortunately, they all knew the music, and later the gowns showed up, but every moment was nerve-racking.

I was still working on the terms of my new contract with Motown as a soloist. Shortly after we got to South America we were notified that Motown did not approve of my taking out another group of Supremes—even though we were not billed as the *Supremes*. Pedro, who'd stayed home to attend to the contract, warned all the promoters and television people we worked with not to announce us as "the Supremes," but as "Mary Wilson *of* the Supremes," a crucial distinction. The name issue was further complicated by the fact that Scherrie and Susaye planned to continue as the Supremes. They were probably sure that when they refused to come with me to South America, I wouldn't go. I could only imagine their surprise when they learned otherwise.

Obviously, they and Motown didn't want a "competing" group out there, which I understood. At the same time, the debt I had assumed on behalf of the Supremes and Motown through the Supremes, Inc., was now hanging over *my* head, not theirs. Nobody offered to help pay off these bills, but

Motown or the booking agent had approved this short tour and had not bothered to cancel it; letting me "borrow" the name was the least it could do. And there was another technicality: both Cindy and I were still under contract to Motown as the Supremes. Confusing? You bet.

One promoter complained about getting only two out of three "real" Supremes. I was quite proud of my command of Spanish, and without Pedro, it fell to me to handle all the business. Some of the promoters were less than gentlemanly, ranting, raving, and yelling at me. By the time Pedro arrived with Herb and Mauna Loa, my spirits were really low. Cindy and Debbie pretty much kept together, which was fine, but I really needed a friend then. At nearly seven months pregnant, I was getting bigger each day and more tired. I still hadn't fully recovered from the tour of Europe, and before long I contracted a severe case of pneumonia.

July 1977

Small money, small club. It was all so small and cheap. Don't get me wrong: the club was first-rate by today's standards. Everyone who came were of the upper-class population of Caracas. It's just that when we were on top we never would have taken these gigs.

I thought Europe was the end. Here I am in it all over again. One thing made it worth it. It's now very clear that I am a soloist, not a Supreme. I sang lead on all tunes. They were all strange, but when we finished, I felt proud of myself. So as a group it was sloppy, but my future was what I was interested in; my development as a solo artist.

Despite everything that was wrong about this tour—Motown trying to stop it, the small clubs, my first time singing all the lead vocals, and forgetting many of the lyrics to our Supremes songs—one of the shows there proved to be the greatest performance I'd ever given. It's hard to describe the magic when you are onstage and know that every note, every gesture, every nuance is perfect. This particular night in Buenos Aires, Argentina, the theater was full, and the crowd was very receptive. From our travels, the band was irritable; as I noted in my diary, all of us were "ugly, tired people." Still, onstage the magic took over, and, as usual, that made all the problems seem unimportant. I *felt* every song and was beginning to feel truly comfortable in my new role as soloist. No longer was I the shy, sweet background singer of the past.

My baby was very heavy and kicked all the time, especially when I was onstage. Right before the show I had such pain I couldn't even move, but we went out there, and even though I knew everything was going against me, I drew on my sickness, my baby, everything. I was on my own now; I had to make it work. Somehow, it did. For the first time in years I could stand onstage without feeling I was cheating the audience.

"Bravo! Bravo!" the crowd shouted. I smiled graciously, but my exhaustion and pain were so great, Debbie and Cindy had to help me offstage. My body ached, my mind was numb. If I only could have slept for several days. Instead, I had to play a private party at a nearby hotel. The room was small, the lighting and sound awful. I was miserable, but I'd had my first triumphant moment as a soloist, and I would cherish it forever.

We gratefully returned home. The house, though, was a mess; Willie had been "entertaining," and our money problems were looming larger than ever. Because Motown had misinterpreted my intentions for taking the South American tour, I was now in a full-fledged lawsuit with them. I certainly didn't have enough money to continue, so my best bet was a quick settlement. Life is funny: one minute they were giving me a solo contract, and the next they were cutting off my lifeline. To prepare for the possibility that there would be trouble, Pedro and new attorney Mark Turk had gone to work gathering up all of our old contracts, back from the very beginning, and putting together a case against Motown.

The company had sent a barrage of threatening letters and telegrams to all the South American promoters, warning them about using the Supremes name in any form. The only way I could fight back was to report its actions to the California State Labor Commission. Under California law, the Labor Commission offered us the best relief. Because so much of the world's entertainment industry is based there, California has very strict laws regarding contracts for performers. Since we were under contract to Motown in California, Motown had been subject to these laws since the early seventies, and possibly earlier.

In September 1977 I filed my complaint against Motown with the labor commissioner. In it I made a number of allegations against Motown Record Corporation, Multi-Media Management Corporation, International Management Company, and Berry Gordy, Jr. The case fell under the labor commission's jurisdiction in part because in California it is illegal for a single person or entity to function as both manager (an adviser) and agent (someone who finds work and negotiates contracts for work). Motown managed us through its Multi-Media Management Corporation, even when we hired outside managers, and functioned as an agent through its International Management Company as well.

The fact that these were all interrelated subsidiaries of Motown and all under Berry Gordy, Jr.'s control presented a clear conflict of interest. Furthermore, because they had the same address and were controlled by the same people, they were in effect a single entity, which violated California law.

In addition, all managers and agents in California must be registered and licensed, which Motown was not. In fact, these Motown-related companies were not even qualified to do business at all in the state, since they were not corporations organized in California, or in any other state, as we later found. The name the company was doing business under at the time, Motown Record Corporation of California, Inc., was not a corporation. Since it wasn't even listed in the telephone directory, it may have been a fictitious company altogether.

I wasn't surprised to learn that Motown's setup constituted a conflict of interest. The company managed us, booked us, provided us with legal advice, made all our career decisions, and invested our personal money for us. Even when Motown made a show of finding us so-called independent managers, they were all culled from a list that met label approval, and were paid by Motown. Any correspondence between us was also sent to Motown. Having spent so many years in the industry, however, I knew there were few options. Either you played by the record company's rules, or you didn't play. Those were your "choices."

As annoyed as I was with Motown, I was still very reluctant to leave, because it was my family, because it was black-owned. To me, that was extremely important, though the people actually handling contracts and running the business were mostly white. Yes, most of the artists fault Berry, and, yes, he graciously accepts the blame. But he still says, "I don't know anything about the legal aspect. I let the legal department handle that. I'm too busy being creative."

Throughout the years, whites such as Barney Ales, Mike Roshkind, Tom Noonan, George Schiffer, Ralph Seltzer, brothers Harold and Sidney Novack, and others have run Motown, with Berry out front as chairman and a few other blacks in seemingly important positions. I'm surprised that we artists never addressed these issues back in the late sixties and seventies. There were blacks in creative areas, and there had been some black executives back in Detroit, but once we moved to L.A., Motown was white-run.

For all his personal flaws and unpopular business decisions, Berry accomplished what no black man had before him. Though the old "Motown family" had no contemporary relevance to me, it still held a place in my heart. Whenever something went wrong, or some Motown executive treated me disrespectfully, I automatically thought back to when I was one of four girls giggling in Hitsville's lobby, or swooning over Marvin Gaye, or getting a lecture from Berry. What broke my heart was the realization that while Motown had changed immensely over the years, its strength—and the artists' weakness—was our clinging to memories of those old days, those happy, happy times.

The final decision to proceed against Motown and Berry took me a long time to reach, and I resisted it every step of the way. But now I was forced to fight. Berry's accomplishments weren't his alone; they were shared by the other artists, writers, producers, musicians—everyone who worked at Motown—and, symbolically, by black people the world over. Motown was so much more than a record label, a roster of artists, a sound. It was a shining beacon of possibilities realized, talent rewarded, and, yes, dreams come true.

Returning to reality, I asked myself, *What had Motown really done to other artists like Flo? Or the lesser-known but no-less-talented singers and musicians the company unceremoniously abandoned in Detroit?* I often thought, *What will those people do?* There was nothing for them in Detroit. I saw the toll the financial inequities took on my fellow artists. People think artists file these lawsuits just to make a financial killing. They don't realize how little money most artists have. Sure, you wear great clothes and ride around in a fancy car. It's all part of the image. Some of the performers I'd come up with couldn't buy health insurance for their children or keep their modest homes. It was morally wrong, but a very real part of show business.

Now I found myself facing the possibility of losing my own house and having my career imperiled by an overreaching and possibly illegal series of contracts. I didn't set out to get revenge against Berry and Motown, or to spend the next dozen years in exorbitant litigation. All I wanted was to keep them from shattering my life.

As I later learned, Motown conducted business just like every other record company. Large or small, black or white, they all treated their artists as commodities. That is the story of the record business. Today's young artists have the benefit of learning from what happened to their predecessors, people like Little Richard and countless others who lost everything to unscrupulous record companies. But even with special attorneys and advisers far more savvy than the advisers Diane, Flo, and I had when we signed to Motown in January 1961— our parents—there are traps no one escapes. In other words, even if my mother had been a lawyer, I'm pretty sure Motown would have worked its way around her.

For one thing, the record company is always in the most advantageous position. Of course we should have asked the right questions and protected our interests, but at that time our interests were simply to get a record deal. When someone offers you what is probably the chance of a lifetime, is it really human nature to look for all the strings attached? Besides, we were idealistic teenagers, with no experience in the cutthroat world of business. Motown certainly wasn't as shrewd with us in 1961 as it would be later with Flo and me. But it was smart enough to get what it wanted from us for next to nothing. The question I'm asked most often is what advice I'd give up-and-coming artists. My answer is, Understand the nature of the business. It's not you the business loves—it's your money and you as long as you make it. So learn how to handle and control it yourself.

My official complaint against Motown was lengthy and

extremely complicated, boiling down to several crucial points: that Motown had illegally acted as both my manager and agent; that because of various aspects of my contracts, the label could not record another act under the name the *Supremes;* and that, as the sole remaining original group member, I should be granted full ownership of the name.

There was also the question of whether or not my contracts with Motown were even legally valid. Because I was a minor in 1961, my mother signed my contract on my behalf. Motown asked her to sign an addendum to that contract, stating that she had read and understood the agreement and, further, guaranteed my performance under it—despite the fact that everyone knew my mother was functionally illiterate and could not read the papers she was signing! Because all our subsequent Motown contracts were essentially extensions of the original, if the original proved unenforceable for *any* reason, the consequences for Motown would be great.

All through the talks that took place that spring between Motown and my attorney, the issue of who owned the Supremes name was never settled. Back in 1974 Ewart Abner convinced me to sign the deal giving me 50 percent of the name. Now I still was entitled to 50 percent. The catch was that even though I technically owned half the rights to the name, Motown retained all the right *to exploit* the name. What Motown was trying to do—make it impossible for me to build upon my past sixteen years of my career by denying me *any* use of the name—was exactly what it did to Florence.

There was also the fact that regardless of Motown's claim, it did not have another group of Supremes waiting in the wings, a group whose reputation would somehow be compromised by my identifying myself as a Supreme. As of fall 1977, Scherrie and Susaye still had not found a third girl, although the press mentioned several candidates, among them Joyce Wilson of Tony Orlando and Dawn. Technically, Scherrie and Susaye were still under contract to perform for my corporation, Supremes, Inc.

As with most legal matters, there were endless postponements and delays, leaving me in limbo for months. Since Motown knew I wasn't earning a great deal of money, we suspected it was trying to wear me down. Pedro and I had just bought the new house, record sales were very slow, there were no concert dates in sight, and we were paying an attorney nearly $1,000 a day to pursue my case. It's very easy for a large corporation like Motown to just drag things along, knowing that eventually you will be bled to death financially by legal fees. One of the main reasons that artists, or anyone, challenging a major company are destined to lose is that for all the lip service we give the idea of justice and fairness in this country, the cost of getting what is due you is beyond most people's reach.

The stress got to me. I was told in late August, a month before my due date, to stay off my feet, or the baby could be born prematurely. I was bored stiff and worried about so many things. We had to lay off some employees. Hazel volunteered to work without pay, and we had no money to even buy groceries.

In his depression and desperation, Pedro continued spending money, feeling he had failed me and the group. We contemplated selling the house and moving to a small apartment. Neither of us could bear the thought of how far we had fallen. One day my life was working, and I was happy; now that seemed so long ago. And, worse, I knew in my heart that part of it was my fault.

I wanted so badly to hate Motown for everything, but I had to face the facts: I was responsible for where I was. I just hadn't had the right advisers, and I didn't have all the answers. Now I was truly paying the price. It was like the line in the song "Send in the Clowns" that laments, "Isn't it rich, isn't it queer, losing my timing this late in my career." When I was afraid to step out front in the act, I had everything I needed except for the nerve. Today I was ready to take on the world, but without any resources to draw upon. Every now and then I'd start to think that maybe I wasn't meant to have this solo career, but I just wouldn't believe that. So, I dove into the deep end and held on for dear life.

Once the press began covering the complaint I'd filed against Motown, people I hadn't seen or spoken to in months started dropping by. Cindy started coming over often. She told me that she had been going to church and had been saved. I went with her the next Sunday. My life was in such shambles—maybe it was because I had strayed too far from God and from the things that meant so much to me when I was younger. I started attending church regularly and read the Bible.

Everyone was thrilled that I'd taken a stand against the label. Jean Terrell was the biggest surprise, since I hadn't seen or spoken to her since she quit the group. "It's the right thing to do," she said supportively, "and I'm glad you're doing it."

When I phoned Scherrie about it, she was surprised to hear from me. "I just want you to know that there are no hard feelings," I said, "and I hope you have none toward me."

"Mary, it wasn't you that I was angry at, it was Pedro," she responded. "Especially the way that he treated you." Not long after that I learned that she and Susaye were going to release an LP as a duo. I was relieved. There would be no more Supremes. My prayers had been answered. I also knew I had been right about Motown.

Soon after, on September 29, 1977, my second child and first son, Pedro A. Ferrer, was born. Again the delivery was by caesarean; in those years it was believed that once a caesarean, always a caesarean. Complications kept me in the hospital for over two weeks. I was overjoyed to have my little son, and yet very sad. A couple of times I sat in my hospital bed and cried my eyes out.

Once I regained my health, I had to get right to work. While Cindy and Debbie had been great on the South American tour, I needed new girls for my solo act. Many vocalists tried out, including soul singer Merry Clayton, whom you might know from *Dirty Dancing*. Before that she'd worked with such greats as Joe Cocker, the Rolling Stones, and many others. As we sat in my house, she said sweetly, "Mary, I'd be honored to sing with you."

"Girl, *I* am the one honored," I said. "You sing too good to be just a backup singer." And with that, I turned her down. She and I sang and chatted for the rest of the afternoon in between other auditions.

In the end, I found two wonderful ladies. Karen Jackson, who was to be with me for the next eight years, worked as a telephone operator and had sung with a few local bands. Kaaren Ragland was an actress and singer from Virginia. Both were single, attractive, and dedicated. Cindy and I rehearsed them, so that by the time we stepped out, I was a full-fledged soloist, and they were great backups.

Dates for my first tour kept getting moved around, and some were even canceled, as Motown brought its weight to bear on promoters, threatening who knows what if they billed us using the Supremes' name. It wasn't hard to imagine Motown killing my solo career if this kept on much longer. We called our booking agent and got started. As always, my English promoters Barry and Jenny Marshall stood by me every step of the way, and we prepared to leave for a year-end tour of Europe.

It was early December, around six in the morning, and I was asleep in bed when Pedro came home after being out all night. He opened the bedroom door, then stormed through the large room, looking in the bathroom and in the closet, like he expected to find someone there. As I lay there, taken aback by his bizarre behavior, he came to the bed and tore the covers off me.

"Who is here?" he demanded angrily. His eyes were wild. When I didn't say anything, he grabbed me and pushed me into the bathroom, forcing me to look at myself in the mirror.

"Tell me who was here!" He slapped me hard across the face, and I felt my eye swell up immediately. Then I saw the gun, which Pedro kept in the house for protection. He pushed it against my face. I kept thinking how insane he looked, and I felt the cold metal graze my forehead. Over and over again he asked me who had been there. I felt that if Pedro truly believed I'd been with a man, he would surely kill me. I'd never been more frightened in my life, yet inside I was strangely calm. It was as if time had stopped, and I remember thinking, *This is my life, and if this is the end, I have to accept it. But no, this can't be the end.* In that split second I thought about how silly I had been all my life to be so afraid of everything else. The things I thought I should fear, I could now laugh at.

After several moments of me insisting that there was no one else, I saw his face change. I had seen this often. I would stare at Pedro, and it would be as if I were watching a dissolve in a movie; his face would change, and he became someone else.

I kept thinking how afraid Pedro would get too when he realized how far he'd gone. He finally put down the gun, then told me to feed little Pedro because he was crying. I said to him, "You will never find another woman like me," and for the first time I believed it. Pedro tried to get me to stay, but I had to get away. After camouflaging my freshly blackened eye with makeup, I went to stay with my mother, now living in Los Angeles. She was sad but asked no questions.

My mind was flooded with ideas of what to do next. Stay with Pedro, because of the children? Get a divorce? Stay but withhold my love? Get revenge somehow? In the end I went home and prepared dinner. Pedro's repeated threats to take away my babies if we split was the most frightening thought I had to deal with. I couldn't see how to get away from him and take my children without him either hurting or killing me, or getting Turkessa and Pedrito.

Why did I go home to my abusive husband? Pedro gave me something I needed: I was learning to be strong in the trenches. No matter that it was gained through such destructive, violent means. I had come full circle, and while I still felt we would eventually divorce, it wasn't something I could deal with just then.

CHAPTER 14

In early 1978 things were so desperate financially that we couldn't pay our bills. Payroll taxes were due, the musicians were again threatening to quit, and everyone wanted a raise.

But where would the money come from? Pedro had an idea: "If we can just come up with some immediate cash, work will come in, and we can cover everything. Why don't we pawn your heart-shaped diamond ring?"

Of all my possessions, my four-and-a-half-carat heart-shaped diamond ring signified everything that the Supremes meant to me. In 1965 when we had each received one of our first royalty checks—after paying off our debts to Motown—I had bought the heart-shaped diamond ring. Eddie and Brian Holland had told me about a wonderful jeweler in Highland Park where they purchased all their diamonds. Since this was my first diamond, they told me that they would assist me in picking it out. The moment I saw the pure white diamond for $20,000, I gasped. Here it had only been a year since our first hit record had hit the charts, and we were still living in the projects, but to me this ring meant that I had made it. I had accomplished something, and this represented my achievement.

The money Pedro and I needed would come from somewhere, anywhere but my ring. We racked our brains for another solution, but it finally came down to either hocking the ring or filing for bankruptcy.

Someone Pedro met on the nightlife circuit said he would front us a few thousand dollars and hold the ring. When we repaid him the loan plus interest, I'd get my ring back. The man was Ron Levin; he made headlines in the eighties, disappearing without a trace, presumably murdered by members of the so-called Billionaire Boys' Club.

Several weeks later, some money came in, and I asked Pedro to get my ring. "Oh, I meant to tell you," he replied a little sadly, "I already called Ron, and we waited too long. He sold the ring." I was crushed. No one would ever know what that ring meant to me, and now it was gone forever. At that moment, I knew I hated Pedro.

Once again I was back on the road, working just to pay the bills. The only good thing about all this ridiculous touring was that I was gaining more confidence on stage.

Cindy had done a fine job of training Karen and Kaaren, so we were ready for our tour of Germany and Europe, where we performed at officers' clubs and a few swank discos. The trip became awkward, because Motown was still threatening promoters. We were supposed to have gone on to England, but Motown quashed that tour and caused various cancellations in several other countries. Each cancellation dealt another financial blow, but, fortunately, our loyal staff and many of the people we worked with stayed with us.

Pedro was constantly on the phone with our attorney Mark Turk and Motown's in-house counsel, Lee Young, Jr.

In the end, Motown succeeded in getting injunctions against me. At the time I was satisfied with the way Pedro stood up to Motown. Looking back today, I realize I needed a top professional manager to deal with this complex, delicate situation.

Another depressing aspect of this tour was the schedule. We'd do two shows nightly, but usually in two different clubs, so there was a lot of travel. Often these places had no dressing rooms, so we changed in the public bathrooms. It was like going out in the early sixties with the Motown Revue and having to change in high school gyms or on the bus. I had hit rock bottom.

The bright side was singing for the American servicemen, who were always a great audience. One evening a serviceman approached me. It turned out he was one of the boys who'd promised me the moon and the stars one night long ago in the Brewster Projects. We had a laugh.

My nineteen-year-old son Willie was with us. He'd dropped out of school in the eleventh grade. He came along to work the sound and lights for us, having learned from the pros we'd had throughout the seventies. He was great at his job. We were still a traveling family—me, Pedro, the two children, Mom, Willie, the band, Karen, and Kaaren—a situation that would continue well into the eighties.

After Europe, we went to Spain, where an Englishman arrived at our hotel in Madrid with some legal papers. Motown was suing Pedro and me for, among other things, using the name *Supremes*.

The company continued harassing almost everyone we worked with. Promoters again were told not to use us because we weren't really the Supremes and I wouldn't be any good. That was odd, since I had been picking singers ever since 1973 and running the group since 1970. How was it that all those years, Motown had no problem with the quality of the group, yet now it was an issue? We fought, but eventually Motown prevailed, and shows were abruptly canceled. We found out later that Motown's people not only said that we weren't the Supremes, but that I was not the real Mary Wilson! If I had ever wondered how low they might stoop, now I knew.

One night in February 1978 I found myself in a fifteenth-century hotel in Wales called the Royal Oak Inn. It was a magnificent place, with a roaring fireplace, a pub, and very friendly innkeepers. There I started writing my first book. I felt calm and relaxed, and I recall it as a sort of magical place. I had a brief respite from Pedro, which I needed. I feared him more and more. As things went against us, he became increasingly irrational, more intent on hurting me.

While in Wales I decided to ask Pedro for a divorce. I thought back over everything that had happened between us, all the abuse, the insults, the black eyes and bruises, the constant control. It had reached the point where he was so suspicious, I couldn't use the rest room without leaving the door open.

When Pedro called early one morning from London, I told him that I was leaving him. He replied that he was tired; that he'd given me everything, and I'd given him nothing. He called me a "a cold, dull piece of meat." He threatened to take the children, maybe not Pedrito, but definitely Turkessa.

The whole night I lay in bed, tormented. For the first time in my life, I could understand how people committed suicide, though it was never a possibility for me. I prayed to God and hoped that he heard me. I hadn't slept all night, so I was up at eight when a telegram from our lawyer arrived. It contained a strange reference to "a lower price." I asked

Pedro about it, and he broke the bad news: we were selling the Hancock Park house. He, all our accountants, and Hazel saw no other way out unless we filed for bankruptcy. I tried to figure out a plan to save my beloved house, but we simply couldn't afford it anymore. In one day I felt that I'd lost my husband, my daughter, my house, and my career. While still in Wales, conductor Teddy Harris and another musician left. The only thing that distracted me from my problems was playing chess with my bass player, Duke Billingsley. I could only pray that I wouldn't have to endure this emptiness forever.

Within the week Pedro and I were back together again, but as desperately unhappy as ever. On March 8, 1978, just two days after my thirty-fourth birthday, our house was sold. I remember lying on my bed in London and crying and crying. Would I always be fighting a losing battle?

Before this tour started, I'd sent Turkessa to Santo Domingo. The longer I was away from her, the more I thought about how she must feel. Even though I know that my mother gave me to my aunt and uncle because she was doing what was best for me, I never outgrew feeling like an abandoned child. With my own baby thousands of miles away, I began feeling sad and guilty. More than anything I wanted my whole family together. Once the tour was over, we flew to Santo Domingo; I couldn't wait to hold my Turkessa.

While I was in England, Hazel had called to tell us that Motown wanted to settle and offer me a solo contract. We were off on a six-week summer tour of New Zealand, Australia, and the Orient. Pedro stayed behind to finalize some business details. We were fighting all the time, and by now everyone who worked for us knew about the beatings. Meanwhile, in the press writers and fans attacked Pedro for "butchering" my career.

Coming home from the tour in Australia and not having a home was one of the biggest downers I've ever felt. Pedro took an apartment in Westwood that cost $900 a month. I hated it. They didn't allow children, but thank God for Mom. She loved having them with her until we found a place. I stayed many nights at Mom's, as Pedro and I started having some terrible fights.

One evening when Pedro had gone to Mexico City I decided to go out with some friends. I don't know what got into me; I just rebelled. I got home very late, and Pedro had been calling all night and not getting an answer. By the time he reached me, he was so furious he flew home. The next thing I knew, at six in the morning he was standing in the room, as mad as I'd ever seen him.

"Where were you?" he demanded.

Feeling like a child, I lied and said I'd been somewhere I hadn't. Why did I lie? Whenever we had these scenes, it was as if I lost control. Pedro beat me as I tried to run from the apartment, then he pulled out the gun again. I was so frightened I could barely move, but I had two children to think about. I had to live.

Before I got too far Pedro caught me and dragged me down the hallway. I screamed as loudly as I could, but, our neighbors just looked at me and did nothing. I felt like I could read their minds: *Oh, they're black.* I couldn't believe it. I managed to break away from Pedro and run outside to the parking-garage attendant, screaming, "Please! Please call the police!"

As if in a nightmare, Pedro grabbed me from behind, and I fell to the ground. He dragged me back upstairs. The police came, but because this was a domestic dispute, they did nothing. "He tried to kill me!" I said. "He should be in jail and charged with attempted murder."

"It's a civil case, ma'am," one of the cops replied. "There's nothing else we can do."

I stood there, half-naked, bruised all over, crying. "What am I supposed to do? Just stay here and be killed?"

The police offered to escort me out of the building, to the street, where I could get a cab. I was so angry at them for not helping me, and I was furious at Pedro for reducing me to some kind of tramp; I knew that was how people saw me that day. I walked up and down Wilshire Boulevard, barely dressed, in a daze. Cabs in Los Angeles are as rare as snowflakes, so it was nearly an hour before I found one to take me to my mother's house. Later I thought maybe I should have said, "Hey, I'm Mary Wilson of the Supremes. Can you do something for me now?" But I wonder if it would have made a difference.

Mom and my sister Cat were so wonderful. They put me in a tub of hot water and cleaned all my cuts and bruises, never once saying anything about my marriage. All they did was care for me. I stayed for a week and again decided, *This is it.* But one evening Pedro came over, and I went home with him.

It was over a year since I'd officially left the Supremes. Scherrie and Susaye had not been able to revive the group and were at work on a duo album, *Partners*, which was released in 1979 to mixed reviews. Scherrie filed a lawsuit against Pedro and me, alleging that we had withheld an accounting of the Supremes' income from her. This case was later settled amicably out of court. Bit by bit we were finally able to negotiate my solo deal with Motown. One condition of the contract was that Motown and I agreed to drop our suits against each other. By dismissing our respective charges "with prejudice," we each legally forfeited our rights to bring up those charges again in the future. In other words, Motown could never contest my using the Supremes name again, and I could never bring them back to court on any of my charges.

All along I'd been told that my Labor Commission case was very strong. I didn't fully understand everything about my case. It was proceeding fine, then suddenly my attorney and my husband were telling me to drop everything. I did, partially because again I needed to be recording, and Motown was offering that. Years later I would learn that I had a stronger case than I knew.

Right then, all I could think about was making my solo career work and strengthening myself emotionally and financially so that I could finally leave Pedro and get on with my life. All this was complicated by the fact that I was pregnant with my third child.

For many women, their abuse is a "well-known secret." Friends and relatives might suspect or even know what's going on, but no one says anything or acknowledges the truth. Too many people find it impossible to understand the battered woman's plight; they can't sympathize with her until she does what they think she should do: leave her abuser.

I was fortunate during this period to be surrounded by several very supportive people. Among those who were really on my side were Hazel, Gill Trodd, and Barry and Jenny Marshall, the promoters who kept me working overseas. The Marshalls have since gone on to well-deserved success in their field, promoting shows for, among others, Lionel Richie, Tina Turner, and, most recently, Paul McCartney. Barry Marshall offered to manage me, but my husband would never allow it.

Ironically, one of the saddest moments in my life was one of my happiest. I was in London, and Barry, Jenny, Hazel, Gill, Karen, and Kaaren gave me a surprise party for my thirty-fifth birthday. They had balloons, champagne, a beautiful cake, and all the trimmings. And there I was, a pound of makeup covering my latest black eye. I remember feeling so touched and happy. These people really did care about me and believed in me. This love and support of fans and friends gave me the extra encouragement that let me know that I was on the right track.

By now Pedro seemed unconcerned about who might know that he was beating me, especially Hazel. He'd beat me up right before a show, and I'd have to go on stage with a pound of makeup to disguise the bruises. He would go for several days or weeks and not touch me—then he'd explode.

The constant fear and worry about when his temper would erupt constantly kept me on pins and needles. Onstage I projected an aura of cool confidence and control. Offstage I was living a nightmare of total degradation.

Finally, in early 1979, Pedro, my lawyers, and Motown came to terms, and I got my solo record contract. The next thing I knew I was back in the Motown studios recording my first solo album with Hal Davis, the staff producer who was responsible for the Jackson 5's "I'll Be There" and "Dancing Machine," Diane's recent Number One hit "Love Hangover," and Thelma Houston's "Don't Leave Me This Way." It felt odd being in the Motown studio—because of my problems with Motown I was being portrayed as a rebel or an outcast.

Hal and his staff of writers worked diligently to come up with the right material to make my album a hit. Although I felt that my strong point was ballads, the majority of the songs I recorded were up-tempo dance numbers, which were the rage at the time. I viewed this album as a beginning to my solo recording career, and planned to develop from there. We finished the LP just two weeks before I gave birth to my youngest son, Rafael.

The album *Mary Wilson* was released in August of 1979,

and I was quite pleased with it. On the cover I was draped in fur and looking every bit the star. Because I had taken the photos only weeks after Rafael was born, the fur concealed the weight I had gained during my pregnancy. I was also thrilled to see the album cover blown up into a huge mural in front of Tower Records on Sunset Boulevard. The record garnered a lot of press, and most of the album reviews were enthusiastic. I was especially happy when the single "Red Hot" became very popular with the fans, especially with disco enthusiasts from Fire Island to Key West. I heard it in clubs wherever I went, from Studio 54 to Studio One. I immediately added the song to my live act, and always got a fabulous response when I performed it. It was recognized around the world as my solo signature song.

On August 28, 1979, I made my true American solo debut at Manhattan's hot nightclub New York New York. The date was very exciting for me personally. The press came out in full force, and the room was packed with celebrities and fans.

There were all kinds of stylists running around backstage helping me. One came in, obviously excited. "Girl, guess who just came in? Miss Ross! And I think she's on her way up here."

Well, everyone went crazy.

"Here, girl, put on some lipstick! Put this in your hair! Hurry!"

Just then, Sammy Davis, Jr.'s wife, Altovise, came in with the guys from the Village People. Andy Warhol stopped in and gave me a good-luck kiss, and Geoffrey Holder and his wife dropped in to tell me to "break a leg." When Diane and her first husband, Bob Ellis, got there, they both made it clear that they were really supportive of my solo debut. The minute she walked in the door she embraced me, and was very warm and expressed genuine happiness over my debut.

She looked great, wearing a pink two-piece silk outfit and a glittering decoration painted on her face. That night she wasn't playing the star. She stood back and allowed me to be the center of attention. I felt that she was content and happy, and it was a pleasure to have her there.

Out front there were klieg lights, and the club bubbled with the excitement of a Hollywood premiere. "The whole town's talking about your opening tonight," Randy Jones, the Village People's cowboy, said enthusiastically. The excitement was mounting, and I was glad to be back, basking in the limelight.

Then it was showtime, and it was off to a brilliant start. The evening's funniest moment occurred a few minutes into the set, when my costume split open down the back. One of my assistants rushed to my dressing room to grab a cape, which was draped over me. I kept right on singing—without missing a single beat. Naturally I had several costume changes, so by the next number I was in a new gown, and the show was flowing along very smoothly.

While I was onstage, Diane held Turkessa on her lap, in the audience. When the spotlight hit Diane, she couldn't stand up, because the tables were crushed in so tightly together. I began the set with a medley of "Everybody Gets to Go to the Moon" and "Corner of the Sky," then jumped into "Midnight Dancer" from my solo album.

"Thank you," I said after the loud round of applause. "It's so wonderful to be in New York. I love it! I'd like to say hello to everybody, and welcome you to my show. Wow! 'My show!' " People cheered, and I thought, *Just two years ago, about twenty blocks from here, I was booed out of Madison Square Garden. Now here I am.*

"Before we go any further, I would like to sing a medley of my greatest hits."

"All right!" someone shouted as the band played the

opening chords to "Come See About Me." I sang only my background parts: "Boo hoo . . . for you . . . to tears . . . the fears . . . hey, hey, hey, hey, hey . . . hey, hey, hey, hey, hey . . . come see about me." Everyone cracked up, then I did the same for "The Happening" and "Reflections."

"Wow, so you guys really did listen to the backgrounds!" I said, laughing. I introduced Diane, "my very, very dear friend for twenty-one years." As I sang the opening lines to "The Way We Were," I thought about all those years when there had been the three of us. Now it was just me. And I felt wonderful.

I sang a medley of Supremes hits that included "You Keep Me Hangin' On," "Where Did Our Love Go," "Baby Love," and "Stop! In the Name of Love," followed by "Stoned Love," "Can't Take My Eyes off of You," "Quiet Nights," "You're What's Missing in My Life," "I've Got What You Need," "Red Hot," and "A Song for You." When I hit the final notes of "How Lucky Can You Get" and heard the audience's applause, I knew they really wanted me to make it.

Naturally, I finished with "Someday We'll Be Together." I was so lost in thought by then, though, that I forgot the lyrics! Laughing, I asked Teddy Harris to start it over again, and this time I really put my heart into it. I asked audience members to sing along with me on the chorus. Then I got to Diane.

"You think that the stars don't do anything," I said, making my way to Diane's table. "They don't wash dishes or whatever. But Diane is out here baby-sitting my daughter tonight. Sure she's asleep—you're a good baby-sitter, honey. With three children, you should be.

"You look so beautiful. Give me some of that glitter you got on you, girl," I said, leaning forward to kiss Diane's cheek. "Diane, would you sing this song with me, please? Now, remember, I'm singing the background. You sing the lead, okay?" We traded off a couple lines of the songs, sharing the microphone, and the crowd went absolutely wild.

"First, I want to say, Mary and I have never left each other," Diane said. "Of course we haven't, darling. We're sisters. Let the world think we fight. It's all right."

With that, the house came down. After the show everyone streamed upstairs for a party that lasted all night. Before I joined them, Diane and I had a few minutes of private girl talk in the club kitchen. This was one of our rare moments together. She was really there for me.

The reviews were positive. The surprising thing was that so many writers expressed surprise that I could sing. *Gee,* I wondered, *what did they think Flo and I were doing all those years? Just moving our mouths?* Other critics were quite rough, saying I had a lot of nerve, with little talent. To me, they missed the point. I perform because I like to perform. I work hard, and I'm getting better all the time. Hit records, Grammy awards—all that stuff is great—but in the end it's the joy of entertaining that keeps me doing it, not the reviews.

After a six-day engagement, we left for England, where we toured through October before leaving for the Middle East. We were in England around Christmastime. My mother was with us, watching the children. Even though Pedro had become crazier, there were still those nice, quiet times. One evening after one of the shows we were just sitting around in our room, talking, mostly about business. We were having a little champagne, and it was very late.

We seemed to be having a great conversation, so I took a chance and started talking about our problems, which we never discussed. I felt that this was the right time to work some of them out because Pedro seemed so open and amenable. However this proved to he a huge mistake on my part. Suddenly a creative conversation turned into a hot verbal confrontation, and he started going off on me. Before I knew what was happening he thrust his champagne glass toward me, intending to smash the glass directly into my face. Instinctively I turned my head in the nick of time, just as the glass shattered against the side of my face. It had happened so fast that I didn't know what had been cut. *Has he destroyed my face?* was my first thought, as I felt the warmth of blood running from my face. When I put my hand up to the wound, part of my severed ear was hanging in my hand, barely attached by a strand of flesh.

Suddenly Pedro was very concerned, running around the apartment, getting a towel to wrap my head in. He quickly gathered me up, and we dashed around the corner to a hospital. The whole time Pedro comforted me, and I remember thinking that he was behaving as if someone else had done this to me. He really had become two people. In the emergency room, no one questioned our story. We simply said that we'd had a fight. Pedro was so attentive and loving that no one suspected that he had really "meant" it. No reports were filed. No one even asked me if something might be wrong.

My mother and Cat, who were upstairs with the kids, came running down as we left for the hospital. My poor mother! Seeing all the blood, she assumed that Pedro had finally killed me. All the years I was with him, she never said anything to me, though she knew full well what was going on. After this Pedro was very attentive, and we both brushed this horrible incident into the background.

Throughout this period I had been touring exclusively in Europe. Overseas I was recognized as a solo star instead of just an ex-Supreme, and I could earn many times more money than I might expect in the United States. I'd need a huge hit record in America to be booked in the kind of venues I played regularly everyplace else in the world. In 1980, after having performed in Asia, Poland, Tunisia, Italy, and the

Middle East—with my husband and three children in tow—I started working on my second solo album.

My contract with Motown called for me to record two LPs per year over five years. Pedro thought it would be good for me to work with someone from outside Motown, and he and Motown's English representative found Gus Dudgeon, the producer responsible for virtually all Elton John's seventies hits. We chose four songs: "Love Talk," "You Dance My Heart Around the Stars," "Save Me," and Creedence Clearwater Revival's "Green River."

I was very excited about these four songs. It wasn't the formula disco of my first album. Two of the songs were big ballads, and the other two were rock and roll in the style of Tina Turner's mid-eighties hits; I was certainly ahead of the time. Motown didn't like any of it, saying that no one was doing ballads then and that it could release only dance music. With that, the company showed me the door, giving me the tapes and dropping me from the label at the end of the year. This was the first time Motown, which has a policy of controlling all its artists' master, or original, recordings, ever gave an artist her masters back. It seemed that the label had given me a solo deal just to get me to drop my lawsuit against it.

Leaving Motown was one of the saddest events in my life. I had long since ceased being a member of the "Motown family." What foolish little girls we must have been to believe that Berry and Motown would always take care of us.

Now I had no record label and, because of all the years I'd spent overseas, no track record in the States. American record companies are interested in you only if you are a success here. That I had sold out the London Palladium, that I had collected piles of great reviews for my performances—all this meant nothing.

In my personal life things were changing too; I was

stronger now. In late 1979 I had given Pedro one year to clean up his act. If he didn't, our marriage would be over. He made some attempts to change, but couldn't. Throughout 1980 the abuse continued, and his violent sexual aggression became unbearable. Pedro always viewed sex as an expression of power, and violence became a big part of that. He was getting rougher and rougher with me. Out of desperate fear, I gave in to wild nights of cocaine and champagne— anything to numb the pain of the inevitable degradation. He then went one step further, humiliating me in front of my own children. That was the last straw.

I knew that if I could just hold on a few more weeks, it would soon be all over. The sheriff was going to serve Pedro with divorce papers on New Year's Day 1981. The week before, Pedro beat me so badly that my face was bruised and swollen beyond recognition. When little Pedrito first saw me, he exclaimed, "Mommy! Do you know who you look like?"

"No, honey," I replied.

"The Incredible Hulk! Mommy, you look like the Incredible Hulk!" Despite everything, I had to laugh. We both looked at my face in the mirror, and my baby was right.

The few days before New Year's, I hid in the house with the children, afraid that someone might come by and see me. New Year's Day I heard a knock at the door. I stood in another room, half relieved, half terrified. Pedro answered the door, and when they handed him the papers, he was totally shocked. He never, ever believed that I would carry out my threat. He had finally learned that while I may not say much, when I do say something, I mean it. Still, the sheriff wouldn't be moving in with us, and anything could go wrong. Again my biggest fear was that my husband would try to keep the children.

Pedro said nothing until the sheriff left. I stood, tense,

waiting. "Get out!" he shouted. I had started to gather up the children when he stopped me. "No, no, you are not taking my children. I'm keeping the children."

I panicked and started crying. Then I thought for a moment: Pedro wasn't the kind of man to change his ways for his children, though he loved them very much. He wouldn't be able to cook, clean, and care for them the way I did, no matter how much he loved them. So I called Cat to come get me. It killed me to see my three babies standing against a sliding glass door, waving good-bye, crying. Pedro stood in the middle of them, like the father-protector. I got into the car, hoping and praying that I was right.

I was with my mother only a few days before Pedro returned the children to me. It was one of the happiest days of my life. He must have realized what a job it was to be a parent. My mother told me how much she had worried about me and that she loved me. Despite everything, I felt like the luckiest person alive. From that point on, I was really on my own.

CHAPTER 15

January 1981

I am now a free woman: free of my husband, free of Motown, and free of the weight of the Supremes. Now I can *finally* be myself. I'm on my own, my solo career is now a reality, and the only way for me to go is up. This is the beginning of the rest of my life, and so what if I don't have a house of my own. Sitting here in my mother's house, I can truly say that there is no love like a mother's love. You can always come home to Mom when things go wrong.

My mother, who had always been my greatest inspiration, came up with the perfect solution. Now that I had filed for the divorce, I needed a down payment on a house I had found for me and the children. This was a dilemma, because all my cash was tied up in my marriage. I didn't want to stay in my mother's house for the rest of my life, so I tried to come up with a plan.

Mom said, "Why don't you call Diane and ask her to loan you the money?"

As the realization hit me, I thought to myself, *Why not? Who else could come up with that amount?* I was damn lucky to have a friend like Diane, whom I could call at a moment like this.

But still I had too much pride. "I can't do that," I said to Mom.

"Mary, if Diane was in trouble, you know that you would help her. And you know that she will do the same for you."

My timing was perfect. Diane was playing Caesars Palace in Las Vegas. So, I picked up the phone and called her, telling her that I really needed to talk. We made plans for me to come to Vegas and talk one night after her show.

I arrived there and saw the show. She was great as always. I went backstage afterward, and she introduced me to everyone. Then we went back to her private dressing room, where I told her of my plight. She was very sympathetic.

In a completely honest voice she said to me, "I'm so surprised. I really thought that you and Pedro made such a great couple."

We spent over an hour just talking about our lives, the children, and how things had changed—it was a wonderful reunion. Diane had recently surprised everyone by leaving Motown Records, and I told her I was glad.

"Diane, I told you years ago that Berry wasn't doing any more for you as a girlfriend than he was doing for us. If he gave you a fur coat, Flo and I each got one too. When you got a diamond ring, we got diamond rings. Think about it. Frankly, I'm glad you left Motown."

"Really?" she asked, surprised.

Once Diane got to RCA Records, I think she must have realized that after a certain point almost any other label would have taken better care of her financially than Motown. However, it was Berry Gordy who was totally responsible for making Diane the star she is today. She agreed to give me the loan, and later Hazel and Diane's business people drew up the papers. Over the next two years I repaid the loan with interest, as she had requested.

My marriage over, I turned my full attention to my career and my children. Without a record label and with a family to support, I was back working all over the United States and the rest of the world. My backup singers were now Karen Jackson and Gloria Scott. We were billed as the Supremes' Mary Wilson.

We toured such exotic, far-off places as Bahrain, Sharja, Muscat, and Saudi Arabia, where we were guests of nomad families who lived in tents in the desert. We passed our time petting camels and dancing in the clubs, where native women were forbidden. Arab men continually approached us, whispering, "Come to my room, I will pay you well." At buffet tables they tried to touch, pinch, and proposition us shamelessly. One New Year's Eve I committed a real faux pas when I asked, "Where's the champagne?" Alcohol is not allowed in the Arab countries, but that doesn't stop people there from hiding it under tables in Coca-Cola bottles. Several sheikhs even put necklaces around my neck.

Karen Jackson, one of my most faithful background singers, reminded me of myself when I was a young Supreme. Several others came and went, including Robin Alexander and Debbie Crofton. Teddy Harris stayed with me, as did bassist Duke Billingsley and drummer Jerome Spearman. I always appreciated their loyalty. It made my job a lot easier.

In October 1981 a booking agent asked me if I wanted to perform at Studio 54, New York's premier disco. I said yes, of course, and my friend John Christy quickly designed, printed, and covered Manhattan with posters of me, announcing the date. Unfortunately, the deal fell through, but before long people were asking about when I was coming to New York. Randy Jones of the Village People and my friend Mark Bego threw a party in my honor at another New York club, Bolero.

My self-confidence wasn't at its highest, so I was excited when the club rolled out the red carpet for me. The party was packed full of friends, fans, and well-wishers that night at Bolero, including Geoffrey Holder and Grace Jones. The four songs that I sang were a huge hit, and it was extremely gratifying for me to have an endless stream of people coming up to me and telling me how much they loved me and wanted good things to happen in my career. I remember hanging out for hours on the cushions of one of the cubicles talking to everyone.

At one point late in the evening—about 3:00 a.m.—I was sitting down surrounded by friends, and Grace Jones, who was sitting next to me, said, "I'd like to propose a toast to the star of the night," as everyone lifted a champagne glass. "It's long overdue, Mary," Grace said, "and it's only the beginning of good things that are going to happen to you."

I was still figuring out what to do with the Gus Dudgeon–produced masters. The record business had changed in the wake of disco. Before, the label did everything for you when it came to making records. Disco showed the labels that they could save a lot of money if they purchased completed masters from independent producers. Now an artist needed a finished product in hand in order to be signed. I met with various label executives, once even auditioning for Merv Griffin's new record company, but no luck.

In the spring of 1982 I was just days from signing a deal with Casablanca Records and Boardwalk Records founder and chairman Neil Bogart when he died of cancer. In many ways, Neil reminded me of Berry Gordy. In the sixties he was a driving force behind the bubblegum-music trend, and in the seventies he built an empire with such varied acts as Kiss, the Village People, and Donna Summer, and, later, Joan Jett.

After Neil heard my four-song tape, he invited me to his house. Gill Trodd went with me. Neil was in his robe, and he and his wife, Joyce, said they loved my voice. "After the bad experience I had with Donna Summer, I swore I'd never work with a female artist again," Neil said. "But we're not only going to sign you, we're going to turn you into a huge star." He promised to have my contracts ready in a few days.

Gill and I acted very cool, but once we were around the block, we pulled my Rolls-Royce over to the curb and let out a scream. It was too good to be true. I knew that Neil was ill, but I didn't realize he was dying of cancer. Besides being a great personal disappointment for me, Neil's death at age thirty-nine was a tremendous loss to the record industry. By the early eighties megacorporations had taken over the business altogether, devouring independent labels such as Boardwalk.

Even though I was no longer with Motown, the family feelings among the artists endured. We all kept in touch. While a few acts returned to the company, including the Tempts and the Four Tops, more were gone, including Marvin Gaye.

Marvin, who had so often felt that Motown was against him, was living in Belgium then, cut off from his audience. When we were teenagers, Flo, Diane, and I loved Marvin. He was so sweet and *so* sexy.

I shared a delightful evening with him in London. From traveling so much for so many years, I had made little groups of friends in every town. One such friend, Omar, lived in London. Soon after I arrived, I phoned him just to say I was back in town.

"Guess who's here?" he asked me, a trace of mischief in his voice.

"Who?"

"Marvin!"

"What?! I'll be right over."

It was wonderful to see Marvin. We had all heard about his various personal and professional problems. Everyone always felt very protective toward Marvin; there was something about him that made you want to take care of him.

Marvin and I were sitting alone in the living room. "I've got these great tracks I want you to hear," he said. "I want you to listen to this."

He slipped a cassette in the tape player, and the songs that would make up his 1982 comeback album, *Midnight Love*, filled the room. "Marvin," I said, "this is *it*, you know. This is really great." Even though several of the songs were just backing tracks, without the vocals, they were very powerful.

"Which one do you like best?" he asked.

"I like the last one, Marvin. That was really hot."

"Yeah, everybody seems to like that one." The song was "Sexual Healing," which was to be his last Top 10 hit record. "Baby, do you really think they'll make it?"

It pained me to hear the doubt in his voice. Marvin was clearly bracing himself for disappointment. It seemed such a pity that someone so creative and brilliant could feel so insecure, so undeserving. It struck me that a lot of us came out of Motown feeling that way about ourselves.

"Oh, Marvin, of course they'll make it," I said. "These are great. I mean that. You know, everybody's dying for you to come back to the States. Everybody, all the fans everywhere, want to know what you're doing and when you'll have something new out."

"Do they really miss me?" he asked softly.

"Are you kidding, Marvin?" On the one hand, I couldn't believe I was hearing him say these things, but on the other, when I thought about how I felt sometimes, faced with the industry's—the world's—indifference, I understood it. Without current hits, an artist disappears. Marvin knew he had to make the comeback, and this was his big chance. When you're an artist, you have to believe in yourself, even though you know that belief may not be rewarded. It hurts, but you have to go on.

"People love you, Marvin."

"Really?" It was as if he couldn't believe it. He responded as if someone had just told him he could fly. Lying there on the floor, we were like two hopeful teenagers dreaming about our futures.

There has been a lot written and said about where Marvin was in his personal life during these years. The evenings I spent with him, he looked great. He was happy, if cautiously so, and during the next couple of days that we were together, we went out with Omar and Marvin's wife, Jan, and had a grand time.

Once Marvin asked, "Do you really think that people love me, Mary? I mean really love me?"

"Marvin, everybody loves you. The women love you. I've always loved you."

He smiled shyly as I continued. "You know, Marvin, you are the kind of guy that women want to take home and baby. *I'd* take you home and baby you." I laughed. We were always comfortable together, and even though I had a huge crush on him when I was younger, there was never anything romantic between us, despite some writers' allegations. Our relationship was much more than that.

When "Sexual Healing" took off, I was very happy for him. Marvin was one of the few Motown artists to leave the label and succeed someplace else. Sadly, his comeback and a richly creative life were cut short in 1984 when his father shot him to death. I still miss him.

When I saw Michael Bennett's Broadway play *Dreamgirls* in New York, I had no doubt that it was based on the Supremes. I sat motionless as I watched our life story unfold. When the first act ended with Jennifer Holliday (as the Flo character, Effie) singing "And I'm Telling You I'm Not Going," tears streamed down my face. The producers changed many details, but I knew, as they did, that the "Dreams" were the Supremes. Of course, in the play Effie emerges triumphant, which Flo did not.

I went to see it again in Los Angeles and, unknowingly, was seated behind one of the show's chief writers, Tom Eyen. At intermission someone tried to introduce us, but Tom appeared upset and declined. I've never understood why. I only wanted to tell him how much I loved the play, which I've now seen nine times. Diane, however, was so infuriated by *Dreamgirls* that she publicly announced that she refused to see the show and wouldn't let her daughters see it, either. People are entitled to their own opinions—I loved it.

After battling with Motown and Pedro for all those years, I was spending a great deal of time returning to Manhattan to hang out with all my New York friends. All anyone had to do was tell me about an event and I'd fly in. Everyone there made me feel so warm and wanted at a time when I needed it the most.

Marvin's and Diane's leaving Motown and the success of *Dreamgirls* seem like three disparate events, but they worked together on the people at Motown. No matter what you might say about Berry, he has a sentimental streak. He wooed back the Four Tops and the Temptations, and in the spring of 1982 launched a much-publicized reunion of all seven living Tempts. Included were not only the originals—

Melvin Franklin, Eddie Kendricks, Richard Street, and Otis Williams—but David Ruffin, Dennis Edwards, and Glenn Leonard.

Around this time someone at Motown figured that it would be a good idea to get the Supremes back together too. The difference between the Supremes and the Temptations was that the general public seemed to have accepted every edition of the Tempts, despite their having gone through seven different lineups since signing to Motown. It was interesting that even though the Supremes had endured a mere five lineups since Diane left, reporters always referred to the group as a "revolving door," an "employment agency," or something else that suggested we'd become an assemblage of faceless singers.

Suzanne dePasse and I talked about Motown's plans for a possible Supremes reunion. Although I have not always agreed with Suzanne over the years, she is fair. At one point she said that she really liked my voice and that she thought they could "do something with it." That was the first time anyone at Motown had ever complimented me. I found that encouraging, and so I dropped my guard long enough to see what was going on. There was never any plan to ask Diane to join; it was out of the question. If the group re-formed, it would be Cindy, Scherrie, and me.

For years Suzanne would go on and on about what good friends she and Diane were. Diane was even quoted in the press as saying that Suzanne was her best friend. However, Suzanne later told me, "I was thrilled when Diana finally left Motown." She should have been, because with Diane out of the way, she was the top-ranking female at the company.

Suzanne described some very elaborate plans, including an album and a tour, à la the Temptations reunion. It all sounded good enough, but my first priority was my solo career, and I knew that Motown had to do more than make promises. Another condition, which I felt very strongly about, was that I sing leads. Not surprisingly, there was some hedging on that point. Motown wanted Scherrie to do all the leads. No one seemed to care that I had put the Supremes ahead of my life for over twenty years. My request was, I believe, very fair.

We set up a meeting at Berry's house. It was to be Berry, ex-Supremes manager Shelly Berger, and me. Shelly didn't show up, and when I arrived, there was Berry in his bathrobe. "Berry," I said, "here you are, receiving me in your bathrobe. Don't you think you could put something else on?"

We laughed, and the whole meeting was very congenial. Finally I said, "What do you feel about this reunion idea? I'm not going to do anything unless you're involved, Berry, because if you're not in it, it's not going to happen. For me to give up what I've accomplished as a solo just isn't worth it to me."

"Well, Mary, the truth is, somebody else brought the idea to me . . ."

"So, in other words, you really aren't interested, are you, Berry?"

Instead of answering me directly, Berry went off on a long digression, saying, "I'm doing this and that. I'm into the movies. You see what I did with Diane?" It was going to be the same old story I'd heard a hundred times.

"That's fine, Berry, I understand. I don't want to do it anyway."

He seemed a little relieved; then we switched subjects, among them Diane's leaving the label. "I just don't understand why she left," he said, visibly hurt and confused.

"Well, you know you created a monster, Berry, don't you? And the monster turned on you."

"I never thought about it like that," he answered.

The Motown-produced television special "Motown 25: Yesterday, Today, Forever," taped in April 1983, was a once-in-a-lifetime event. As a live show, it was definitely the grandest edition of the Motor City Revue. Martha Reeves, Stevie Wonder, the Temptations, the Four Tops, and the Supremes would all be sharing the stage, just like in the old days at New York's Apollo or Detroit's Fox Theatre.

Billed as "the night everyone came back," it was truly magical. The show's most talked-about and eagerly anticipated event was the promised Supremes reunion. It would be our first appearance together in over thirteen years. This event was a big feather in Suzanne dePasse's cap, because she had done the impossible: coaxed dozens of acts to return to Motown, even those, such as Marvin Gaye, the Jacksons, Mary Wells, the Four Tops, the Temptations, Diane, and me, who at one time or another had left the label. With the exception of Gladys Knight and the Pips, we all came "home," happy to bury the old feuds in the joy of seeing the Motown family back together again.

When Suzanne called, she said, "Mary, Smokey Robinson is getting together with the Miracles, and Michael and Jermaine are going to rejoin the Jackson 5. Mary Wells is going to be there, and so are Marvin and Martha. The event will raise money to fight sickle-cell anemia.

The details were finally settled. I agreed to sing a medley of four Supremes hits with Diane and Cindy. It promised to be a tremendous historical moment, and I was looking forward to it. When I arrived at the Pasadena Civic Center for a brief rehearsal that day, things were already going awry. Diane greeted Cindy and me with a cocktail party hug and quick pecks on the cheeks, as if we were acquaintances she'd just run into on the street. For the rest of the evening, Cindy and I might as well have been invisible, but she and I did have some time alone to go over a few things. For one thing, we decided to sing softly at soundcheck, because our microphones were always turned down to half the volume that Diane's was set at.

Diane claimed she wasn't feeling well, so our rehearsal consisted of about a minute of "Someday We'll Be Together." With that she retired to her dressing room. I was to give a brief speech saluting Motown's musicians and songwriters. The minute I read the self-serving text prepared for me, I knew what I had to do: write my own. There were some things that I felt ought to be said, and I was going to say them.

At the pretaping cocktail party for executives of Motown and other key entertainment corporations, Diane was the only artist. My escort was Jim Lopes, then an MCA executive who was among the invited. He came out of the cocktail party and announced, "Come on, Mary, you're going with me to the 'A' list party."

Before I took a step, the chaperone Motown assigned to keep tabs on me said, "I'm sorry, but Miss Ross is the only celebrity allowed to attend."

"That's too bad," I said, taking Jim's arm and heading toward the party.

"No, you don't understand," the chaperone blurted in fear. "If *you* show up there I'll be fired on the spot."

"Really?" I asked. He nodded, looking very frightened. "Okay, then, I'll stay out here." After all, the cocktail party wasn't the big stakes tonight.

The taping began, and the show was magnificent. Marvin, in the last major television appearance of his life, was inspiring. The Tempts and the Tops were fantastic together, and Michael Jackson brought down the house with "Billie Jean."

For my speech I wore designer Tony Chase's tight black

dress that glittered with long silver beads. Gorgeous—and impossible to sit down in. Ignoring the TelePrompTer, I ad-libbed my own heartfelt message. "I couldn't be here tonight without mentioning some of the people who are not with us," I began, and then named Paul Williams, Berry's parents, "Mom" and "Pops" Gordy, and, of course, Flo.

"She's not here with us tonight, but I know that wherever she is, she's up there—whoo!—doing it!" My speech was directly from the heart, and I received a thunderous round of applause.

Before the last number, our reunion, I took Cindy aside and said, "Remember, this is a reunion, and for once all three of us are going to get equal play. Whenever Diane takes a step forward, we step forward as well."

I'd changed into another Tony Chase number, a fire-red beaded gown that was slit up the back. I was waiting in the wings. Diane sang her solo, "Ain't No Mountain High Enough." She was wearing a short black skirt, a silvery top, and a white foxtail fur. Sashaying across the stage, she dramatically flung the fur downstage. By this time everyone was fed up with her prima-donna attitude.

"Step on that fur, Mary!" Richard Pryor hollered from backstage.

"Kick it!" Martha Reeves said venomously.

I have to admit that I was amazed at the overwhelming feelings of animosity that Diane had brought upon herself. I wanted this show to have the kind of dignity that was befitting the Supremes. I refused to let a fight happen. The music to "Someday We'll Be Together" started.

"Mary? Cindy?" Diane called, as if wondering where we were.

Cindy entered from stage right to a huge round of applause. I let her get to the middle before making my entrance. When Diane announced, "This is Cindy Birdsong, and *that's* Mary Wilson," the crowd went crazy. At last, the Supremes were together on stage again. I was so proud and thrilled. We started singing "Someday We'll Be Together." Then something went wrong.

Diane seemed genuinely confused. Attempting to distance herself from us, she took two steps closer to the audience. As agreed, Cindy and I stepped two paces forward too. Diane again moved forward; we followed.

The third time it happened, Diane turned and forcefully shoved me aside. The audience gasped, appalled. Diane's eyes widened in shock at the realization that I wasn't about to back down, and that all these people had just witnessed her little tantrum. She got so flustered she lost her place in the song, so I sang a line, thinking Diane would compose herself and assume the lead again in a few seconds.

I kept singing lead. The only thing that she could think of doing was to begin to talk while I sang. She proceeded to speak to Berry, out in the audience.

"Berry, come on down," I called while the music continued.

With that comment, Diane grabbed my microphone and pushed it away from my face. "It's been taken care of!" she snapped at me with fire in her eyes.

The audience gasped again. I was told later that Suzanne dePasse panicked and sent out Smokey Robinson to defuse the crisis. In seconds the stage filled with other artists, and the Supremes "reunion" was over.

Diane had given the media the cat fight they were praying for, and they licked their collective chops in delight. I have never been so mad at her in my entire career. Just when I thought that we were at a stage where she was going to bury the hatchet, she went and pulled something like that. I was hurt and stunned.

Naturally, when the television special was edited, all but

about ten seconds of "Someday We'll Be Together" was snipped out of the special. And they billed this debacle as the reunion of the Supremes? What a sad travesty. To further get my goat, they also scissored out my entire speech.

The press had a field day when they wrote about the taping of "Motown 25," and *US* magazine ran photos of Diane pushing and shoving me on stage. If I live to be a hundred I will never figure out what prompts her to act this way. The funny thing is that the next time I ran into her, she pretended like this incident had never happened. I am told that to this day the full finale footage is locked up in a vault and that only Suzanne and Berry have access to it.

Later that year, I got a call from Motown saying that the "Motown 25" special had been such a success it now wanted to distribute it as a videocassette. At first, I was excited. The label wanted me to sign a release with a "favored-nation clause," meaning that all artists would get minimum scale for their appearances, plus a tiny percentage. Immediately, I grew suspicious. It seemed that everyone had signed their releases already—everyone but me. It made me think that while taping "Motown 25" the company had intended this all along. The more I thought, the more I felt that it was trying to take advantage of everyone.

The original performance had been a charity event to raise money for sickle-cell anemia. Doing a TV special was one thing, putting out a video for profit another. I felt the artists should be compensated; after all, it was we who had donated our services. I said I wanted to negotiate my agreement on the video; the label flat out refused. I sued Motown, and it in turn countersued me. This started a lawsuit that continued until 1990.

My separation from Pedro did not always protect me from his jealous rages. As many battered women can attest, court orders of protection are not worth the paper they're written on if somebody really wants to get at you. Even after our divorce, there were confrontations between me and my ex-husband.

One evening my good friend Mark Bego and I were getting ready to go see a show at L.A.'s Roxy when Pedro showed up at my house unannounced. The minute he walked in, I sensed his rage. I had to get Mark out of the house before Pedro blew up.

"Where do you think you're going?" Pedro demanded, staring at Mark and me.

"What do you want?" I asked as coolly as I could. "I don't have time to stand here and argue with you. Mark and I are late for a meeting with a record company. Now, will you please leave?"

Surprised, Pedro turned on his heel and stalked out. I hurried to my bedroom to get my lipstick, thinking, *That ought to leave us just enough time to get out of here before he changes his mind and comes back.*

Mark and I climbed into Grace. Unfortunately for us, my 1959 Rolls was badly in need of a tune-up, her door locks were broken, and one of the windows didn't shut completely. I didn't want to alarm Mark by explaining what might happen. I quickly got behind the wheel and backed out of the drive and onto Ventura Boulevard. I pressed the accelerator to the floor, but we were still going too slow. I glanced in the rearview mirror.

"Darn!"

"Something wrong?" asked Mark.

"Yes. Pedro is following us, and I'll have to lose him. I haven't told you this, but Pedro goes into insanely jealous rages."

I tried zigzagging through traffic to lose Pedro, but Grace was so big and slow, it was hopeless. I shouted, "Mark, find a police car. There's no telling what he'll do if he catches us!"

"Where's a doughnut shop?" Mark screamed. "You can always find a policeman at an all-night doughnut shop. There's one! Quick, turn in!"

We pulled into a Winchell's Donuts, and, sure enough, three police cars were parked there. Mark hopped out and told the cops what was happening. Pedro must have seen this, because he sped off down Santa Monica Boulevard. The policemen promised they would detain Pedro if they saw his car again in the area. We thanked them and left, detouring through a residential neighborhood with winding streets, as a precaution.

Just when we thought we were home free, Pedro's car pulled in front of us and stopped, blocking the narrow street. He jumped out of his car, jerked open my door, and reached across me to grab Mark by the throat. Then he smacked Mark in the forehead, causing him to crack his head against the windshield.

"If I ever see you with my wife again," Pedro growled, "I'll kill you!" He slapped me five times in about five seconds. "And if I ever catch you with another man, you know what I'll do."

Before either of us could react, Pedro was gone. Mark and I looked at each other as if to say, "Did that just happen?" My makeup was smeared all over my face, and Mark was seeing stars. We freshened up at my friend Jim Lopes's nearby apartment and then went on to the party. Pedro was not going to ruin our evening.

Afterward, Mark came to my house for a nightcap. It was four in the morning by the time we'd stopped talking and laughing about the evening's events. Mark had a huge welt on his forehead, so perhaps it wasn't really funny, but finding whatever humor there was in these situations helped me keep it together. We decided it would be better for Mark to stay over, so I prepared the sofa for him.

No sooner had I gotten into my bed than I heard Pedro screaming in the front yard. "Mary, if Mark is in there, I'm going to kill both of you!" He pounded on the front window, and Mark and I called the police. While we waited, Pedro circled the house. Not knowing what he would do, I took out a pistol that I kept in the house for protection. I don't think Mark understood the gravity of the situation until he saw the gun, then he went to get a weapon—a silver-plated champagne bucket.

The police finally came and ran Pedro off the property, but he continued calling and threatening us for hours. Mark and I were in the kitchen making breakfast, waiting for a police officer to come and take our formal complaint. Mark looked at the gun and said, "You'd better unload that pistol, Mary, before someone gets hurt."

"Don't worry," I said, pointing the gun toward the kitchen cupboard, "it isn't loaded." Just then a gunshot went off, and a bullet pierced a hole in the ceiling molding.

In the spring of 1983 I came to New York City to sing a jingle for an ice cream company that was introducing its line of Tuscan Supremes flavors. I enjoyed working with the musical director, Paul Shaffer, from the David Letterman show. During the eighties I came to New York often to work and to audition for shows and plays. Friends in the business introduced me to people they thought I should know; Mark Bego especially did all he could to help me.

One evening I met an up-and-coming club DJ and record producer named John "Jellybean" Benitez. Jellybean had a hot reputation for remixing hit singles and turning them into blockbuster disco hits. We chatted for a few minutes, then Jellybean played me a song he wanted me to sing.

I listened carefully, trying to envision myself singing it. There weren't a lot of lyrics; the words "holiday" and "celebrate" seemed to be repeated over and over. It was cute and catchy, but I didn't think it was right for me. I passed on it, thanked Jellybean for his time and interest, and wished him luck. Mark kept telling me I could sing it, so I changed my mind and called Jellybean back, but it was too late. He'd already given the song to someone else.

Several months later I was listening to the car radio when the disc jockey announced a new song by a new singer called Madonna. It was "Holiday," the very song Jellybean had handed me on a silver platter. I thought I would die. It went on to become Madonna's first Top 10 hit, and . . . well, you know the rest of the story.

I was working constantly: performing, auditioning for Broadway parts, and expanding into other areas. That summer I sang the National Anthem in the Disney film *Tiger Town*, starring Roy Scheider. At the suggestion of my good friend Bill Cosby, whom I opened for in Las Vegas, I auditioned for the part of his wife on *The Cosby Show*.

One of my tours that year took me to Key West, Florida, where my two background singers and I spent a fun-filled five days basking in the sun and performing to hundreds of party-loving people at night—the people who come to Key West *really* love to party. One afternoon, while I was dining with the promoter who had brought us there, he asked, "Would you like to have lunch with Tennessee Williams?"

He said that Tennessee had been at my show the night before and had absolutely loved it. By coincidence, our promoter, Gary, was working with Williams on what was to be his last play. Gary told me that Tennessee had been very down, but listening to my music helped to give him some happiness. Tennessee had said that he would have loved to meet me after the show, but since it had been so hectic, he didn't get the chance.

I told him that I'd be thrilled to meet the famous playwright, and the next afternoon Tennessee joined me and my background singers for a wild luncheon at an oceanside restaurant. What was to be a simple lunch ended up to be a five-hour fete. We were absolutely flying on great wine, raw fish, and Tennessee's wonderful stories. The man was truly fascinating.

Because of the warm tropical air, the outfit that I had chosen that afternoon was a beautiful bright-orange and yellow two-piece sun suit with a wild orange straw hat. At one point in the evening, as the sun began to set, Tennessee looked at me and said, "There is only one other woman who can wear colors like that, and that is Liz Taylor. My dear, you are in her class."

As always, I took part in celebrity charity events. I have always wanted to save the world, and thanks to my friends, particularly Dionne Warwick, I have been able to lend my name and my time to a wide range of causes, including substance abuse, sickle-cell anemia, the homeless, AIDS, and such organizations as the Heart Foundation, the Starlight and Make a Wish programs, the United Negro College Fund, the Bill Cosby Illiteracy Program, and the Dionne Warwick AIDS Foundation.

I've performed at concerts for Dionne's foundation and visited people with AIDS, including little babies, in hospitals and hospices all over the country. While performing recently in Chicago, I went to an AIDS ward. One patient was extremely ill, and I was told that he was an avid Supremes fan but that for medical reasons I could not enter his room. The poor young man had lost most of his sight and was nearly in a coma.

"I'm sorry," I said. "but I *have* to see him." I approached his bed and gently took his hand.

"You're Mary Wilson," he said weakly, smiling. "You're just like I pictured you to be. You're like an angel of mercy."

Through my charity work I made new friends, among them Rita Coolidge. She is truly a beautiful person, both inside and out. We found that we had so much in common, like single-parenthood, and whenever we get together we have a ball. After years of feeling that I didn't have a close girlfriend in the business, she came along. In 1989 I joined her in a march on behalf of the homeless in Washington, D.C.

Today in America tens of thousands have no place to live. These people are not criminals, or strung out on drugs or alcohol. They're just people who ran into hard times or hard luck. Having grown up in the Brewster Projects, I know that even though we didn't consider ourselves poor, my family just got by financially. I also know that if Diane, Flo, and I were growing up today instead of back in the fifties, our families might very well be homeless.

When I heard, in 1984, that Diane was booked at Caesars Palace the same week I was appearing at the Sands, I became so excited. Her name loomed above the Vegas Strip in huge letters on her hotel's marquee, and my name topped the massive marquee at my hotel: "MARY WILSON Now Appearing at the Sands." At last I had made it all the way back to the top—and this time I did it as Mary Wilson. Not as "one of the girls who sang in the background in the Supremes." Not as "one of the girls who sang with Diana Ross." I was Mary Wilson, headliner.

Diane and I had had no contact since the "Motown 25" special; our relationship has run hot and cold over the years, and I never know what to expect. As odd as this might sound to most people, though, there is still a part of her that I love, the person she was when we first met as young girls, a part that I believe is still there.

It's always been my custom to call up any Motown act appearing in the same town just to say hi and catch their show. When I found out Diane would be in Vegas too, I decided to wait and see if she called me. The days passed, and it seemed like everyone in the world was stopping by, including Sister Sledge and some of Diane's band, but still no Diane.

Finally one night I said to my friends John and Tony, "What the hell, why don't we just go to see her at Caesars?" We were walking from my dressing room to the casino when I heard, "Mary! Mary!" It was Diane, on her way to see me.

We embraced, and she said, "My dad and a friend of mine and I are on our way to a club and Italian restaurant Dionne Warwick owns. Would you like to join us?"

John, Tony, and I went to the restaurant, an intimate place on the strip, and joined Diane and her party. Her date for the evening was a car dealer. I was wearing a jumpsuit and a punk-style wig.

"I love your hair, Mary," Diane remarked. "Wait until you see the billboard on Sunset Boulevard for my new album. I have a punk cut as well!"

When I lit up a cigarette, Diane acted surprised. "Are you still smoking, Mary?" she asked.

"Yes, Diane," I answered coolly. "It's my only bad habit. How about you?"

"Well, I'm alone, and sometimes I may drink a little too much."

I laughed to myself, knowing that for Diane more than two drinks was "a little too much." She was never a big drinker. There wasn't much to say to that. The rest of the evening was pleasant enough, but I remember that all through dinner Diane's father kept talking about his other daughter,

Barbara, who is a doctor. When we finished, Diane and her father got into her limousine, while John and I rode back to the Sands with the car dealer. That was the last time Diane and I were together as friends. Never once was her shoving me during the "Motown 25" special ever mentioned. It was as if it hadn't happened. I wasn't going to bring it up, and she wasn't going to apologize, so that was that.

Shortly after this friendly evening, Diane apparently decided—long before my book *Dreamgirl* came out—that I was her rival.

In 1985 Motown produced a television special, "Motown Returns to the Apollo," a tribute to all the Motown and other r&b acts who'd performed there over the years. The Supremes played the Apollo many times, beginning in 1962 when Florence, Diane, and I sang "My Heart Can't Take It No More" as part of the original 1962 Motown Revue.

Smokey Robinson and the Miracles, Martha and the Vandellas, Stevie Wonder, and the Four Tops were also on the bill in 1962, and on this night they and Diane were all invited back by Motown to relive the old days; I, however, was not, because of my "behavior" during the "Motown 25." I attended as the date of Jim Lopes, an invited guest, and, as luck would have it, our seats were in the front row.

When Bill Cosby, the evening's master of ceremonies, spotted me, he said, "What are you doing down there? You should be up here!" I laughed when during breaks in the taping Bill, who's always been a good friend, made pointed but funny comments about the fact that I wasn't on the show. He hinted several times that he would do something to "rectify" the situation.

Late in the show Bill introduced Stevie Wonder, who was performing his new single, "Part-Time Lover," backed by what they called an all-star backup group: the Four Tops, Boy George, and Smokey. Bill looked out over the audience and asked, "Are there any more background singers out there?" Then he pointed at me. "How about you?" He came down and helped me up onstage, where I joined the other six. When it was over, one of the Tops escorted me back to my seat.

Of course, except for a tiny glimpse of my face that couldn't be edited out, none of this appeared in the final show. A friend of mine who works at Motown told me they were going crazy trying to edit me out altogether. During the big finale, I was again invited up, to join other celebrities from the audience in a number. As I approached the stage, Diane looked at me and said, "Want to pick a fight tonight, Mary?"

I ignored her comment and, hugging her, said, "Diane, I love you."

In the summer of 1989, Diane was performing at the Universal Amphitheatre in Studio City; she was on her "Working Overtime" tour. Jay Schwartz, my publicist, had arranged for Turkessa and me to accompany him to the concert. Jay had also made arrangments for us to visit her.

When the show was over, we went backstage and chatted with Bobby Glenn and some members of Diane's band I was friendly with. Diane was still sequestered in her dressing room, and because my Rolls-Royce was parked near the backstage door, I was obviously around. One of Diane's employees came up to Jay and said to him, "You'd better leave, because Diane doesn't want Mary here."

I'd had just about enough of her nonsense and informed Jay, "I'm not leaving until I'm ready to leave."

With that, the Motown executive who had given the tickets and the backstage passes was becoming uncomfortable and implored us to go before an ugly scene ensued. I was a guest of Motown's, and I wasn't about to leave.

Jay then told me that we had best leave. With that I

decided to return to the car, and Turkessa stayed with my friend Ian Lawes, because she wanted to see her godmother, Diane. Turkessa went into a small lounge outside Diane's dressing room and stayed there about ten minutes until Bobby Glenn came by and said to Ian and Turkessa, "I'll do what I can to get you into the dressing room."

A half hour passed, and finally Turkessa told Ian, "Oh, let's just leave."

Jay then escorted Turkessa and Ian to my Rolls. As Turkessa was leaving, someone approached Jay and again mentioned that Diane wouldn't come out until I left. I was quite upset over this display of childish nonsense. I have seen her act like this time and time again, but for a forty-five-year-old woman to act like a spoiled child really affected me emotionally. After this, I knew that we could never be friends again.

Turkessa was crushed by the way her godmother was acting. She had never believed that Diane was anything less than benevolent, but her image of her was shattered.

Jay wanted to go out for a drink to smooth over what had become an upsetting evening. "Let's go to Le Dôme," he suggested. "Or should we just go home?"

"Let's just go home," I said wiping away a tear.

Turkessa was so let down that she conceded, "Let's just go to Carlos's and Charlie's."

With that, I decided that after this slap in the face, we should go to Spago, where Diane was holding an afterconcert party in part of the restaurant. I have been there several times when private affairs are being held in the back, and the front restaurant is still open to the public.

We arrived at Spago, and as Turkessa and I got out of the car and were on the way to the front door, we were surrounded by photographers, reporters, and television camera crews. The manager of the restaurant, who had obviously been instructed to keep the press away, started to yell at them, "Get off my property!" This only encouraged them to want to get a statement from me.

We started walking closer to the door, and the camera crew from *Entertainment Tonight* was a few feet behind us. We went up the two steps to the door, and the woman greeting people said, "I'm sorry, but you can't come in." I never even told her my name. She then said curtly, "You are not on the guest list."

I was stunned by this rude display, which was evidently on orders of Diane. With that, the camera crew from *Entertainment Tonight*, which had witnessed this scene, jumped at the opportunity to film my comments.

That was the last time I saw Diane, or had any desire to. She wanted a feud, and now she has one. I have never been so insulted and hurt by someone I once considered to be a friend.

EPILOGUE

One thing that's kept me going is knowing that there are people around the world who love the Supremes. Not the Supremes as an institution, or the Supremes at our mid-sixties height, but each and every Supreme. In terms of fans and friends, I have been truly blessed. I knew they were out there, but the real proof came when my first book, *Dreamgirl: My Life as a Supreme*, was published in 1986. After years of talking about it, and almost as many years writing it, it was finally real. It was a thrill to see the name Mary Wilson and the word Supreme back in the Top 10, only this time on the national best-seller list.

The book's success afforded me the opportunity to do many things, for which I am thankful. I purchased a huge house in Hollywood, sent my children to school in England, and we all took a long-overdue family vacation in Hawaii.

Dreamgirl was a real turning point in my life. Writing it and later talking about it forced me to look at both the positive and negative aspects of my life and myself. It also gave me the confidence to try new things. I did some acting on television *(227)* and onstage, in a production of *Beehive*, a tribute to the women of rock and roll, including the Supremes. I even got the chance to audition for songwriter Stephen Sondheim.

So much had occurred in the last couple of years. In 1987 the old Hitsville building in Detroit was officially acknowledged with a state historical marker. The Motown Historical Museum was finally a reality. Berry didn't bother to attend the ceremonies, but legions of fans did.

When I got to visit the museum in the fall of 1989, it was a mixed experience. It was an unusually warm autumn day, and I was starring in *Beehive* in Windsor, Canada, site of the first semiprofessional singing contest Diane, Flo, Betty, and I won, back in 1960. I remembered pleading with Diane's father to let her go. Had it really been thirty years?

I arranged to meet a local reporter, a camera crew, and several fans at the museum. One of the first things I noticed was that the Supremes were conspicuously absent from the front-window display of artists' pictures. There were photos of Diane, the Smokey-less Miracles, the current Temptations, and *Bad*-era Michael Jackson (over fourteen years after he'd left the label), but no Supremes.

As I walked through the rooms and hallways that had been my second home, I felt very hurt and sad. The tour guide referred to the Supremes as "Diana Ross and Her Supremes," and as I looked at the walls, it was obvious that someone had made a very determined effort to erase Flo, as if she had never existed. One displayed photograph of the Supremes, taken on our 1966 tour of the Orient, showed just Diane and me. In the original, the three of us are standing side by side, with Flo in the middle. Visit the museum, and you will see that someone has crudely cut Flo out of the picture!

MARY WILSON

Many of the photos were mislabeled, and there was a makeshift air about everything. Motown's lack of respect for its artists extended even to cutting "troublemakers" out of photographs. I looked around the museum and can honestly say I felt no sense of nostalgia being there.

But not everyone had forgotten Flo. In 1987 Florence's fan club held the first annual Florence Ballard Exhibit, a tribute to Flo in pictures and memorabilia, in Hollywood. Among the people who attended were Flo's youngest daughter, Lisa Chapman, as well as Scherrie Payne, Gladys Horton of the Marvelettes, Mike Warren, Fuller Gordy, Janie Bradford of Entertainment Connection, and fans from all over the world.

In October 1987 it was announced that the Supremes were to be inducted into the Rock and Roll Hall of Fame. I was excited and honored that the group should receive such a dignified and prestigious homage from its peers. This was only the third year of the Hall of Fame's existence, and the Supremes were going to be honored along with the Beatles, Bob Dylan, the Drifters, and the Beach Boys. Since the Supremes had never even won a Grammy, I wasn't about to miss this big event.

It was also a wonderful coincidence that our induction would occur in early 1988 because later that year I had the very special honor of presenting Brian Holland, Lamont Dozier, and Eddie Holland with their induction certification from the Songwriters' Hall of Fame. It was great to give Eddie, Lamont, and Brian an award in return for all those terrific songs they gave the Supremes.

As the date for the ceremonies drew closer, I began thinking about my acceptance speech. Music history and the record business in general still accord the Supremes far less respect than I believe we deserve. I'm sure part of it is because, as women, we were viewed as not being "creative"; that is, we didn't write our own songs. But another part of it was Motown's doing. For years and years Motown had sought to make the Supremes disappear in Diane's shadow, and, I was sorry to admit, it had nearly succeeded.

On January 20, 1988, I flew to New York City and checked into my room at the Waldorf-Astoria on Park Avenue. The whole place was already buzzing with excitement over the fact that the inductees were going to be honored by the Rolling Stones, Little Richard, and Bruce Springsteen.

I checked into my suite—and in classic Supremes fashion laid out several beaded and sequined gowns—so that I could figure out which one, or ones, I would be wearing. I was hardly at a loss for dates that evening. Five minutes after the announcement came about the Supremes being inducted into the Hall of Fame, Mark Bego was on the phone asking if he could be my date. I instantly agreed, but explained that I was also going to be meeting a lawyer friend of mine, Mitchell Ware, and that my publicist, Jay Schwartz, would also be with me. Mark was undaunted.

That evening I dressed in a shoulderless, tight-fitting beaded white gown, designed by my godson.

Just then I heard a knock on the door. It was Jay, and he had a list of press people who wanted to talk to me. I explained to him that Florence's daughter had not yet arrived and I was concerned. He agreed to wait in the room until she checked into the hotel and said that he'd come downstairs to get me when she got there.

At the appointed hour Mark and Mitchell Ware escorted me downstairs to the cocktail party, where I was nearly blinded by the flashbulbs of dozens of paparazzi from every major newspaper and magazine in the country. Since I was the only female inductee to arrive, I was treated like the belle of the ball.

"Is Diana coming this evening?" one reporter asked me, shoving a microphone in front of me.

"I really couldn't say," I answered. "I can only speak for myself and say that I'm thrilled to be accepting this honor tonight." All of a sudden, every photographer ran to greet Yoko Ono as she arrived to accept for John Lennon. Thank God there was another woman besides me.

Also at the ceremonies that night was Berry Gordy, Jr., who was being honored as a "nonperforming inductee" for having formed Motown Records.

The room that the cocktail party was held in was packed so full of people that maneuvering around it was nearly impossible. Just then I spotted Berry, who was being accompanied by the humorless Michael Roshkind.

While we were still at the cocktail party, a publicist who represents Paul McCartney announced that Paul wasn't attending because he was still mad at George Harrison, Ringo Starr, and Yoko Ono, because of a pending lawsuit over royalties from the Beatles' former record company, Apple Records. On Diane's behalf, her publicist showed up and said that she had "a personal family reason" for declining the invitation to attend. For a moment, my heart sank. I was surprised at how much I had really wanted to share that moment with Diane one last time. If only just to say thanks and to acknowledge that dreams do come true.

The cocktail party ended, and we all filed into the ballroom to find our places for the $1,000-a-plate dinner and ceremony. I shared the table, located off to stage right, with another of the evening's inductees, guitar innovator Les Paul. They began to serve dinner—a Liverpudlian specialty in honor of the Beatles, bangers and mash (sausage and mashed potatoes)—but still no Lisa. Jay Schwartz rushed to our table to say that Lisa had arrived, but the airline had lost her luggage. I excused myself and ran to help her. She was standing in the hallway outside the ballroom, very upset.

"Auntie Mary, what am I going to do? I don't have a thing to wear!" I, naturally, was never at a loss for an outfit. "Just come upstairs with me. I have the perfect thing for you," I said as we rushed up to my suite.

She looked wonderful in the simple black dress I gave her. She had Flo's statuesque bearing, long, pointed chin, and steady gaze. As I looked at Lisa, I hoped that her mother could see her.

"All set? Now let's go back downstairs," I said. "You're going to look great onstage. Your mother would be so proud."

"I have to go up there?" Lisa asked nervously.

"Don't worry. Let's get something together for you right now. I'll be onstage with you, so don't worry. You loved your mom very much, didn't you?"

"Yes."

"And you are very proud of her accomplishments, aren't you?"

"Yes."

"Well, let's take those two thoughts, embellish them, and put them down on paper. You're going to be just fine."

We hurried back to the table, and I was just sitting there, looking around, when I spotted Berry making his way across the room. As I watched him move toward us, my first thought was, *Why should I stop him?* It could only be embarrassing for me and for Lisa. Then I thought, *Right is right, and there is no way I can let Berry go the whole evening without acknowledging my existence or paying his respects to Lisa. He's not going to get out of this ballroom without looking me in the eye.*

"Hi, Berry. How are you doing?"

"Oh, hi," he said. "You look beautiful tonight."

"Thank you. Berry, this is Lisa, Florence's daughter."

"Nice to meet you," he said. I wondered if he saw the resemblance. After a few more words, he returned to his table. We did not speak again for the rest of the evening.

The presentations began. Berry was the first inductee, followed by a few more nonperformers. The first of the other five inductees were the Beach Boys. Following the Hall of Fame's standard procedure, they were inducted by someone who had been inspired by their work, Elton John. Elton had always been one of my favorite people, so it was nice seeing him.

As the rest of the group was leaving the stage, Mike Love suddenly began criticizing Paul McCartney and Diane. He just went off on them, proclaiming, "I think it's sad that there are other people who aren't here, and those are the people who passed away [referring to John Lennon, Beach Boy Dennis Wilson, and Flo], but there are also . . . people like Paul McCartney, who couldn't be here because he's in a lawsuit with Yoko and Ringo . . . that's a bummer, because we're talking about harmony . . . in the world. It's also a bummer when *Miss* Ross can't make it."

The audience howled, hissed, laughed, and booed. Mike's tirade obviously struck a nerve. Bandleader Paul Shaffer cut him off by cuing the band to play, ironically, "Good Vibrations."

Next Billy Joel inducted the Drifters. I was so happy for them. In the early years, Diane, Flo, and I had shared many bills with the Drifters, and we considered them our friends. They had inspired us as young teenagers. It was wonderful to see Ben E. King, Johnny Moore, Bill Pinkney, Gerhart Thrasher, and Charlie Thomas acknowledged for their accomplishments. Artists like the Drifters, who meant so much to so many performers who followed them, should never be forgotten. Bruce Springsteen inducted Bob Dylan, who got a standing ovation. Then it was our turn.

Lisa and I stood backstage as Little Richard began making his speech about the Supremes. Since the Hall of Fame ceremony, many people have asked me how I felt about Little Richard's induction statements. Some people thought he was fantastic; others felt that his asides were inappropriate. He had been among the first artists inducted, in 1986, but couldn't attend because of injuries from a car accident. He spent a good deal of his speech thanking the Hall of Fame for his own award, and just being himself.

Little Richard was one of my idols, so it didn't bother me that he went off on tangents and talked over his time. I had to laugh when he said, "I love the Supremes so much, 'cause they remind me of myself. They dress like me. Diana Ross been dressin' like me for years. You all know that! And they also do my holler: *Whoo!*"

He had the crowd laughing, but he also said some very kind things about the group and about us as individuals. "You know, Miss Ballard passed away, but she was a great singer too." The whole room burst into applause. "The first women in rock and roll are the Supremes, to me. There's never been anything like them, and I don't think there ever would be. They are the greatest, and I just love the Supremes.

"I am proud to present to you Miss Mary Wilson of the Supremes." The band struck up "You Keep Me Hangin' On," and I walked across the stage to the podium with Lisa, stopping once to do the "Stop" gesture.

"First of all," I began, "I'd like to talk about the fact that I was really privileged to have sung with two really wonderful people, Diane and Flo. [I'm sorry] that Florence could not live to be here to know that what we as three little girls—three insecure little girls—had dreamt of could possibly come true. It saddens me to know that, but that's life, and there's nothing we can do about it. We're very proud that everyone has given us this honor so that her daughter could be here to see how much we loved her.

"Now I'm gonna read my speech. Since I've written my book I had to get glasses, but I'm not wearing them tonight.

"It was my wish, of course, that Diane be here, but we must all recognize that people have to live their lives. And there comes a time in a star's life when you have to really assess what's important to you. And I would say that perhaps since Diane has received so many, many accolades in life and so much success, she probably has felt that—she's married, she has a child—that this is something that is very, very important. And I respect the fact that maybe she saw fit to stay with something very personal, a personal achievement more than a public achievement.

"This is one of those rare moments in a person's life and in history that we all dream of. And like I wrote in my book, dreams do come true. Sometimes people have to just keep dreaming. We all hope that the world is looking in when we receive our award, and that the world can share in the moments of happiness we each receive. I'm told that in order to be eligible to receive an award from the Rock and Roll Hall of Fame, you had to have recorded some twenty-five years ago. Well, I was six when I started. It's very obvious, I'm sure.

"It was because of one young man, Berry Gordy, who was there for us. We had a place at Motown Records to go. And I'm very happy to say he gave us the opportunity. And we cannot forget Holland, Dozier, and Holland, whose music still lives on today.

"Florence, Diane, and I shared a success that you were all looking in on, throughout the world. And I certainly hope that you . . . were able to see the hopes and desires that we had and that it helped your lives along the way. I'd like to thank the directors of the Rock and Roll Hall of Fame for honoring us at this moment. And we can all remember that rock and roll will never die as long as we, the people, out there make it. I thank you very much."

Before Lisa got up to the podium, "You Keep Me Hangin' On" started, but was cut short. She spoke softly but with such dignity, saying, "I would like to say that I'm very pleased to be here tonight representing my mother. I'd like to thank the Rock and Roll Hall of Fame for inducting my mother. Thank you."

We posed for photographs with Little Richard and Atlantic Records chairman Ahmet Ertegun; then everyone sat down for the final induction, the Beatles.

After that began a large and initially unorganized jam session. Among the dozens of people onstage, in addition to the inductees, were Elton John, Billy Joel, Mick Jagger, Bruce Springsteen, Neil Young, Nile Rodgers, Jeff Beck, Peter Wolf, Dave Edmunds, and Julian Lennon. It seemed so symbolic of the record industry, and rock and roll in general, that the only two women onstage were Yoko Ono, there to accept her late husband John Lennon's award, and me. I noticed her standing a bit off to the side and looking a little left out, so I went up to her and got her to join me. I felt so funny being the only other woman up there, but the jam turned out to be the highlight of the evening for me. I sang "Stop! In the Name of Love" with Ben E. King and Yoko helping on background vocals. I got her to join me in the traffic cop "Stop" choreography, making her a Supreme for the night. Then I did a lot of backup singing with Mick Jagger. It was fun.

While it was a very special evening, it was also one of the saddest in my life. Except for a few friends I'd known for many years, such as Ringo, George Harrison, Elton, Paul Shaffer, and the Drifters, hardly anyone spoke to me that evening. It drove home something I had always known, which was that despite all my efforts and through all those years, the record industry recognized only one Supreme: Diane.

As I stood at the podium giving my speech, I could see that many people in the room, even musicians and singers, probably didn't know who I was, or who Flo was. And didn't care, either. Literally and figuratively, we were history. In many people's minds, we were three people: the big star who made good, the one who died in poverty, and me, the background singer. For so many years I had dreamed and hoped that I might one day change that, but it's probably impossible, and that's probably the only thing I've stopped dreaming about.

Maybe it's because I'm a Pisces that I can have two totally opposing reactions to the same situation. That evening I felt like two different people. One Mary Wilson was hurt and mad because of how she was being treated; the other was happy, thrilled, and honored to be saluted. The Supremes were taught to always behave like proper ladies, with class and breeding. That night I checked my hurt feelings at the door. I could have predicted how the evening would go, but I was determined to enjoy it for what it was. I don't ever want anyone to cry for me, because I don't.

What I felt that night was deeper, and more important to me. It had taken me a lifetime, but I finally knew in my heart that no one could make me feel like less than I was. Did it hurt to be snubbed? To be regarded like somebody's secretary sent to pick up an award in her boss's absence? Of course. It was like being six years old again, looking out my parents' picture window at the other kids playing in the street and not being allowed out to join them. I had to learn to be happy all alone, and I have.

The lesson that came from all I'd been through that night was that it had nothing to do with me, or how I thought about myself. Whatever hurt I felt, I acknowledged and accepted.

The difference between it and so much of my life before was that I didn't let it push me or frighten me. I knew who I was and what I'd done, and, at last, I could honestly say that was all that mattered.

For me the seventies and eighties were a time of growth and learning. In the sixties, with the Supremes, I went from having nothing to having it all. These past two decades taught me that just being the "sexy one" wasn't enough. There were things I had to fight for, like my self-respect.

After the huge success of my book *Dreamgirl* and being inducted into the Rock and Roll Hall of Fame, I decided to start my life over. My ongoing lawsuit over the ownership of the Supremes' name was coming to trial soon. And to be honest, I was tired of fighting a losing battle.

In the first days of 1990, before I turned forty-six, I called Berry Gordy and said, "Look, after nearly sixteen years of arguments and lawsuits, I'm tired of fighting over the Supremes' name."

He agreed that we should talk, and we met several times to discuss the matter. Not once did Berry ever apologize for what he or Motown did; he couldn't even acknowledge that Diane had pushed me during the "Motown 25." *Fine*, I thought. *If this is how it is, that's how it is.*

There was never any question in my mind that I would have won had the case gone to court. But that seemed so far away, and I knew that even if I won, there would be endless appeals. The fight had already cost me more than $1 million and would cost probably hundreds of thousands more before it was all over. Realistically, I had to consider the financial needs of my family before setting off on what might have been another legal wild-goose chase.

It was a hard decision, but I made it. We finally came up with a satisfactory agreement, and I signed away my rights to the name—forever. Yes, I was sad, but I was also relieved.

Motown's action back in the 1970s made it so that I had to work very hard to keep a roof over my children's heads, which is unforgivable. But I go to sleep every night with a clear conscience; I doubt many of those who had a hand in creating this situation can say the same. For the first time in years, I didn't have to fight.

I'm still traveling the world, singing and performing. Of course, we're all raised to believe that there's only one place to be, and that's on top, but I feel so fortunate to be doing what I love. As long as I'm making people happy, I'm proud to be wherever I am. I try new things all the time, but I never tire of singing the great old songs. There's always going to be a place in my heart for the Supremes. I stayed with the group through all the ups and downs, and as much as I often felt hurt and defeated, I've reached heights few of us dare dream of. For that I feel blessed.

With the Hall of Fame induction and the success of *Dreamgirl*, the Supremes finally received the recognition we long deserved. No, it didn't all turn out the way I expected, but that was okay too. My promise to Flo—and myself—had been kept:

I'd taken care of it.

DISCOGRAPHY

Mary Wilson, Cindy Birdsong, Jean Terrell

1970

February | "Up the Ladder to the Roof" b/w "Bill, When Are You Coming Back" [Motown 1162]

April | *Right On* [Motown MS–705]

April | *Farewell* (Diana Ross and the Supremes) [Motown MS2–7088]

July | "Everybody's Got the Right to Love" b/w "But I Love You More" [Motown 1167]

September | *The Magnificent 7* (with the Four Tops) [Motown MS–717]

October | "Stoned Love" b/w "Shine on Me" [Motown 1172]
| *New Ways . . . but Love Stays* [Motown MS–720]

November | "River Deep—Mountain High" b/w "Together We Can Make Such Sweet Music" (with the Four Tops) [Motown 1173]

1971

April	"Nathan Jones" b/w "Happy (Is a Bumpy Road)" [Motown 1182]
May	"You Gotta Have Love in Your Heart" b/w "I'm Glad About It" (with the Four Tops) [Motown 1181]
June	*The Return of the Magnificent Seven* (with the Four Tops) [Motown MS–736]
	Touch [Motown MS–737]
September	"Touch" b/w "It's So Hard for Me to Say Good-bye" [Motown 1190]
December	"Floy Joy" b/w "This Is the Story" [Motown 1195]
	Dynamite (with the Four Tops) [Motown M–745L]

1972

April	"Automatically Sunshine" b/w "Precious Little Things" [Motown 1200]
May	*Floy Joy* [Motown M–751L]
July	"Your Wonderful, Sweet Sweet Love" b/w "The Wisdom of Time" [Motown 1206]

Mary Wilson, Jean Terrell, Lynda Laurence

October	"I Guess I'll Miss the Man" b/w "Over and Over" [Motown 1213]
November	*The Supremes Produced and Arranged by Jimmy Webb* [Motown M–756L]

1973

March	"Bad Weather" b/w "Oh Be My Love" [Motown 1225]

Mary Wilson, Cindy Birdsong, Scherrie Payne

1975

June	*The Supremes* [Motown M6–828S1]

Supreme Faith

295

June	"He's My Man" b/w "Give Out, but Don't Give Up" [Motown 1358]
October	"Where Do I Go from Here" b/w "Give Out, but Don't Give Up" [Motown 1374]

Mary Wilson, Cindy Birdsong, Scherrie Payne, Susaye Green

1976

April	***High Energy*** [Motown M6–863S1]
May	"I'm Gonna Let My Heart Do the Walking" b/w "Early Morning Love" [Motown 1391]

Mary Wilson, Scherrie Payne, Susaye Green

October	"You're My Driving Wheel" b/w "You're What's Missing in My Life" [Motown 1407]
	Mary, Scherrie & Susaye [Motown M6–873S1]

1977

February	"Let Yourself Go" b/w "You Are the Heart of Me" [Motown 1415]

1978

July	***At Their Best*** [Motown M7–904R1]

Mary Wilson Discography

1979

August	***Mary Wilson*** [Motown M7–927R1]
October	"Red Hot" b/w "Midnight Dancer" [Motown 1467]

1980	"Love Talk," "You Dance My Heart Around the Stars," "Green River," "Save Me" (produced by Gus Dudgeon) [Unreleased; recorded for Motown]
1986	"My Lovelife Is a Disaster" [Unreleased; demo only]
1987	"Don't Get Mad, Get Even" [Nightmare Mare 39]
1989	"Ooh Child" [Nightmare MOT-C7]

Album Guest Appearances

With Neil Sedaka

"Come See About Me," from *Come See About Me*

With Paul Jabara

"This Girl's Back," from *Dela Noche Sisters*

With Dionne Warwick

"Heartbreak of Love" (Unreleased)

Supremes Compact Discs

Meet the Supremes
I Hear a Symphony
Supremes A Go-Go
Supremes Sing Holland-Dozier-Holland
Diana Ross & the Supremes with the Temptations Together

Right On
Touch
Floy Joy
Anthology
25th Anniversary (two-disc set)

Two Albums Per Disc

Love Child/Supremes A Go-Go
More Hits by the Supremes/The Supremes Sing Holland-
    Dozier-Holland
A Bit of Liverpool/TCB (with the Temptations)

Available on Compact Disc Only

Never Before Released Masters
The Rodgers & Hart Collection
Motown Around the World
Love Supreme (England Only)
Every Great #1 Hit

PEOPLE WHO HAVE WORKED WITH THE SUPREMES OVER THE YEARS

Comedians

Herb Eden
Rodney Dangerfield
Stiller and Meara
Rip Taylor
Skiles and Henderson
George Carlin

Back-ups for Mary Wilson

Debbie Sharpe and Cindy Birdsong
Karen Jackson and Kaaren Ragland
Gloria Scott and Karen Jackson
Debbie Crofton and Karen Jackson
Karen Jackson and Robin Alexander
Silvia Cox

Elizabeth Fields
Anna Beaumont
Rhonda Trodd
Linda Levine
Damia Satterfield
and numerous other ladies

Wardrobe Mistresses–Chaperones

Mrs. Powell
Esther Edwards
Mrs. Morrison
Margie Wooden
Doris Postles
Ardeena Johnson

Designers

Pat Campano
Michael Nicola
Bob Mackie
Mike Travis
Stephen Burrows
Allen Poe
Barnard Johnson

Hair Stylists

Gregory
Winnie Brown
Jan Dochier

Bob Cousar
Teddy Harris
Duke Billingsley
Mel Brown
Phil Upchurch
Gil Askey
Curtis Kick
Napoleon "Snaps" Allen
Jerome Spearman
Lorenzo Brown
Travis Biggs
Darrell Smith
Joe Harris
Louis Spears
and many others

SEVENTIES SUPREMES FAN CLUBS

There were many Supremes fan clubs, but these lasted the longest:

Jerry Jaco
SUPREMES FAN CLUB
U.S.A./Texas

Russ Bart
SUPREMES FAN CLUB
Scotland

Randy Taraborrelli
Carl Feuerbacher with
    Wayne Brasser assisting
SUPREMES FAN CLUB
U.S.A./Pennsylvania

Mario de Laat
SUPREMES FAN CLUB
Holland

David Barrie
SUPREMES FAN CLUB
Canada

Mark Douglas
SUPREMES PUSH FAN CLUB
U.S.A./New York

Ernie Brasswell
SUPREMES FAN CLUB
U.S.A./Los Angeles

Carl Feuerbacher
MARY WILSON FAN CLUB*
International

*still operating now

FLORENCE BALLARD
FAN CLUB*
P.O. Box 36A02
Los Angeles, CA 90036

Danny Williams
Harold Winley, Jr.
FAN CLUB

*still operating now

Dave Godin
TAMLA-MOTOWN
APPRECIATION SOCIETY
London, England